Northwest Vista College
Learning Resource Center
3535 North Ellison Drive
San Antonio, Texas 78251

D1557040

THEATRICALITIES OF POWER

Theatricalities of Power

THE CULTURAL POLITICS OF NOH

Steven T. Brown

STANFORD UNIVERSITY PRESS
Stanford, California

Stanford University Press
Stanford, California

© 2001 by the Board of Trustees of the
Leland Stanford Junior University

Printed in the United States of America
on acid-free, archival-quality paper

Library of Congress Cataloging-in-Publication Data

Brown, Steven T.
Theatricalities of power : the cultural politics of Noh /
Steven T. Brown.
p. cm.
Includes bibliographical references and index.
ISBN 0-8047-4070-4 (alk. paper)
1. Nō—History and criticism.   I. Title.
PN2924.5.N6 B76   2002
895.6'2009—dc21   2001032267

Original Printing 2001

Last figure below indicates year of this printing:
10   09   08   07   06   05   04   03   02   01

Typeset by James P. Brommer in 10.5/12.5 Bembo

Contents

PART THREE
PERFORMATIVITIES OF POWER

Acknowledgments

Numerous encounters figured into the materialization of this project. I owe an immeasurable debt of gratitude to my teachers at Stanford, especially Tom Hare and Hans Ulrich Gumbrecht. As readers, mentors, and friends, they gave me the much needed support that helped get the project off the ground, as well as the critical feedback that kept me from going astray. Tom Hare was an exemplary reader from start to finish, helping to bring into focus the vision of the project while encouraging me to explore new avenues of research. His own work on noh sets a very high benchmark to which I have always aspired, if not yet attained. It would not be an exaggeration to say that every student who has had the good fortune to study closely with Sepp Gumbrecht has been inspired by his relentless drive toward critical self-overcoming. Special thanks are also due to John Bender, Herbert Lindenberger, David Wellbery, and Marsh McCall for their generous encouragement and sage advice at crucial stages during my studies at Stanford and after. At Stanford University Press, I wish to thank Helen Tartar, Elizabeth Berg, and especially Andrew Frisardi for his meticulous editorial advice.

Thanks to all the participants who have commented on my work at various conferences, especially the *Ominameshi* colloquium (University of Pittsburgh, October 3–5, 1997), "The New Historicism and Japanese Literary Studies" conference (University of Michigan, October 24–26, 1997), and the "Theatricalities of Power: New Historicist Interventions into Japanese Drama" panel at the Association for Asian Studies Meeting (Hawaii, April 12, 1996). Special thanks to Susan Klein, Mae Smethurst, Karen Brazell, Susan Matisoff, Lynne Miyake, Wakita Haruko, Nishino Haruo, Takemoto Mikio, Royall Tyler, Kate Saltzman-Li, and Beng Choo Lim for critical advice and inspiration.

At the University of Oregon, I would like to thank my colleagues in East Asian Languages and Literatures for their generous support. Special thanks to Mike Fishlen, Steve Kohl, Wendy Larson, and Yoko McClain. Bob Felsing, Aimee Yogi, Paul Atkins, Yamamoto Takashi, and Chōnan Ariko provided valuable assistance in locating materials. Thanks also to the many students whose questions have inspired me over the years, especially Sudeshna Sen, Michael Wood, Yamamoto Takashi, Yoshida Junji, Asahara Masako, and Kusakabe Madoka. Portions of this study were written with the assistance of two University of Oregon Summer Research awards and the support of the Office of Research and Faculty Development.

During my studies in Japan in 1992–93, the staff of the National Noh Theater Library offered generous assistance in locating obscure materials. Bruce Batten and the entire staff of the Inter-University Center in Yokohama were also most supportive of my efforts. I owe a special debt of gratitude to the incredible generosity of Yanagisawa Kiyoko-sensei at the Inter-University Center for enabling me to attend innumerable noh performances over the course of my stay. An even more profound and unrepayable debt is owed to Nakaya Hiroko-san, whose tireless enthusiasm and support insured that my first extended stay in Japan in 1984–85 would forever remain etched in my memory as among the best years of my life.

Heartfelt thanks go to my entire family, especially Maryanne and Verlin Brown, Henrietta and Louis Kovarik, Carrie, Brandon, and Matthew Harnack, and Kay, Bill, and Jon Hokanson. Many close friends offered assistance and encouragement along the way: Kinch Hoekstra, Patrick Murphy, Kerstin Behnke, and Leslie Brown were always willing to discuss matters ranging from the quotidian to the philosophical. They have inscribed their signatures onto this project in unforeseen, though singular, ways.

Since the writing of this book was enframed by both the birth of my son Gabriel and the deaths of my close colleague Alan Wolfe and brother-in-law Allen Harnack, it seems only fitting to dedicate its publication to my son's future and my friends' memories. I shall always feel a profound sense of gratitude to Alan Wolfe for the generosity of his friendship and the intensity of his critical spirit.

It is for my wife Katya that I reserve my deepest gratitude, whose unfailing patience, ceaseless enthusiasm, and keen editorial eye were the true conditions of possibility for the realization of this project. Without her, this study might never have seen the light of day.

S.T.B.
Eugene, Oregon

THEATRICALITIES OF POWER

The History in Noh

According to philosopher Gilles Deleuze, there are two types of reading: one that conceives of the text in terms of signification or representation, another that approaches it as a nonsignifying assemblage.[1] The former asks what a text means, the latter what a text does. The present study approaches noh texts in this second manner, examining how they work within their historically specific social and political contexts.[2]

Instead of reading the noh performance text as a space for the free play of poetic signifiers, such an approach positions noh as a site of conflict framed by the mechanisms of patronage within which poetic, religious, political, and economic discourses are brought together in complex and innovative ways. The task of such an analysis is to ferret out the power relations and tensions at play between noh texts and their institutions of support, opening noh to extra-dramatic linkages with contemporaneous figurations of authority, changes in legal codes, and sexual politics.

Neither reducing noh to its theatrical conventions nor abstracting its style and poetics from its performative materiality, this study attempts to open the performance text of noh to its historically specific outside. In short, I attempt not merely to recount the history *of* noh, which has been discussed elsewhere at great length, but rather to investigate the history *in* noh.

Through an extended reading of the play *Aoi no Ue* (Lady Aoi), as well as briefer interventions into *Ominameshi* (Damsel flower), *Yumi Yawata* (Bow

of Yawata), *Tomoe*, and the series of *Taikō nō* (Retired regent noh) plays written for and starring Toyotomi Hideyoshi (1536–98), this study sheds new light
on the circulation of power and desire in the middle and late medieval periods, engaging specific sociopolitical issues and problems. Rather than simply
mirroring the sociopolitical contexts in which they were performed, I argue
that these plays constituted an active, productive force in the theater of the
medieval cultural imaginary. Other plays could certainly have been chosen
for this task, but I have resisted the urge to fabricate an artificial unity an-
chored in a single author, period, or genre of noh, instead selecting diverse
plays from each period of noh's premodern history, from early Muromachi
(1338–1573) to late Azuchi-Momoyama (1568–1600).

Although the Hideyoshi plays obviously lend themselves to an analysis of
the history *in* noh, the ruler himself does not necessarily have to step on stage
in order to make such reading strategies worthwhile for the study of noh. In
the remainder of this prologue, I will outline the theoretical positions and
stakes involved in reading noh in terms of a "micropolitics"[3] of culture.

Dōmoto Masaki has suggested somewhat polemically that noh was the
"newspaper" of its day.[4] Although I do not think that noh is as linguistically
transparent as Dōmoto's analogy suggests, such an interpretation serves as a
useful corrective to dehistoricized readings of noh, which reduce it to the expression of some timeless lyrical or aesthetic "essence."

Reading noh as a nonsignifying assemblage involves ferreting out the
power relations and tensions at play between various performance texts of
noh and their institutions of support. Such an approach undertakes to break
the study of noh theatricality out of the prison house of aesthetic autonomy,
which all too often pays scant attention to the social, political, and economic
contingencies surrounding its production, performance, and reception.

Of course, it goes without saying that much invaluable work has been
done on the poetic (Itō, Tyler, Matisoff, Goff), stylistic (Yokomichi, Kitagawa,
Takemoto, Hare), performative (Yokomichi, Brazell, Bethe, Emmert), aesthetic
(Yokomichi, Omote, Katō, Takemoto, Hare, Nearman, Rimer, Thornhill), biographical (Kobayashi, Omote, Dōmoto, Nishino, Hare), and historical (Nose,
Gotō, Omote, Nishino, Amano) aspects of noh. By laying the groundwork for
later studies, such scholarly riches make the analysis envisioned here possible.
Micropolitical readers of noh necessarily stand on the shoulders of more traditional scholars, even while questioning the discursive boundaries of their
scholarship.

This study departs from more traditional noh scholarship in its attempt to
analyze critically the complex linkages and interchanges between different
discursive zones without privileging one zone over the other. Correlatively,

approaching noh in terms of its micropolitics of culture also involves unpacking the power plays and techniques involved when one discursive zone *is* privileged over another by particular performers, patrons, audiences, or scholars.

Rather than restricting the performative text to the hermetically sealed internal readings of formalism, a micropolitical approach opens that text to extradramatic linkages, whether intertextual, institutional, or merely circumstantial. Without attempting to define the "truth" or "meaning" of a sociocultural artifact, such an approach maps the strategic force-values, or effects of power, produced by a particular sociocultural artifact as it is contingently traversed by the discourses, institutions, and practices of a certain discourse network (or assemblage). The terms "discourse network"[5] and "assemblage" are deployed interchangeably in this study as shorthand abbreviations for the historically specific, differential web of power relations linking sociocultural, economicopolitical, and ontoepistemological codes, discourses, and institutions, along with their associated procedures, rituals, and practices. Although few noh plays lend themselves to an explicitly political treatment—"political" in this instance being understood in the restricted sense of relating to affairs of government—the "politics" of noh begins to make more sense once one conceives of the "political" in a more generalized sense to refer to the power relations and effects associated with figurations of authority, gender, subjectivity, naming, and patronage.

In addition to analyzing the contingencies inscribing the development and mutation of sociocultural artifacts within a certain discourse network, a micropolitics of culture also examines the mechanisms of legitimation and naturalization used to efface such contingencies. By historicizing sociocultural artifacts, such an analysis attempts to denaturalize and de-essentialize the grip of discursively constructed "necessities," bringing into focus the contingencies of "necessity" and the constructedness of sociocultural authority.

In an effort to avoid reducing the interrelations between sociocultural artifacts and their discourse networks to a unidirectional cause-effect relationship with sociocultural artifacts in the subordinate position, a micropolitics of culture gives attention to the multidirectional and mutually constitutive exchanges and "refashionings" structuring their relations. To ignore this constitutive reciprocity by reducing the sociocultural artifact to a mere product of historical influence or the ideological reflection of economic infrastructure is to efface the active, constructive force of the sociocultural artifact. A micropolitics of culture endeavors to situate sociocultural artifacts within their historical matrices without effacing their potential for *artifice* or reducing them to passive mimetic or allegorical reflections of such totalizing, universalist hypostatizations as "reality," "history," "society," "culture," or "man."

Even when such an approach stresses the importance of "power" and "discourse," it attempts to avoid the vacuity of Power and Discourse by investigating the particular micropolitical mechanisms and strategies, the meticulous rituals and infinitesimal techniques, operating in a historically specific field of shifting discourse-power relations.

Though a micropolitics of culture makes no pretense of empathetically recovering (or reliving) the full plenitude and presence of some self-evident "authentic" past, it does, nevertheless, presume to map out the contingent relations and linkages between sociocultural artifacts and their discourse networks, which have survived in the form of documentary and institutional traces. Perhaps the most difficult question for any reader of noh has to do with the historiographical status of such "linkages" and "traces."

In the case of Hideyoshi and his Taikō noh, the linkages between theatricality and politics seem relatively well defined, but one will look in vain for official policy decrees issued by the Hideyoshi regime (or any other, for that matter) that *explicitly* disclose the political strategies and objectives of powerful patrons and their forays into the world of noh. Indeed, all the archival research in the world will not make up for the fact that such "evidence" is rarely unambiguous. What makes a micropolitical approach to noh so challenging is that linkages between the cultural, the political, and the historical are rarely, if ever, straightforward or self-evident.

Given the evidentiary indeterminacy of such linkages, one might well ask whether a micropolitics of culture is not an "unacknowledged branch of fiction."[6] To this I would respond that such readings are neither more nor less prone to the writing of academic fiction than other literary critical approaches. Indeed, a Foucauldian cynic might respond that all academic writing is an unacknowledged branch of fiction, to the extent that interpretive links are always in some sense "fictioned."[7] Or perhaps more to the point, I would suggest that even if my questioning of the academic boundaries partitioning the study of culture, politics, and history into separate compartments is itself a fiction, then the micropolitics of culture should at least be viewed as a counterfiction to the formalist fiction of aesthetic autonomy to which some readers and viewers of noh continue to subscribe.

A micropolitics of culture may evade the reductiveness of linear, teleological, and metanarratival explanations, but it cannot go beyond the imposition of power enacted by its own contingent descriptions, which occupy the status of interpretive interventions and selective engagements: that is, power maneuvers operating within a specific discourse network, contingently *performing* the past rather than actually *restoring* it.[8] Nagao Kazuo has offered a provocative rejoinder to those who seek (or presume) to disclose the "essence" of noh, arguing that the entire history of noh could be viewed as an extended and productive series of "misunderstandings" (*gokai*) of an *unrecoverable* past. The essentialization of noh thereby comes into view as a historical exercise and power maneuver in its own right.

This is neither to authorize the abuse of the text nor the fabrication of evidence; it is merely to own up to the performative force enacted by every practice of reading in the process of engaging a text. But just because micropolitical analysis acknowledges its status as a form of power/knowledge does not mean that its analyses are uncritical or uninformed. On the contrary, a micropolitics of culture attempts to render visible contingent events that have been concealed by various discursive mechanisms, strategies, and techniques of power.

Such a venture requires both the courage and the competency to venture across disciplinary boundaries in search of linkages that are at best oblique and refracted—not the "smoking gun" that would provide indisputable evidence for micropolitical claims. But the fact that one rarely proves beyond a reasonable doubt that cultural artifacts inscribe and are inscribed by the historically specific power relations across which they circulate does not mean that analysis of the micropolitics of noh culture is doomed from the start. Indeed, I would argue that it is both the promise and the challenge of a micropolitical approach to explore "the indecision as to the limit" between the performance text of noh and its other.[9]

PART ONE

Theatrical Technologies of Power, Self, and Signification in Medieval Japan

CHAPTER I

Instituting Noh

Although noh is thought to have derived, in part, from various forms of entertainment performed at court, such as Chinese dance (*gigaku*,[1] *bugaku*) and music (*gagaku*), imported into Japan in the seventh and eighth centuries, its beginnings were more popular than courtly. The early popular dramatic forms that seem to have exerted the greatest influence on the development of noh include various sacred and shamanistic rituals and entertainments, such as *kagura*, *shushi*, and *ennen*, performed for commoners at Shinto shrines and Buddhist temples. Festival performing arts, such as *dengaku* agricultural performances and *sarugaku* mime, magic, and acrobatic acts, also played a constitutive role.[2] Although these early beginnings are significant, here I am more concerned with what noh eventually became than with what it originally was: the "origins" of noh interest me less than the contingent intersections and mutations of the *institution* of noh from the Kitayama epoch (1367–1408) of the Muromachi period, when noh flourished under the patronage of Shogun Ashikaga Yoshimitsu (1358–1408), to the Edo period (1603–1867), when noh was transformed into the official state-sponsored form of entertainment (*shikigaku*) for the Tokugawa *bakufu* (shogunate).

The focus of this chapter will be the *institutionality* of noh.[3] Instead of proposing a normative discourse that would prescribe what noh generically *is* or *should be*, I will describe the linkages binding noh to its institutional and discursive apparatuses of support. Toward this end, I consider the following is-

sues: Who sponsored the production of noh during Muromachi and later periods? What was the demographic composition of the audiences attending noh
performances? How do the contingencies of authorship and attribution define the reception of noh? What parameters of theatricality (including theater
architecture, chorus and actors, choreography, music, and costume) constitute
the staging of noh? How did medieval conceptions of dramatic impersonation
inscribe noh performativity? Finally, what sociopolitical functions, if any, were
served by Zeami's (1363?–1443) conception and practice of *yūgen* (aesthetic
ideal of "mystery and depth" used with varying connotations in association
with *waka, renga,* and noh)?

The Theater of Kyoto:
Patronage, Competition, Audience

If asked to single out the most important turning point in the patronage
history of noh, few scholars would hesitate to name the performance at Imagumano (a district in southeastern Kyoto), where the young shogun Ashikaga
Yoshimitsu first attended *sarugaku* noh by the Yūzaki troupe in the year 1374
(or 1375). During the early fourteenth century, both Hōjō Takatoki (1303–33),
the shogunal regent of the Kamakura *bakufu,* and Ashikaga Takauji (1305–58),
the first shogun of the Ashikaga *bakufu,* were enthusiasts of *dengaku* noh, but
their interest in it never compared to Yoshimitsu's patronage of *sarugaku* noh.[4]
Yoshimitsu was so impressed by the performance at Imagumano that he soon
established shogunal patronage for the Yūzaki troupe from Yamato province
(led by Zeami's father Kannami, 1333–84), and later added other troupes to
the shogunal payroll, such as the Hie troupe from Ōmi province (led by Inuō
Dōami, ?–1413).[5]

Although it may be going too far to say that after the establishment of
shogunal patronage, noh's "ostensibly religious purpose was clearly subordinated to that of entertainment,"[6] Yoshimitsu's sponsorship certainly made it
possible for noh to begin to shed its folk trappings and to adopt the more refined style of an aristocratic performing art. The performance at Imagumano
thus marks the beginning of noh's transformation from a popular provincial
entertainment for commoners to an aristocratic art form staged for the military ruling class. Though noh troupes never ceased to perform both at the
capital and in the provinces before popular audiences,[7] the institution of shogunal patronage meant that noh troupes now had to learn to cater to the tastes
of the military elite.

In theory, the Ashikaga shogunate was in a financial position to patronize
multiple noh troupes simultaneously, but in practice, only those troupes that

succeeded in attracting the interest of the shogun were rewarded with patronage. Although Zeami described noh as "a prayer for peace to reign over the entire country" (*tenga taihei no onkitō*),[8] it might also be viewed as a supplication to those elite members of the warrior class who held the reins of political power. Zeami's frequent references to the likes and dislikes of Yoshimitsu, as well as to whether or not the shogun was present at a given performance, indicate just how important shogunal patronage was to the survival and development of noh.[9]

The competition between noh troupes was brought onstage as formal performance contests called *tachiai* ("combined performances"), which were judged by the highest-ranking audience member—in many cases, the shogun himself.[10] *Tachiai* were usually included as part of the program at *kanjin nō*, or subscription performances (see discussion below). Not surprisingly, the winners of such contests stood a much better chance of attracting the shogun's notice and receiving his patronage as a result. Although noh *tachiai* bear some resemblance to the tragic contests held at the Great Dionysia festival in fifth-century B.C.E. Athens, in which individual playwrights vied for victory, *tachiai* involved competition between the performers, not the playwrights, of different troupes. Moreover, unlike the Athenian contests, in which selected tragedians had already received official sponsorship from the polis and were competing more for fame and glory (*kleos*) than for patronage per se, noh *tachiai* held out the possibility that a rousing victory might elicit the admiration and long-term support of the shogun.[11]

Tachiai typically involved the simultaneous or successive performance of a set piece or pieces by various actors from competing troupes. When performers took the stage successively, the order of the performances was determined by the drawing of lots (*kuji wo hiku*).[12] The ultimate victor of the *tachiai* was not merely the most impressive performer, but more importantly the winning performer's troupe, insofar as it was the performer's troupe that stood to gain the most from patronage granted (or maintained) by the shogun in response to an impressive performance. Even when noh troupes were not competing against one another in official *tachiai*, every noh performance was, in a sense, an informal contest against other troupes competing for the same sources of patronage.

In *Fūshikaden* (Transmission of flower through forms; 1400–1418), Zeami makes it clear that although the goal of every performing art should be "to calm the hearts of a wide variety of people and move the feelings of high and low alike" (*geinō to wa shonin no kokoro wo yawaragete jōge no kan wo nasamu koto*),[13] the success of noh in the Muromachi period depended upon the favorable response of the nobility (*kinin*). Zeami's conception of the nobility included members of the military elite (*buke*), such as the shogun and his high-ranking officers, as well as court aristocrats (*kuge*). Zeami advised the noh actor to regard the attendance of the nobility as the foundation of one's performance—going so far as to recommend starting a performance before its appointed time, if members of the nobility should happen to arrive early—since it was of the utmost importance that the actor perform in an elegant, dignified style in accord with the feelings, expectations, and tastes of the nobility.[14] Even after Yoshimitsu's death, when Zeami and his troupe fell out of favor with the Ashikaga shogunate, Zeami never lost sight of the importance of performing in an aristocratic manner in the capital, as attested by his harsh criticism in *Sarugaku dangi* (Conversations on sarugaku; 1430) of provincial noh actors who repulse the shogun with their "countrified performance style" (*inaka no fūtei*).[15]

Although members of the military and court elite were not necessarily in attendance at every performance, shogunal patronage during the Muromachi period and later insured that the general composition of noh audiences often included some aristocratic component. Moreover, given that the shogun's most powerful vassals, the *shugo daimyō* (regional military governors), often followed his example in offering financial backing to selected art forms and artists, noh troupes were effectively performing to please more than one patron.[16] In a diary entry from 1378 (dated Eiwa 4/6/7),[17] Sanjō Kintada (1325–83), a palace minister, offers a scathing attack on *daimyō* who ingratiate themselves with the shogun by showering *sarugaku* actors (such as Zeami) with lavish gifts. Such resentment from a high-ranking court aristocrat underscores the extent of *daimyō* participation in the patronage of art and artists already in the late fourteenth century. Let us look briefly at the demographic composition of noh audiences across the three main contexts of performance.

Audience composition and distribution corresponded, for the most part, to the context of performance. The three principal theaters for noh performance and their respective audiences during the Muromachi and Azuchi-Momoyama periods were as follows: (1) performances staged at Shinto shrines and Buddhist temples before an audience of commoners; (2) performances staged at private residences before an audience of military and court aristocrats; and (3) performances staged at *kanjin nō* ("subscription performance") festivals before a mixed audience of commoners, warriors, and courtiers.[18] Following the institutionalization of shogunal patronage, though noh troupes continued to perform at shrines and temples, performing at private residences (usually the official mansions of high-ranking nobility) and subscription festivals proved to be much more lucrative.[19] Given this shift, it comes as no surprise that Zeami describes the attendance of military and court nobility as the "foundation" (*hon*) of noh performance.[20] Even at subscription performances, where multiple classes inhabited the same theater, the spatial distribution of the audience suggests that the performance was staged primarily for the shogun and his inner circle, secondarily for other high-ranking military and court aristocrats (and perhaps high-ranking priests), and lastly for commoners.[21] Although the best box in the *kanjin* theater was set aside for the gods (*kami*), who were situated immediately opposite the stage in galleries reserved for nobility, a noh troupe clearly stood to gain the most by impressing the shogun and his inner circle, who occupied the prestigious areas immediately adjacent to the gods' box. Generally, the shogun and his closest advisors sat to the left of the gods' box, whereas the shogun's principal wife and family sat to the right.

While the shogun and other high-ranking military and court aristocrats sat in raised and covered galleries (*sajiki*) at the rear of the theater, commoners were relegated to the open, uncovered area below the raised stage and surrounding aristocratic galleries.[22] As with any open-air theater, meteorological contingencies must have played some role, no matter how small, in the constitution of the audience's reception. But insofar as the noh stage, bridge, dressing room, and aristocratic galleries were all covered by an awning or roof, the vicissitudes of weather probably affected the popular audience much more than anyone else.

The mixture of these three audiences—symptomatic of contemporaneous sociopolitical changes taking place in Muromachi society, which allowed for much greater interaction between social classes than had been the case hitherto—was circumscribed by the highly differentiated zones of audience viewing. But such zones of viewing, while they might delimit the degree to which different social classes mixed, could not altogether prevent such cross-class mixing from taking place, since the frequently unruly and sometimes even violent popular audiences were known to intrude upon the enjoyment of the nobility.[23]

The architectural distribution of space in the *kanjin* noh theater makes it clear that the shogun's box was the actor's primary focus. Even when the shogun was not actually in attendance, other aristocrats, seated on either side of the shogun's box, insured that the actor performed for those sitting in the ring of power surrounding the stage. It should be added that, although such patronage mechanisms certainly informed the goals and strategies of noh troupes, it would be a mistake to assume that the existence of such power relations necessarily compromised the artistic aims of noh actors, especially since the fickleness of patronage required that noh troupes be ready to perform before any audience, whether in the capital or in the provinces, whether noble or common, whether cultivated or uncultivated.[24] For example, Kannami in-

sisted on the importance of performing as professionally before popular audiences in the provinces as before aristocratic audiences in the capital. Zeami
seems to have preferred aristocratic audiences but recognized that the consummate actor must be able to entertain any audience on any occasion. Even
after the death of Yoshimitsu, although later Ashikaga shoguns such as Yoshimochi (1386–1428) and Yoshinori (1394–1441) favored other troupes over
Zeami's, it seems that Zeami never lost sight of the importance and desir-
ability of shogunal patronage.

Zeami advised the noh actor, when confronted with a mixed audience of
aristocrats and commoners, always to perform to please the aristocrats first and
the commoners second. Harmonizing one's performance with aristocratic audience members was simply an application of the more general acting principle to attune one's performance to the contingencies of the moment. The
consummate noh actor should be able to perform on any occasion before any
audience, no matter what the circumstances.[25] Only by learning to respond to
the contingencies of the moment would the actor and his troupe be able to
weather the long-term vicissitudes of patronage. In *Shūgyoku tokka* (Gathering
jewels and gaining the flower; 1428), Zeami asserts the importance of attending to and harmonizing with the contingencies of performance marking a
particular occasion (*jisetsu ni kwa suru*), including circumstances pertaining to
the four seasons (*shiki*), day and night (*nichiya*), morning and evening (*chōbo*),
warm and cold (*unki/kanki*), inside and outside (*yanai/teizen*), large and small
theaters (*kōza/shōza*), and aristocratic and plebeian audiences (*kisenkunju*).[26]
Since each of these contingent conditions might give rise to either a successful or unsuccessful performance, the noh actor must be prepared to make
whatever adjustments necessary in order to take advantage of the opportunity
provided by the present performance occasion. Of course, given the unpre-
dictability of chance (*jibun*)[27]—whether divine or natural—Zeami recognized
that even if one possessed an understanding of the complex causality (*inga*) of
fortune, the quality of one's performance would still be influenced in the intervals of time (*toki no ma*) by the frequent oscillations of good luck (*odoki*, or
"male/masculine time") and bad (*medoki*, or "female/feminine time"), which
are beyond one's control:

> In the matter of good luck and bad luck, in every contest there inevitably comes
> a time when the performance becomes more colorful and more relaxed, and so
> a good turn of fortune comes about [*yoki jibun ni naru koto ari*]. An actor should
> look on this moment as one of good luck. In the case of a contest that contin-
> ues on for a considerable time, then luck will of its own accord change hands
> again and again from one side to the other [*ryōbō e utsurikawari utsurikawari*
> *subeshi*]. It is written that "both the god of victory [*katsu kami*] and the god of

defeat [*makuru kami*] are always present to decide the outcome of any contest. Such is a crucial secret in the way of the warrior [*yumiya no michi*]." Therefore, if the *sarugaku* of the enemy's side [*tekihō*] is doing well, the actor must realize that the god of victory [*shōjin*] dwells on the enemy's side and be awed accordingly. However, these two gods decide the fortune of cause and effect only for brief intervals [*toki no ma no inga noni*], so that luck switches again and again from one side to the other [*ryōbō e utsurikawari utsurikawarite*]; thus, if an actor is convinced that his turn of fortune [*wa ga kata no jibun*] will come, he will be able to perform noh with confidence. Such is the law of cause and effect within the place of a performance [*zashiki no uchi no inga nari*].[28]

Zeami advises the actor to look upon his performance in terms borrowed from the Japanese military arts: in order to emerge victorious on stage, the actor must learn to take tactical advantage of the contingent opportunities of good fortune as they present themselves during the course of doing battle with "enemies" from opposing troupes, as well as with various contingencies of the moment, whether natural or divine. Of course, on some occasions, the contingencies of the moment favor one's opponent so overwhelmingly that it is nearly impossible to be successful. In such situations, Zeami advises the actor to bide his time until the gods of victory and defeat turn the wheel of fortune back in his direction. Such military tropes serve not only to underscore the constitutive and often unpredictable contingencies of performance, but also to call attention to the fierce competition that pitted troupe against troupe in the struggle for patronage.

Noh Theatricalities:
Authorship, Performance, Impersonation

Extrapolating from the available evidence is perhaps the greatest difficulty facing any attempt to analyze the theatricalities of noh in its medieval contexts of performance: although the noh performed today offers some guidance, historical changes during the medieval and early modern periods make it difficult to imagine precisely how noh was performed in its premodern contexts. Certainly, Zeami's aesthetic and dramaturgical treatises provide us with a much greater wealth of practical performative knowledge for the study of noh than, say, Aristotle's *Poetics* does for the study of Greek tragedy, but in relation to numerous issues of performativity we are still in the position of having to read between the lines.

It goes without saying that the study of any premodern theatricality is made more difficult by the vicissitudes of its manuscript tradition. In the case of the manuscript history of noh texts (*yōkyoku*), since editorial accretion and revision have become part of the texts over time, it is often quite difficult to distinguish earlier textual layers from later ones. Moreover, the history of noh's transmission and reception is complicated by medieval conceptions and practices of noh authorship and attribution.

The issue of authorship and attribution in relation to the noh manuscript tradition is a matter of great complexity and debate. For example, a play such as *Aoi no Ue* has been attributed variously to Konparu Zenchiku (1405–70?), Inuō Dōami, and Zeami. Contemporary scholars generally agree that it is extremely unlikely, if not impossible, for Zenchiku to have composed the original text of *Aoi no Ue*, since the earliest extant performance record of the play is Zeami's mention in *Sarugaku dangi* of a performance by Dōami, which must have taken place in or before 1413, the year of Dōami's death. This means that Zenchiku would have been, at the most, eight years old at the time that he supposedly composed *Aoi no Ue*. Since this is extremely unlikely, many commentators have taken Zeami's high praise for Dōami's performance as evidence that Dōami himself was the original author of the play. But Zeami says only that Dōami performed the play, he never claims that he composed it. Thus it is probably a bit hasty to assume that Dōami was the original author. Another piece of evidence relating to the authorship of *Aoi no Ue* is in *Go on* (Five sounds; ca. 1432), in which Zeami quotes a passage from *Aoi no Ue* marking the entrance of the *shite* (primary actor) and suggests it is his own. But this could be interpreted as meaning simply that Zeami revised portions of the play (its words and/or music), such as the section quoted, *not* that he originally composed the entire play.[29]

Perhaps more interesting than an attempt to resolve the question of who originally authored *Aoi no Ue* is to pose the question of how the Muromachi conception of authorship is radically at odds with traditional Western conceptions of authorship, which remain bound up with metaphysical notions of authorial originality, intentionality, and property. This is not to say that no conception of authorship existed or that authors were of little or no importance; it is simply to suggest that the "author-function" in medieval Japan needs to be considered in its own context.[30] As the noh play *Tadanori* amply demonstrates with its dramatization of the eponymous hero's suffering over not receiving official recognition for his poem's inclusion in the seventh imperial poetry collection, *Senzaishū* (Collection of a thousand years), the authorship of *waka*—medieval Japan's supreme cultural form—was no trifling matter. However, it would be a mistake to assume that the authorship of *yōkyoku* was necessarily as proprietary as that of *waka*. As Monica Bethe and Richard Emmert have noted, a distinction needs to be drawn between those plays that were considered "general property," which any mature actor or playwright could modify to create new effects, and those whose performance rights were in some sense "protected" by virtue of their established association with a particular school, playwright, or style of performance and passed on by means of selective transmission.[31]

Zeami's own remarks in *Sandō* (Three ways; 1423) on the continual process of writing and rewriting by different authors, which most noh plays underwent to varying degrees, provides us with a unique perspective from which to approach the vertiginous contingencies of authorship and attribution during the medieval period, especially in relation to those older plays that were regarded as "general property":

> On the whole, many of the plays that have been written recently are actually based on older plays in which a few changes have been made in order to create new artistic effects [*sukoshi utsushitoritaru shinpū nari*]. . . . Depending on the varying taste in different periods, words are slightly altered, the music is renewed, and a new flower is created in response to changing times. In the future as well the same principle will continue to apply.[32]

According to Konishi Jin'ichi, during the medieval period "the modern concept of authorship did not exist. Remodeling, even outright appropriation, was done quite freely."[33] As a result, it is often difficult, if not impossible, to distinguish the so-called original text composed by the original author from the layers of revision, adaptation, and appropriation that have accumulated during the course of its circulation among subsequent troupes, playwrights, actors, and editors. Although the mechanisms of canonization would eventually put a damper on such revisionist spirit, as attribution lists centered around unifying authors began to proliferate during Edo (probably in response to the shogun-ordered standardization of noh), during Zeami's day, revision was not only acknowledged as a compositional practice: such rewriting was actively encouraged in order to produce "new artistic effects" (*shinpū*) that would better correspond to the specific demands and expectations of different audiences on different occasions.

Attributing a noh play such as *Aoi no Ue* to a *single* author, whether that author be Zenchiku, Dōami, Zeami, or some other playwright, effaces the multifarious contingencies of collective composition and reception in favor of the proprietary authority of a single, original author, who is thought to have produced a self-identical, autonomous work beyond the threat of contingent change and becoming. Such a conception of the author-function not only anachronistically domesticates the otherness of medieval Japanese cultural artifacts and textual practices, but also prevents us from seeing their linkages to artifacts and practices of earlier periods in Japanese literary history.

The pluralist conception of textual production and reception is not unique to the medieval period, but stretches back at least as far as the Heian period (if not earlier), in which the "participatory textual production" and revision of *monogatari* by multiple readers implied that "reception (*kyōju*) also meant creation (*sōsaku*)."[34] Indeed, such processes of collective textual production and reception, which blur the boundaries between literary composition, reception, and revision, probably also played an important role in the history of the earliest extant text of Japanese literature, the early-eighth-century mythopoetic historical chronicle of the *Kojiki* (Record of ancient matters), which seems to have been a product of collective authorship, involving multiple poets, reciters, and editors.

Medieval practices of authorship and revision meant that noh plays were open to the contingencies of restaging and rewriting that divided the singularity of a play's initial performance and created room for future innovations. Although the rest of this study attempts to map the singular traces that link the staging of specific noh plays to their respective, historically specific discourse networks, my interpretive performances in no way exclude the possibility of other performativities at other times and on other stages.

Other paradramatic contingencies influencing the reception of noh include editorial differences concerning the distribution of individual roles and lines, and the lack of specific information about staging practices and techniques in the medieval period. Role and line distributions, although they often can be inferred from the text, were not—until long after the Muromachi period—rigorously or consistently specified according to the current system:

1. *Shite*: primary actor; sometimes differentiated into *maejite* and *nochijite* to distinguish between the roles assumed in acts one and two of a two-act play

2. *Tsure* or *shitezure*: attendant actor accompanying the *shite*

3. *Waki*: secondary actor

4. *Wakizure*: attendant actor accompanying the *waki*

5. *Ji* or *jiutai*: chorus (typically composed of eight members)

6. *Ai* or *aikyōgen*: interlude actor

In the early texts of many noh plays, only the roles of *shite, waki,* and *ji* were originally indicated (if at all), leaving unspecified the roles now assigned to the *tsure, wakizure,* and *ai*. As a result, the two main noh manuscript traditions, the *kamigakari* and *shimogakari* recension lines, and the respective schools associated with the former (Kanze and Hōshō) and the latter (Konparu, Kongō, and Kita), differ not only in terms of textual and performance variants (*kogaki*) but also in terms of role and line distributions. However, such indeterminacies notwithstanding and despite our ignorance of many details relating to medieval noh theatricality, we are much better off than in the case of classical Greek theatricality because of the relative perdurability of noh as a performing art up until the present time. In what follows, I will give a brief overview of the most important elements of noh theatricality, and then follow this up with a closer look at the complex relations between actor, role, and character in noh.

Noh is a complex theatrical tapestry, intertwining intricate sequences of song, music, dance, and costume. The performance of noh involves a highly stylized configuration of the following elements:

1. *Utai*: vocal music (various forms of chant and recitation) performed by *shite, waki*, or *ji*[35]

2. *Hayashi*: instrumental music (which is rhythm- not melody-centered) played by an orchestra composed of flute (*fue* or *nōkan*), small hand drum (*kotsu-zumi*), large hand drum (*ōtsuzumi*), and sometimes large stick drum (*taiko*)[36]

3. *Kamae, kata*, and *katachi*: acting techniques consisting of fixed postures, movements, and forms

4. *Mai* or *shimai*: choreography (patterned body movements and dances accompanied by *utai* and *hayashi*)[37]

5. Costumes: robes (*kosode*, etc.), wigs (*kazura*), and masks (*omote*)[38]

6. Props: fans, swords, huts, boats, etc.

7. *Butai*: theater and stage architecture[39]

An enormous range of human affects and desires can be evoked on the noh stage through the multifarious interplay of music, song, dance, and poetry. The accomplished noh actor is able to suggest subtle affective nuances and finely hued gradations of psychological tonality through different body postures, mask movements, and dance patterns. For example, the ambiguous *hyō-gen*, or expression, of a noh mask can be altered in numerous ways by changing its angle vis-à-vis the play of light and shadow within a theater. Tilting the mask upward (*omote wo terasu*, "to illuminate the mask") creates a suggestion of joyfulness; whereas tilting it downward (*omote wo kumorasu*, "to cloud over the mask") places a shadow over the mask that suggests sadness. Likewise, the actor can simulate strong anger by quickly shifting the mask (*omote wo kiru*, "to cut the mask") from one side to the other.

According to Zeami, the ordering principle and process that interweaves all of these theatrical elements is *jo-ha-kyū*: *jo* refers to the slow tempo of a beginning, introduction, or preface; *ha* marks the temporal break into a medium tempo with correlated changes in tone and topical development; *kyū* is a rapid tempo that explodes into a climax until the cycle resumes again. In Zeami's usage, *jo-ha-kyū* is that which inflects the rhythmic composition and flow of an entire day-long program of plays, as well as each play within that program, each section and subsection within each play, each line or syllable of text, each measure or note of music, each bodily movement, gesture, or step.[40] Indeed, Zeami even extends *jo-ha-kyū* to the cyclical rhythms of transformation that differentiate time-space intervals in both the natural and human worlds.[41] From the macroscopic level to the microscopic level, everything is defined by the timing and spacing of *jo-ha-kyū*: in principle, even the individual phases of *jo*, *ha*, and *kyū* are animated by the overlapping cyclical rhythms of *jo-ha-kyū*.

Now let us turn to a discussion of medieval conceptions of performative impersonation and the relations between self and other in noh. Like other forms of staged drama, noh is a performative event, not merely a genre of literature.[42] To cut off noh from its various performative elements and patterns of combination is to sever its lifeline. Unfortunately, this is what happens every time we read a noh play as literature, insofar as the *kamigakari* and *shimogakari* textual lines function primarily as scripts to guide the singing, not the staging, of noh plays. Given that little precise information about the staging of noh during the medieval period can be extrapolated from the manuscripts themselves, it would be anachronistic to assume that noh was performed in the same manner during the medieval period as it is today. Therefore, wherever possible, I have drawn upon historical accounts of medieval performances in my remarks on the staging of noh, rather than projecting modern performance conventions onto the scene of its Muromachi and Azuchi-Momoyama enactments. Before turning to a more detailed analysis of role types and classifications, acting techniques, and the body of the actor, it should be useful to discuss from a comparative perspective that concept that has served as one of the ordering principles for most classical and medieval forms of Western drama: mimesis.

Most forms of drama presuppose some conception of the relations between actor, role, and character. In the history of Western theatricality, the way in which that performative triangle has been configured, enacted, and received is largely a function of how it has been situated in relation to the problem of mimesis and its related practices of imitation, impersonation, simulation, and identification. In a by now famous footnote in "La Double Séance," Jacques Derrida outlines the positions and consequences associated with Platonic mimesis, which he suggests forms a kind of logical machine, churning out all the propositions of the Western tradition and its "clichés of criticism."[43] According to this interpretation, later inscriptions of mimesis such as *imitatio*, *verisimilis*, *simulatio*, and so forth, are in some sense preprogrammed variations of Platonic mimesis.[44]

Although emerging from a completely different discursive and institutional history, noh playwrights such as Zeami also conceived of acting practices and processes in relation to a Japanese concept akin to mimesis, called *monomane*. Indeed, it is probably because of the similarities between *monomane* and mimesis that Western scholars of noh have often (mis)translated *monomane* as "imitation." Although "imitation" describes some of the effects produced by *monomane*, it drastically reduces the term's wide range of meaning and usage (which includes mimicry, miming, impersonation, and simulation, as well as nonrepresentational forms of becoming-other), and thereby conceals the alterity of medieval noh theatricality.

In the remainder of this section, I attend to the otherness of medieval conceptions of performative embodiment in noh by posing the following questions: What happens when a noh actor takes the stage and assumes a role? How does noh theatricality conceive of the space of acting? What is the relationship between acting in noh and the staging and scripting of the body? How does the actor-audience relationship figure into the space of noh acting?

Ever since the Edo period, when the Tokugawa shogunate adopted noh as the official state-sponsored form of entertainment and ordered the strict codification and formalization of every aspect of noh theatricality, noh has been identified with the taxonomy of plays, roles, and characters known as *gobandate*.[45] *Gobandate* differentiates the noh repertoire into a taxonomy of five play types (rather than "plots"), each centered around the principal character played by the *shite*, in the order in which they were ideally to be performed during the course of a day-long program of plays:

1. First-category pieces (*ichibanmemono*), or *kami noh* (also referred to as *waki noh*): "god plays" (e.g., *Takasago*, *Oimatsu*, *Yōrō*), involving the felicitous, celebratory manifestation of a divinity, initially disguised as an old man or woman, who bestows "auspicious blessings" (*shūgen*) upon the nation and present government, praying for "national harmony and peace"[46]

2. Second-category pieces (*nibanmemono*), or *shuramono*: "warrior plays" (e.g., *Atsumori*, *Sanemori*, *Tadanori*), involving the ghost of a warrior slain during the Genpei War (1180–85), who, in an attempt to attain release from his bad karma and obsession with vengeance, recounts the circumstances surrounding his own death, reenacting his death scene in a highly stylized dance

3. Third-category pieces (*sanbanmemono*), or *kazuramono*: "wig plays" (e.g., *Nonomiya*, *Izutsu*, *Matsukaze*), involving the ghost of a woman who tells a tale of unrequited love, having pined away after she could wait no longer for the return of her absent lover (other plays in this category include those about the spirits of nonsentient beings such as plants)

4. Fourth-category pieces (*yobanmemono*), or *kyōjomono*: "mad-woman plays" (e.g., *Aoi no Ue*, *Kinuta*, *Dōjōji*), involving a woman (or, in some cases, a man) who is driven mad by the violent emotions of love, jealousy, or yearning (this category is also referred to as *zatsumono*, "miscellaneous pieces,"

because it includes plays about vengeful female spirits, living warriors, and Chinese characters)

5. Fifth-category pieces (*gobanmemono*), or *kichikumono* (also referred to as *kiri noh*, "end noh," because it is the final play of the day): "demon plays" (e.g., *Rashōmon*, *Tōru*, *Kappo*), involving a being with a human body and a demon's heart, or a demon's body and a human heart, who terrorizes those it encounters until the very end, when it attains release from its karmic chains and enters Nirvana

According to this Edo-period taxonomy, 17 percent of the current repertoire of approximately 250 plays falls into the first category, 7 percent into the second, 18 percent into the third, 36 percent into the fourth, and 22 percent into the fifth.[47]

Though the five-play cycle was the Tokugawa ideal, it certainly was not the typical Muromachi reality: a Muromachi program often consisted of as few as two or three performances, or as many as seventeen, in addition to the farcical *kyōgen* interludes that were performed between noh plays in order to provide comic relief.[48] Moreover, it has been calculated on the basis of documented examples of fifteen- and seventeen-play programs, performed between dawn and dusk during the Muromachi period, that, whereas individual plays presently take between an hour and two hours to perform, the Muromachi performance average could have taken no more than forty to forty-five minutes.[49]

The most common taxonomy in use today, which was developed in the 1950s by Yokomichi Mario,[50] divides the noh repertoire into two broad categories:

1. *Genzai* noh: "contemporary noh," involving a historical figure who appears (usually without a mask) as a person who is presently living in the world and who is placed in a conflictual relationship with one of his contemporaries

2. *Mugen* noh: "phantasmal noh," involving a supernatural figure (usually wearing a mask), such as the ghost or spirit of a vanquished hero or unrequited lover, who returns to the site of battle or courtship disguised as a local inhabitant in order to recount[51] his or her personal tragedy to the *waki* (usually a traveler or itinerant priest[52]); at the end of the play, the *waki* awakens from the phantasmal spell as if from a dream

Although most people today conceive of noh in terms of these two taxonomies (*gobandate* and *genzai/mugen* noh), they should be used with some caution since neither was employed as such during the Muromachi period, but only came to be codified and formalized much later. Indeed, such codification and formalization, which was actively encouraged during the Edo period by the Tokugawa shogunate, is largely responsible for turning noh into the anti-

quarian museum piece it is today.[53] Perhaps the greatest danger of such antiquarianism is the myth of metaphysical preservation that it fosters: that is, the
presumption that it is possible to shield the "essence" of noh from the change
and becoming that invariably alter, whether explicitly or imperceptibly, the
form and function of every cultural practice during the course of its history.[54]

Over two hundred years before the introduction of *gobandate* and *genzai/
mugen* noh, a very different practice of categorizing plays and roles was in use
during the Muromachi period—when most noh plays were being written—
one that presupposed a nonrepresentational conception of *monomane*. According to Zeami, noh consists of "two arts" (*nikyoku*), which are dance and song
(*buga*), and "three bodies" (*santai*)—the "old person's body" (*rōtai*), the "woman's body" (*nyotai*), and the "warrior's body" (*guntai*). Zeami considered the
three bodies to be the main types of dramatic enactment that must be mas-
tered by an actor if he is to perform the wide variety of roles encountered in
the noh repertoire. The three bodies pertain to the specific dramatic decorum
associated with performing the roles of beneficent gods and tranquil old men
(in the old person's body); jealous, mad, and forlorn women (in the woman's
body); and fierce warriors and frightening demons (in the warrior's body).[55]
What precisely is the object of *monomane* according to the theory of the three
bodies? When a noh actor enacts one of the three bodies, does his *monomane*
merely imitate that body? Or does something else take place?

Although *santai*[56] has often been translated as "three modes," "three styles,"
or "three types," I have translated it as "three bodies" in order to preserve its
distinctive corporeality. The *tai* of *santai* is a Chinese graph—also pronounced
karada in Japanese—which can refer to bodies, physical organisms, or corpses,
as well as to forms, shapes, appearances, styles, or modes.[57] Zeami underscores the corporeality of *santai* by stating right at the outset of *Shikadō* (Way
to attaining the flower; 1420): "What I call *santai* are the human bodies of
monomane" (*santai to mōsu wa monomane no jintai nari*).[58] Here Zeami's usage
of the term *jintai* (human bodies) suggests that *santai* are more corporeal
than mere "modes," "styles," or "forms." This emphasis on corporeality is also
readily apparent in the sketches of unclad bodies found in *Nikyoku santai nin-
gyōzu* (Human-figure sketches for the two arts and three bodies; 1421), where
Zeami emphasizes the physicality of bodies, postures, and movements associated with the old person, woman, and warrior.[59] Though the medieval audience never had an opportunity to see the naked body of the actor on stage,
concealed as it was under so many layers of costume, the point seems to be
that the actor must *become* the body of the character to such a degree that the
audience imagines just such a body underneath the actor's elaborate costume
and mask.[60]

In *Shūgyoku tokka* Zeami provides us with his most interesting reflections on the corporeality of the three bodies as objects of *monomane*. The first object of *monomane* is the body of the old person, described as "calm heart, distant gaze" (*kanshin enmoku*):

> The actor must learn to keep his mind calm and to look off into the distance. (As the eyesight of old persons is hazy, the suggestion is that the old person looks off vaguely into the distance.) Such is the elegant appearance [*fūtei*][61] of the old person's body. If the actor can put both his body posture [*minari*][62] and mind into this and then perform both chant and dance correctly, while carrying the figure of his body [*jintai*] in an appropriate manner, he will enter into the essence of the role he is playing and so achieve the sphere of accomplishment appropriate for an old person's body [*rōtai no gaibun*].[63]

The second object of *monomane* is the body of the woman, described as "body-mind, abandoned strength" (*taishin shariki*):

> An actor must concentrate his attention on producing an inner intensity and abandon any detailed stress on his physical movements (since, if he infuses the figure with the feminine mind, a relaxation of physical strength will surely come about of itself). If he can carry out these principles in his own performance of the two arts, he will have entered the sphere of accomplishment as concerns a woman's body.[64]

Finally, the third object of *monomane* is the body of the warrior, described as "body-strength, fragmented heart" (*tairiki saishin*):

> (Although a manifestation of strength is the most important element in such a role, the subtle movements of the actor's mind must be fully exploited.) Here, although the actor must show the strength of his outward movements, he must bear in mind the necessity for preserving the subtleties of his inner posture. If the actor can develop this ability in mind and body alike, he can, when he exhibits these skills, enter into the sphere of accomplishment of a warrior's body.[65]

Of these three bodies, Zeami writes that "the performance by a man of a woman's posture is the most difficult accomplishment of all":

> If the actor can take the concept of "body-mind, abandoned strength" as a basis for his performance, and his elegant figure becomes the body and spirit of the woman through and through, he can achieve this sphere of accomplishment of a woman's body. But if he does not take these matters to heart but merely tries to imitate the woman [*tada onna ni nisen to bakari wa*], he cannot attain the sphere of accomplishment of a woman's body. To imitate a woman is not to be a woman [*onna wo nisuru wa onna narazu*]. But if the real essence of a woman comes into being through an actor's internalization of the woman's figure [*nyoshi no ushufū ni shinjitsu narite koso*], then it is the sphere of accomplishment appropriate to the woman's body. (The stage of mere imitation represents a surface copy, mere ex-

ternalization [*mushufū*];[66] becoming the essence of a character represents internalization [*ushufū*].[67] After attaining the level of internalization, it may be possible for an actor to then return and create the external aspects of his performance as well.) These two distinctions—internalization and externalization—must be thoroughly understood. The same concepts apply to the role of an old person. With a full grasp of the concept of "calm heart, distant gaze," the actor becomes one with that part [*sono bun ni nariiritaraba*] and so achieves the sphere of accomplishment of the old person's body. The same applies to each of the three bodies.[68]

The noh actor does not merely imitate, represent, or simulate action or character; rather, the actor *becomes other*—becoming the otherness of the role, becoming the other's body. It is not simply that the actor makes the role his own; rather, he allows himself to be made other, releasing himself into the otherness of the role, allowing his body to be used as a "vessel" or "receptacle" (*ki, kimotsu*) for the body of the other, as Zeami suggests in *Yūgaku shūdō fūken* (Viewpoints on noh training; ca. 1424).[69] Zeami conceives of the corporeality of the three bodies in such a way that rather than breathing life into a character, the noh actor *embodies* a role—becoming the body of the other as if possessed. The noh actor's performance of the role exemplifies an aesthetics of internalized "alterity" rather than of externalized "expression," operating at the level of embodiment (the turning into the body of the other) rather than of representation (the imitation of the other's body). Of course, this is not to say that there is no place in noh for the circulation of representations; it is simply to recognize the importance of nonrepresentational forms of performativity on the medieval noh stage.

Despite its minimalist approach to set design and stage properties, it would be difficult to deny the significant role played by representations—whether iconic, symbolic, or otherwise—in noh, especially given that *monomane* also includes more straightforward examples of imitation and mimicry. But if one follows the implications of Zeami's theory of acting with its immanentist ontology of the other's body, then *monomane*, in addition to representing superficial aspects of the body, also includes the possibility of *becoming* the body of the other.

Pursuing this notion further, one discovers that the corporeality of the actor's body is situated in a rather peculiar fashion: the body of the other is not simply the everyday body of the actor disguised as an other, but rather an *incorporeal* body imago,[70] or *virtual body*. Here I am using "imago" in a Lacanian sense as an imaginary template or configuration, which is not reducible to an image or representation. Though the body-role performed by the noh actor has sometimes been described as a "fictive body,"[71] I would resist labeling the body imago in this way, since Zeami's Buddhist-influenced conception of the three bodies does not so clearly differentiate the "fictive" body from the "real" body. The fact that Zeami's conception does not enact such a differentiation is related to the complex ways in which the noh actor embodies the otherness of the body imago. I think it would be more apt to describe the body of the other on the noh stage as a virtual body, one that effectively transforms the actor's body into an embodied other. Underneath the actor's costume and mask is the body of the actor transformed into the virtual body of the other. When the actor becomes one of the three bodies, he embodies that other's body imago—his physical body becomes a vessel for the virtual body of the old person, the woman, or the warrior. As we shall see below, insofar as the virtual bodies circulating on the noh stage were constructed by the creative gaze of male playwrights and actors in an effort to appeal to the aesthetic tastes and cultural aspirations of their military aristocratic patrons, who were also men, such virtual corporeality is inscribed not only by the mechanisms of shogunal patronage that sponsored it, but also by the gender politics of medieval patriarchal institutions.

In practice, the transformation of the noh actor into the body of the other is accomplished through exhaustive training (*keiko*), involving the internalization and mastery of hundreds of individual body postures, steps, movements, rhythms, and gestures that are linked together into integrated bodily patterns and dances.[72] A veritable grammar of the body—with its own rules of selection and combination—is used by noh actors to guide them in playing different roles. But while the imitation of such body postures and gestures is an important aspect of *monomane*, Zeami insists that the *monomane* of the body's "essence" is more important than the imitation of the body's "surface."

Zeami's theory of acting presupposes an ontology of the other's body: not the word made flesh, but the imago made flesh. When the noh actor embodies the old person, woman, or warrior, he does not possess the body of the other, rather he is possessed by the "essence" of that other's virtual body imago. Among the various terms Zeami uses for the "essence" of the body of the other, perhaps the most interesting is *hon'i*, which can be translated as original essence, primordial substance, or real intention.[73]

Zeami's usage of *hon'i*, like so many of his aesthetic terms and formulas, is derived largely from twelfth-century *waka* and *renga* poetics. Although *hon'i* (Chinese, *pen-i*) was first used in Japanese literary history during the tenth century as an evaluative poetic term to indicate that a given poem had fulfilled conventional, often stereotypical, poetic expectations and codes, twelfth-century poets such as Fujiwara no Teika (1162–1241) redefined *hon'i* to refer to the essential "nature," "form," or "spirit" (*kokoro*) of a given poetic topic. In order to reveal *hon'i*, the *waka* poet had to focus his attention not on superficial aspects of the poetic topic, but rather on the "essence" of the topic as it lay within his own mind. In other words, the poet had to become one with the subject of his poem in order to disclose its poetic "essence" (*hon'i*). This moment of mystical fusion between poet and poem, which Teika refers to as *ushin* (intense feeling and concentration), owes much to esoteric Buddhist conceptions of mystical identification (*shikan*) between a religious practitioner and Buddhist iconographic art.[74]

According to Zeami's ontology of *hon'i*, the other's body imago is not a *transcendental* essence, but rather an *immanent* one that gives virtual shape to the configuration of the actor's physical body. Two aspects of noh theatrical-ity that further complicate this scene of becoming-other involve the donning of masks and reflexive relations between actor and audience, topics to which I now turn.

Before going onstage, the noh performer enacts the aesthetics of alterity in a ceremonial donning of the mask, which takes place offstage in the para-dramatic space of the "mirror room" (*kagami no ma*). Though audience mem-bers do not actually see this preliminary ceremony, they imagine it taking place. Here is a description of the mask ceremony by a twentieth-century noh performer:

> Just before going onstage the *shite* sits before a mirror (in the mirror room) fac-ing his own reflected image and puts on the mask. As he gazes intently through the tiny pupil eyeholes at the figure in the mirror, a kind of willpower is born, and the image—another self, that is, an other—begins to approach the actor's everyday internal self, and eventually the self and this other absorb one another to become a single existence transcending self and other. . . . [T]he functions of mirror and mask merge as a spirit is incarnated and the self transformed by the magic of strengthened auto-suggestion. When the time comes to go onstage, he fixes in his mind the stage as the mirror and himself as the image and then de-votes himself completely to the magic of performance, which is meant to be shared with the audience and its group mind.[75]

The noh mask (*omote*) does not disguise the face of the actor; rather, the ac-tor's face *becomes* the face of the other through the spirit of the mask. The mask is not worn like a hat, but is "affixed" or "joined" (*tsukeru*) to the actor's face, becoming "a part of [his] body."[76] The mirror room is the "space of transformation"[77] where the actor becomes other, possessed by the spirit of the mask and the body of the other. Indeed, it is partly due to the shamanis-tic connotations of this scene of masking that many scholars have interpreted noh as a sort of staged exorcism, a reinscription of the rites and rituals of ex-orcism performed by Buddhist priests and shamans throughout the medieval period.[78] Noh's links to the history of spiritual possession are underscored not only by how often it stages different types of spiritual possession—whether by gods and demons (*kamikuchi*), the spirits of the dead (*shinikuchi*), or the spirits of the living (*ikikuchi*)[79]—but also by the frequency with which it addresses the complaints of dispossessed victims, who haunt their victimizers (or their victimizers' descendants) until they gain release from worldly attachment with the help of a priest or shaman.

In regard to the scene of possessive othering that takes place in the mirror room, Zeami's aesthetics of alterity, rather than simply dissolving the self into the other, produces multiple effects of reflexivity between self and other. It is possible to schematize these multiple effects into three different stages of increasing complexity: (1) The actor sees the image of the other in the mirror as himself in a moment of transcendental self-referentiality (i.e., the self occupies the place of the other). (2) The actor sees himself as an image of the other that is in the mirror, exemplifying the intertwinement of self-referential transcendence and other-referential immanence (i.e., the self as other viewing the self as other). (3) The actor sees himself seeing himself as the other in a moment of transcendental-immanent self-other-referentiality (i.e., the self outside of the self as the other occupies the place of the self).[80] What prevents this dialectic between seeing and being seen from becoming a proto-Hegelian formulation of "pure self-recognition in absolute otherness"[81] is its vertiginous hyperreflexivity, which leads to the utter collapse of firm boundaries between self and other. As soon as the actor-as-other takes the stage, he enters into a similar dialectic with the audience, which Zeami glosses in *Kakyō* (Mirror of the flower; 1424) as "the eyes look ahead and the mind looks behind" (*mokuzen shingo*):

> As concerns the dance, it is said that "the eyes look ahead and the mind looks behind." This means that the actor looks in front of him with his physical eyes, but his mind must be directed to the appearance of his movements from behind. This is a crucial element in the creation of what I have referred to above as the movement beyond consciousness [*buchi fūtei*]. The appearance of the actor, seen from the spectator in the seating area, produces a different image than the actor can have of himself. What the spectator sees is the outer image of the actor. What an actor himself sees, on the other hand, forms his own internal image of himself. He must make still another effort in order to grasp his own internalized outer image, a step possible only through assiduous training. Once he obtains this, the actor and the spectator can share the same perspective [*kensho dōshin no ken*]. Only then can it actually be said that an actor has truly grasped the nature of his appearance.[82]

Here multiple effects of reflexivity and alterity are played out between actor and spectator both in terms of self-referentiality, which Zeami refers to as *gaken no ken* ("vision of self-vision" or "self-reflexive perspective"), and other-referentiality, which he calls *riken no ken* ("vision of separate vision" or "detached perspective"):[83] first, the actor sees himself from his own perspective; next, the actor sees himself from the perspective of the audience; finally, the actor sees himself seeing himself from the perspective of the audience. The various strands of noh theatricality that I have considered here, such as *monomane*, the virtual body, and reflexive oscillations between self and other, are brought together in particularly dramatic fashion in the climactic scene of *Matsukaze*.

Matsukaze tells the story of two ghostly sisters, Matsukaze and Murasame, who pined away after their aristocratic lover, Ariwara no Yukihira (818–93), abandoned them in Suma Bay, southwest of Kyoto. The two sisters have haunted the area ever since, awaiting the return of their lover, who is himself no longer alive. In the climactic scene of the play, Murasame watches in amazement as Matsukaze slips into a state of derangement, donning Yukihira's keepsake cap and robe and dancing as if possessed by the spirit of Yukihira, while the chorus serves as her mouthpiece:

> Kore wo miru tabi ni
> Iya mashi no omoigusa
> Hazue ni musubu tsuyu no ma mo
> Wasurareba koso ajikinaya. . . .
> Wasuregatami mo yoshinashi to
> Sutete mo okarezu
> Toreba omokage ni tachimasari.

> Every time I look at them,
> my tangled thoughts grow in ever greater profusion;
> for even as briefly as the dew clings to the leaf tips,
> if only I could forget—how miserable I am! . . .
> His keepsakes, difficult to forget, do me no good!
> Though I discard them, I cannot let them lie;
> picking them up again, his visage haunts me once more.[84]

The challenge facing the actor of this role is that he must become the otherness of both Matsukaze and her lover Yukihira: in effect, the audience is presented with a scene of double cross-dressing, in which a male actor plays a woman playing a man.[85] Complicating matters even further, at the same time that she assumes the demeanor of Yukihira, Matsukaze also mistakes a pine tree on stage—which earlier served as the two sisters' grave marker—for Yukihira, thus simultaneously embodying Yukihira's otherness and also seeing that otherness projected onto the pine tree. In the phantasmal interchange between Matsukaze and Yukihira, the pine tree oscillates between presence and absence, self and other: the presencing of absence and the othering of the self. As soon as the possessed Matsukaze tries to reach out to Yukihira *as* Yukihira by embracing the pine tree signifying "Yukihira," the pine tree reemerges as a pine tree, dispelling the phantasmic signification of Yukihira and dashing Matsukaze's hopes of reunion.

The net result of the pine tree's duplicitous signification, as well as Matsukaze's transformation into Yukihira, is that even as Matsukaze becomes Yukihira, the prosopopoeia of Yukihira that is conjured up by the pining imagination of Matsukaze becomes the grave marker of Matsukaze, thus oscillating between multiple levels of reflexive alterity. Life and death, self and other, referent and figure, are inextricably intertwined in the figure of the represented, absent Yukihira. Paul de Man defines prosopopoeia as "the fiction of an apostrophe to an absent, deceased or voiceless entity, which posits the possibility of the latter's reply and confers upon it the power of speech."[86] Insofar as the figure posits voice and face "by means of language," it asserts a trope of life that defaces our "linguistic predicament" (what de Man calls "death"): namely, our inability to gain access to the so-called "external" world, or reality "in-itself," outside of the linguistic sphere of tropes. Prosopopoeia reanimates the other self, the self as other—in many cases, an other self long dead.

The elasticity of classical Japanese syntax, with its frequent shifts in perspective and omission of a specified subject, heightens this play of self and other even further. Caught in a vicious circle of karmic attachment and substitution, Matsukaze recites a poem by Yukihira that puns on the encrypted tropes of "pine" and "pining" in the name of "Matsukaze" (both "pine wind" and "pining wind"). Matsukaze thus identifies herself with the prosopopoeia Yukihira—a figure stretched between life and death, simulating a "voice-from-beyond-the-grave"[87]—at the same time that she distinguishes herself from him in her recitation by offering a variation on Yukihira's original poem: "Though we may be apart for awhile, if *I* hear that *you* pine for *me*, I will return" (*tatoi shibashi wa wakaruru to mo matsu toshi kikaba kaerikon*); or alternatively: "Though we may be apart for awhile, if *you* hear that *I* pine for *you*, might *you* return?"[88] Similar scenes of self-other referentiality and becoming-other can be found in countless *mugen* noh.[89] Indeed, it could be said that most *mugen* noh—that is, over half of the current repertoire of approximately 250 plays—stage in some fashion the dynamics of reflexive alterity and the transformation of self into its other.

Reconsidering Yūgen*: From Lyricism to Symbolic Capital*

Although Zeami never wrote in any of his treatises that the characters in noh speak "politically"—as did Aristotle in his *Poetics* (1450b6) in regard to the characters in early Greek tragedy—nevertheless, Zeami's aesthetics of alterity is historically marked by the political ambition to secure and maintain patronage from the ruling military aristocracy upon which it depended. In other words, playwrights such as Zeami recognized that not just any characters should be embodied on the noh stage, but only such as might appeal to the imagination of the audience, especially members of the shogun's inner circle, who sought in noh the symbolic power of *yūgen*.[90]

In *Sandō*, Zeami singles out for special praise plays in which "female bodies of the nobility" (*kinin no nyotai*) are depicted, such as in dramatizations of spiritual possession from *Genji monogatari* (*Tale of Genji*) involving Yūgao, Aoi, and Ukifune, which, in their display of aristocratic appeal, embody "*yūgen* at the highest level" (*yūgen mujō no kurai*).[91] Probably under the influence of the poetics of Nijō Yoshimoto (1320–88), *yūgen* is delineated by Zeami as an aristocratic aesthetic of darkly mysterious and sublime elegance strongly associated with the conduct of the court nobility: their ceremonial rituals, artistic interests, haute couture fashions, graceful manners, distinguished demeanor, and refined speech. Correlatively, Zeami discouraged members of his troupe from imitating *too realistically* the behavior of commoners, even when a particular play called for the portrayal of a lowly salt maker, charcoal burner, wood cutter, or other laborer, since such commonplace subjects were only deemed dramatically interesting to the extent that they could be rendered more poetic than they actually were.[92]

Arthur Thornhill III has argued recently that in comparison with the philosophical profundity delineated by Zeami's son-in-law Konparu Zenchiku in his theoretical treatises, in which *yūgen* is ontologically equated with Buddha Nature (*busshō*), Zeami's notion of *yūgen* is practically "superficial."[93] Without denying the esoteric complexities of Zenchiku's engagement, one could read Zeami's positioning of *yūgen* not only as implying a lack of "depth," but more importantly for a micropolitical reading, as suggesting that it is more akin to "symbolic capital" than to the "lyrical essence" to which it has all too often been reduced by modern commentators, from Nogami Toyoichirō to Kanze Hisao. Although the ontology of *yūgen* is undoubtedly important to anyone interested in studying the theoretical history of the term, in practice the sociopolitical function of *yūgen* as symbolic capital seems to have exerted even greater influence upon the medieval performance of noh.

Here I follow the usage of Pierre Bourdieu, who employs the term "symbolic capital" to refer to the idea, historically inflected by the specific sociocultural field in which it operates, that

> struggles for recognition are a fundamental dimension of social life and that what is at stake in them is the accumulation of a particular form of capital, honour in the sense of reputation and prestige, and that there is, therefore, a spe-

cific logic behind the accumulation of symbolic capital, as capital founded on cognition [*connaissance*] and recognition [*reconnaissance*].[94]

Symbolic capital, as Bourdieu conceives it, is relatively unstable, difficult to transmit, objectify, or quantify, and not easily convertible.[95] Moreover, the specific efficacy of symbolic capital works only when "it is *misrecognized* in its arbitrary [and contingent] truth as capital and *recognized* as legitimate."[96]

Viewed in a Bourdieuian light, Zeami's notion of *yūgen* codifies at the level of aesthetic discourse what had already been operative at the level of material practice: medieval noh troupes vied for support from economically affluent and politically connected patrons by producing symbolic capital that appealed to the imaginations of those who were already culturally "elite" (i.e., court aristocrats), as well as those upwardly mobile individuals who aspired to become culturally "elite" (e.g., the shogun and his *daimyō*).[97] In other words, rather than hypostatizing *yūgen* into an ontological first principle or transcendental signified animating noh performance *in toto*, *yūgen* may be viewed as symptomatic of the field-specific investments of symbolic capital made and renewed by noh troupes in an effort to secure their own future.

By the time Zeami wrote in praise of the *yūgen* of noh, Yoshimitsu's sponsorship had already helped noh become an "aristocratic" art form, or at least an art form possessing "aristocratic" pretensions and "aristocratic" symbolic capital. Even the philosophically recondite Zenchiku seems to confirm *yūgen*'s status as symbolic capital in *Kabu zuinōki* (An account of the essentials of song and dance; 1456), where he writes that the art of noh flourished once Yoshimitsu came into power, insofar as the shogun and his circle demanded performances exemplifying the aristocratic ideal of *yūgen*.[98] Moreover, Zenchiku adds in *Yūgen sanrin* (Three circles of *yūgen*) that if an actor's performance did not manifest *yūgen*, then he could not possibly hope to appeal to the aesthetic tastes of the nobility.[99]

By the late fourteenth century, noh started to function for the first time as a mechanism for the acquisition, circulation, and display of cultural authority, but it is worth recalling that this had not always been the case. Noh had not always been considered an "aristocratic" form of theatricality, nor had it always appealed to an "aristocratic" audience. In response to the popular origins of noh, as well as to the low-ranking status of most noh actors, playwrights, and musicians, court aristocrats initially sought to dissociate themselves from what they regarded as a lowly art form practiced by a disreputable "band of beggars."[100]

After a few years of shogunal patronage, even the snobbiest of court aristocrats could no longer ignore the fashionable new "aristocratic" dramatic form that noh had become. By 1383, more and more court aristocrats began to attend noh performances, both at private residences and at subscription festivals. Though some courtiers continued to denounce Yoshimitsu's patronage of noh, many more came to recognize that they were no longer in a position to turn down an invitation from Yoshimitsu or to openly reject or disapprove of Yoshimitsu's cultural investments without incurring his disfavor.[101]

In a strange turn of events, court aristocrats began to imitate the cultural interests and practices of military aristocrats such as Yoshimitsu, insofar as their continued survival depended to a large extent on the generosity of the military elite. Soon even imperial sovereigns—both reigning and retired—were attending special noh performances at the imperial palace, the retired sovereign's palace, and the shogun's mansion.[102] Given that the military aristocrats' patronage of noh was originally an attempt to imitate the *yūgen* associated with traditional court culture, the court aristocrats' reverse emulation of military aristocratic culture exhibits a rivalry born of mimetic desire.[103] This scene of culturo-political mimetic desire unfolds in the fourteenth through sixteenth centuries as follows: with the economic and political decline of the court aristocracy and the rise of the military aristocracy, the military elite—desiring to become as powerful culturally as they were politically—actively imitated the cultural objects of desire favored by the traditional arbiters of taste: the court nobility. Through their patronage of architecture, painting, poetry, music, dance, drama, and tea ceremony, military aristocrats such as Ashikaga Yoshimitsu and other shoguns in the Ashikaga dynasty and after were able to acquire the cultural prestige and authority they had long sought.[104] Finally, once the military aristocracy became the new patrons of the arts, usurping the position previously held by the court aristocracy, court aristocrats were compelled to follow the examples set by their precocious imitators.

Although Ashikaga Yoshimitsu's institutionalization of shogunal patronage during the late fourteenth and early fifteenth centuries for the country's most accomplished noh troupes was the first time a shogun had ever officially sponsored noh, it certainly was not the last. Indeed, following Yoshimitsu's example, almost every subsequent ruler of the late medieval and early modern periods also extended such patronage, thereby guaranteeing the eventual canonization and monumentalization of noh as Japan's "classical" form of drama par excellence during Edo.

In Part II of this study, "Powers of Performativity," I investigate the micropolitics of medieval culture through a close reading of *Aoi no Ue*. The theatricalities of spiritual possession on the noh stage are situated in relation to the harsh materialities of socioeconomic dispossession experienced by women in the service of the further consolidation of shogunal authority and its differentiation from imperial authority.

PART TWO

Powers of Performativity

CHAPTER 2

The Politics of Exorcism in Aoi no Ue

Framing the Scene of Possession

Before *Aoi no Ue* begins, a stage attendant brings out a folded *kosode* (narrow-sleeved) brocade kimono signifying Lady Aoi, and lays it at the front of the stage.[1] Though the play is named after her, Aoi speaks no lines during the performance and appears onstage only as a mute signifier, lying prostrate and motionless in the form of this empty *kosode* kimono. After the preplay "entrance" of Aoi, the play itself begins with the spoken self-introduction (*nanori shōdan*) of the *wakizure*, an imperial retainer, who wastes no time in identifying himself and the scene of possession at hand:

> Somosomo kore wa Shujakuin ni tsukaetatematsuru shinka nari. Satemo sadaijin no onsokujō Aoi no Ue no onmono no ke motte no hoka ni gozasōrō hodo ni kisō kōsō wo shōjimōsare daihō hihō iryō samazama no onkoto nite sōraedomo sara ni sono shirushi nashi. Koko ni Teruhi no miko tote kakurenaki azusa no jōzu no sōrō wo shōji ikiryō shiryō no aida wo azusa ni kakemōsabaya to zonjisōrō.

> Here before you now is a retainer in the service of Emperor Shujaku. The malevolent spirit possessing the Minister of the Left's daughter Lady Aoi has recently proven to be excessively strong. So we have summoned venerable priests of great virtue to perform various secret rites and medical cures, but there have been no signs of improvement. I shall invite someone here called Teruhi the Shamaness, a well-known and highly skilled catalpa-bow diviner, and have her determine by plucking the string of a catalpa bow whether it is the spirit of someone living or dead.[2]

This opening scene takes place sometime in the middle of the Heian period (794–1185) beside the sickbed of Aoi in the mansion of her father, the Minister of the Left. An imperial retainer describes the worsening condition of Aoi, who is caught in the clutches of a malevolent spirit (*onmono no ke*) that is *motte no hoka*, "excessively strong"—literally, exceeding the boundaries of normality, thrusting her into the realm of the extraordinary. As would have been obvious to most Muromachi playwrights and audiences familiar with *Genji monogatari* (or at least familiar with one of the various plot summaries and poetic digests of *Genji monogatari* circulating at the time),[3] Aoi's sickness was profoundly connected with and complicated by the fact that she was pregnant with the child of her husband, the eponymous hero of *Genji monogatari*, Hikaru Genji (Shining Genji). It was widely believed during Heian and subsequent periods that the emotional and physical distress of pregnancy made a woman more vulnerable to spiritual attacks, and that difficulties suffered during pregnancy and childbirth were caused by the baleful influence of the spirits of living or dead rivals.[4]

In *Genji monogatari*, Aoi's pregnancy is never explicitly mentioned as such, but only alluded to as her "unusual condition" (*mezurashiki koto*), or her "condition of discomfort" (*kokorogurushiki sama*).[5] *Mezurashiki koto* and *kokorogurushiki sama* are conventional Heian euphemisms for the emotional and physical stresses suffered during pregnancy. It is precisely such psychophysical distress that places Aoi in a position of vulnerability in which she is open to attacks by malevolent spirits. Though the references in *Aoi no Ue* to Aoi's pregnancy are even more oblique, such obliquity in no way lessens the importance of her pregnancy as the framework within which the scene of her possession unfolds. Given the extraordinary popularity of *Genji monogatari* throughout the medieval period, it is probably safe to assume that a Muromachi audience would have been well aware of the "unusual condition" informing the tale of Aoi's possession. A variant performance of *Aoi no Ue*, called *Mumyō no inori*, in which Aoi is signified by a white *kosode* robe, makes this connection more explicit, insofar as white robes were commonly worn during the Heian period by women in childbirth.[6]

On the stage of *Aoi no Ue*, the imperial retainer reports that venerable priests have already been summoned to perform various rites and treatments, but it has been to no avail: the empty signifier of Aoi has shown no signs (*shirushi*) of improvement, no signs that she has escaped the grasp of the possessing spirit. Therefore, a shamaness (*miko*) called Teruhi (whose name means "shining sun") has been summoned to ply her skill at catalpa-bow divination and force the spirit to disclose its identity. It was believed throughout the medieval period that a shamaness could, by plucking a bow made of catalpa wood, enter a trance and summon forth an evil spirit, forcing it both to identify itself and reveal its motives for possession. If Teruhi can compel the malevolent spirit possessing Aoi to identify itself and articulate its motives, then she might be able to successfully placate and exorcise it. However, before introducing Teruhi the Shamaness, let us step back for a moment and consider the sociopolitical dynamics enframing this scene of spiritual possession and exorcism. How was exorcism enacted on the stage of medieval Japan?

Sociopolitical Aspects of Japanese Spiritual Possession

Exorcism, or the ritualistic appeasement and expulsion of evil spirits, played a very important role within the discourse networks of early, middle, and late medieval Japanese history. Medieval Japanese history is overflowing with stories of spiritual possession and the rites of exorcism performed both to placate and to drive away malign spirits. Jien (1155–1225), the early Kamakura poet, historian, and archbishop of the Tendai sect of Buddhism, recounts the most frightful sociopolitical ramifications, issuing from encounters with malevolent spirits, in his wide-ranging historical treatise on the principles of government, *Gukanshō* (The future and the past; 1219–20):

> Since ancient times, there has been the principle that vengeful spirits ruin the state and destroy man [*mukashi yori onryō to iu mono no yo wo ushinai, hito wo horobosu dōri no hitotsu haberu*]. The first thing to do about this is to pray to Buddhas and Kami. . . . The main point about a vengeful spirit is that it bears a deep grudge and makes those who caused the grudge objects of its revenge even while the resentful person is still alive. When the vengeful spirit is seeking to destroy the objects of its resentment—all the way from small houses to the state as a whole—the state is thrown into disorder by the slanders and lies it generates. . . . And if the vengeful spirit is unable to obtain its revenge while in this visible world, it will do so from the realm of the invisible.[7]

Jien makes it clear that the destructive force of vengeful spirits is not to be underestimated, since malign spirits of both the living and the dead can bring about the downfall of an entire nation.

Some of the most notorious vengeful spirits were from the Heian period. For example, the dead spirit of the famous poet and statesman Sugawara no Michizane (845–903) was said to have wreaked havoc in the capital, causing a string of natural disasters, because he had been forced into exile by his political opponent Fujiwara no Tokihira (871–909). The living spirit of Middle Counselor Fujiwara no Asahira (917–74) was reported to have possessed Regent Fujiwara no Koretada (924–72) for refusing to recommend him for promotion to senior counselor. The dead spirits of Major Counselor Fujiwara no

Motokata (884–949) and his daughter Sukehime were believed to have possessed Emperor Reizei (950–1011) because he occupied the position that Motokata and Sukehime thought rightfully belonged to Sukehime's son Prince
Hirohira. The living spirit of Minister Fujiwara no Akimitsu (944–1021)
(probably in conjunction with the living spirit of his daughter Enshi) was said
to have possessed Regent Fujiwara no Michinaga (966–1027), the most powerful Fujiwara of all, for preventing Akimitsu's son-in-law Prince Atsuakira
(994–1051) from ascending to the throne.[8] Finally, the vanquished spirits of
Heike warriors from the Genpei War (1180–85) were thought to have haunted
and possessed their enemies in order to exact vengeance.

The list goes on and on, but what most of these tales of spiritual possession and vengeance have in common is *political dispossession*: destructive influence was thought to be exerted by the malign spirits of both the living[9] and
the dead,[10] against their enemies or their enemies' descendants, in order to
exact vengeance for political injustices suffered in the past. Such injustices included politically motivated usurpation, oppression, disenfranchisement, exile,
and murder. The more politically powerful a person was in life, the more his
spirit was to be feared in death.[11] Though the most formidable and frightening evil spirits of all were those of past sovereigns, imperial princes, and high-
ranking court officials who had been the victims of political maneuvers and
machinations, in principle anyone with a grudge, whether male or female,
who thought he or she had been dispossessed of economic, political, or symbolic power, had the potential to wreak havoc as a malign spirit.

Most natural calamities were attributed to the evil spirits of such political
victims. Various rituals of exorcism were officially practiced after earthquakes,
floods, droughts, fires, plagues, and crop failures in order to redirect the malevolent energy of the angry spirits that supposedly caused them. The exorcism
and placation of evil spirits was thus of major political importance both to recover from recent national disasters and to avoid future ones. In short, rituals
of exorcism were performed in order to reinstate both the cosmological and
sociopolitical order of the nation.

Placation could be achieved by the posthumous conferral of rank, the
dedication of shrines or temples, the recitation of *Lotus Sutra* passages, or even
the performance of various forms of art, including music, dance, drama, literature, and poetry. Once placated, malevolent spirits were thought to undergo
a ritual transformation called *tamashizume* (or *chinkon*) and become benevo-
lent spirits that would facilitate rather than hinder the preservation of the political order.[12]

Returning, then, to the opening scene of possession and exorcism in *Aoi
no Ue*, we might pose a number of important questions: Who is the malevo-

lent spirit possessing Aoi and why does it possess her? Does the malevolent spirit possess as a result of its own dispossession? If so, was the spirit dispossessed by Aoi herself, or by her father, the Minister of the Left, who occupied the second most powerful ministerial position in the Heian bureaucracy? To answer these and other questions, we must turn to the catalpa-bow-wielding shamaness Teruhi.

As soon as she is summoned forth, Teruhi sings an evocatively melodious lyric chant (*yowagin*, or "soft chant") in the noncongruent style (*hyōshi awazu*), such that the syllables of the text do not correspond to the beats of music. Teruhi chants the following quasi-Chinese lustration:

> Ten shōjō ji shōjō
> Naige shōjō rokkon shōjō.
> (Yokomichi and Omote, 40: 125)

> Heaven be pure, earth be pure,
> inside and outside be pure, six sense organs be pure.

This formulaic lustration not only prepares Teruhi for her confrontation with the malevolent spirit, but also anticipates, in her purification of the "six sense organs,"[13] the eventual identification of the spirit as that of the Lady of the Sixth Ward: that is, Rokujō no Miyasudokoro. Teruhi then proceeds to call forth the possessing spirit with a conventional incantation delivered in the metrical form of a *waka* poem (5-7-5-7-7) and sung in a highly inflected, noncongruent manner centered on the higher register (*jōnoei shōdan*).

> Yoribito wa
> Ima zo yorikuru nagahama no
> Ashige no koma ni
> Tazuna yurikake.
> (Yokomichi and Omote, 40: 125)

> One possessed
> now along the shore approaches
> on a dappled-gray horse,
> loosely shaking the reins.

Teruhi the Shamaness, in summoning forth the malevolent spirit, effectively transfers that spirit from the possessed body of Aoi into her own body. Teruhi embodies the ambiguous functions of the *yoribito*: both "spirit medium" and "one possessed by a spirit."[14] As the *yoribito* approaches *and* is possessed (*yorikuru* combines both meanings) "on a dappled-gray horse, / loosely shaking the reins," there is no way to determine whether it is the medium who rides the malevolent spirit, reining it in like a horse, or the spirit who rides the medium. Who tugs whose reins? Teruhi's incantation maintains the tension of this ambiguity through puns on *yori-* in *yoribito* and *yorikuru*. Moreover, the "loosely shaking reins" (*tazuna yurikake*) continue the reverberation of the *yori-* and thereby suggest the trembling body of the possessed medium, who must relinquish at least partial control to the possessing spirit in order to serve as a vessel through which the spirit can articulate its identity and demands. The medium Teruhi effectively offers herself up for (dis)possession by the spirit in order to enable Aoi to repossess her own body and spirit.

H. E. Plutschow has argued that spirit mediums in noh are "a more passive kind of medium," who "do not transfer the evil spirits onto themselves." According to this view, the malevolent spirit possessing Aoi identifies itself "not so much by possessing the body of a medium but through disguise."[15] Furthermore, Plutschow concludes, "we may risk reading too much of Heian-period culture into the Noh theater because no plays in Noh present a disguised spirit revealing its agony through a medium's hysteria and contortions."[16] But if I have attended correctly to the equivocalities of Teruhi's incantation, in which *yoribito* marks not only the possessed body of Aoi but also the spirit medium Teruhi offering her own body up for possession, then that would make Teruhi an exception to the general rule claimed by Plutschow: Teruhi is, after all, an example of a medium who *actively* invites the malevolent spirit into her own body in order to release Aoi from possession. Furthermore, the "loosely shaking reins" of the *yoribito* seem to suggest the contortions of both the medium Teruhi and the possessed Aoi. The vision of the malevolent spirit that the audience witnesses in the next scene is one that has been enabled by Teruhi's work as *yoribito*: the malevolent spirit of Rokujō soon seen dancing about the stage is, in effect, a vision summoned forth by the shamaness and channeled through her. We are able to see and hear the malevolent spirit of Rokujō only *after* it has transferred itself from Aoi to Teruhi. As long as the shamaness remains on stage, so too does the channeled spirit of Rokujō.

Soon after Teruhi chants her poetic conjuration, special rhythmic entrance music is performed, and the *shite*, playing the spirit of Rokujō, enters the stage. Wearing the golden-eyed *deigan* mask of a beautiful young noblewoman, whose eye color, facial expression, and slightly disheveled hair over the forehead signify jealous attachment to a lover, Rokujō chants the following highly inflected, noncongruent song centered on the higher register (*issei shōdan*):

> Mitsu no kuruma ni nori no michi
> Kataku no kado wo ya idenuran
> Yūgao no yado no yareguruma
> Yaru kata naki koso kanashikere.
>
> (Yokomichi and Omote, 40: 125)

Riding in three carriages on the path of the Law,
might one pass through the gate of the burning house?
At the ruins of Yūgao's dwelling, a dilapidated carriage:
how sad that there is no way to drive it out!

A famous historical account of a performance of *Aoi no Ue* by Inuō Dōami, recorded in Zeami's *Sarugaku dangi*, gives us some idea as to how this entrance song was performed during the Muromachi period:

Inuō was in the upper three levels, and never fell to the top of the middle level or knew anything about the middle or lowest levels [of artistic attainment]. . . . In the noh *Aoi no Ue*, he rode in a carriage wearing a long, willow-green lined robe which covered his feet. While a female carriage attendant, played by Iwa-matsu, clung to the carriage shafts, he sang the *issei* on the bridge and advanced the carriage.[17]

This historical record is significant not only because it helps us date the play—it must have been performed in or before 1413, the year of Dōami's death—but also because it gives us some idea of how the scene was actually performed during the Muromachi period. Until recently, modern performances of *Aoi no Ue* never employed the carriage, since such realistic stage properties were considered to be lacking in refinement. It was only after scholars began to take note of the account in *Sarugaku dangi* that both the carriage and carriage attendant were reintroduced into contemporary productions of *Aoi no Ue* as a variant performance.

Zeami's historical record is also of interest because Dōami, a prominent actor of the Hie troupe from Ōmi province, regarded as one of the three great noh actors of his time (along with Itchū and Zeami's father Kannami), was actively patronized by the most powerful and ambitious shogun of the Muromachi period, Ashikaga Yoshimitsu. As Yoshimitsu's favorite—even more favored than Zeami—Dōami and his troupe often performed before the shogun, both at large subscription festivals and at smaller private performances. Although the sketchiness of extant noh performance records before 1429 makes it difficult to ascertain exactly when and where Dōami gave his famous performance of *Aoi no Ue*, it is probable, given the extent of Yoshimitsu's patronage of Dōami's troupe, that Dōami performed *Aoi no Ue* before Yoshimitsu. Indeed, I would contend that even if Yoshimitsu were not in attendance, Dōami's performance of *Aoi no Ue* would still have been linked to the patronage provided by Yoshimitsu's shogunate.

At any rate, Zeami's record of Dōami's performance indicates not only his high esteem for Dōami, but also the success of *Aoi no Ue* during the Kitayama epoch of the Muromachi period. Zeami and his Yūzaki troupe actively adopted the techniques of Dōami's Hie troupe both to elevate their art to a higher level of refinement and to achieve similar success in attracting the patronage of powerful members of the military aristocracy.[18] Later I will explore in greater detail linkages between *Aoi no Ue* and the Muromachi discourse network that sponsored its production. I return now to my analysis of Rokujō's *issei*.

Rokujō's powerful entrance song unleashes a string of intertextual citations bound together by the *kakekotoba* (pivot word) *nori*, which homophonically and syntactically oscillates between the verb "to ride or mount," and the noun "the Law of Buddha." In this way, Rokujō associatively links the preceding clause, "riding [*nori*] in three carriages," with the one that follows, "the path of the Law [*nori*]." Leaving no doubt that she is referring to the famous "parable of the burning house" (*katakuyu*) from the second fascicle of the *Lotus Sutra* (*Myōhōrengekyō* or *Hokekyō*), she asks, "Might one pass through the gate of the burning house?"

In the parable of the burning house, a fire suddenly breaks out in a large house owned by a man of great wealth and power. Seeing his house engulfed by flames, the man's first thought is to save his sons still trapped inside. Though he shouts to them from outside the house, the man's sons are too young and too absorbed in their games to pay any attention to the fire raging around them, or to understand what it is their father commands them to do. "Unalarmed and unafraid, they have not the least intention of leaving. For they do not even know what a 'fire' is, or what a 'house' is, or what it means to 'lose' everything."[19] Fearing that his children will be burned to death, the man devises an expedient to get them out of the house. Knowing that the children are most attached to their toys and games, he shouts:

> The things you so love to play with are rare and hard to get. If you do not get them, you are certain to regret it later. Things like these, a variety of goat-drawn carriages, deer-drawn carriages, and ox-drawn carriages, are now outside the door for you to play with. Come out of this burning house quickly, all of you! I will give all of you what you desire.[20]

Fortunately, the children are lured out of the house by this enticement, and are saved from the fire. Upon escaping, the children demand the three types of carriage promised to them by their father. Instead, the father gives to each child one great carriage yoked to a white ox, which far surpasses the smaller goat-, deer-, and ox-drawn carriages he had originally promised them. The burning-house parable is thought to illustrate the efficacy of "expedient devices," or "accommodated truth" (*hōben*), for guiding human beings out of this burning world of delusory attachment (*mōshū*) and toward enlightenment. Moreover, it also allegorically suggests that such multifarious devices are always subordinated to the One Vehicle (*ichijō*) of the One Buddha. According to this view, despite the great variety of Buddhist doctrines, schools, and sects, all the vehicles of Buddhism are meant to bring the believer into an experience with the single Buddha nature residing within every being.

By "riding in three carriages" on the path of the One Law, Rokujō hopes to pass through the gate of the burning house of karmic attachment, but her doubts concerning the success of this endeavor are poignantly articulated by her use of the interrogative particle *ya* in *kataku no kado wo ya idenuran*. *Ya* can be used to raise a question, express doubt, assume an ironic stance, or pose a rhetorical question expecting an affirmative answer. Here the exact force of *ya* seems undecidable. It could be that the spirit of Rokujō doubts she will ever find release from this world of karmic attachment: "Will I ever pass through the gate of the burning house?" Indeed, her doubts may run so deep that any discussion of escape must necessarily be ironic, taking it for granted that release is impossible: "Pass through the gate of the burning house? Of course not!" On the other hand, the question may be rhetorical: "Might I pass through the gate of the burning house? Certainly, as long as I receive the prayers of the living and the assistance of various bodhisattvas." Without resolving this indeterminacy, let us go on to consider Rokujō's response.

"At the ruins of Yūgao's dwelling, a dilapidated carriage: how sad that there is no way to drive it out!" (*Yūgao no yado no yareguruma, yaru kata naki koso kanashikere*) laments Rokujō. In modern performances of *Aoi no Ue*, as Rokujō intones this lament, she raises her right hand and sleeve to her eyes in a highly stylized weeping gesture (called *shiori*), which underscores the depth of her sadness. Moreover, Rokujō's response is made phonetically conspicuous by its extended alliteration of semivowels (*y*) in "Yūgao," *yado*, *yareguruma*, and *yaru*, which seem to echo the undecidability of the interrogative *ya* particle in the previous line. This alliterative repetition is balanced by the accumulation of velar consonants (*k*) in *kata* and *kanashikere* in the fourth line of the *issei*, which reverberate off of the cluster of velar consonants in the first and second lines (*kataku* and *kado*). Though any interpretation of the assonance produced by such alliterative chains is necessarily speculative, such phonetic play probably helps shape the almost incantatory emotional tonality of Rokujō's lament in the present passage, which is summed up by her sadness that "there is no way to drive it out."

Though the neuter pronoun included in my translation, "there is no way to drive *it* out," is nowhere to be found in the Japanese text, nevertheless it aptly evokes the ambiguities of the phrase *yaru kata naki koso kanashikere*, "there is no way to *yaru*, how sad!" Translating such a passage is an extremely difficult task, both because of its almost indecipherable figural density, which consists of layer upon layer of intertextual inscription, and because of its ever shifting syntactic looseness, which prevents one from pinning down its various pivot words and puns.[21] Since noh syntax is generally characterized by parataxis—the loose, side-by-side juxtaposition of clauses without well-defined or necessarily logical connections (as opposed to hypotaxis: the forward-pressing, architectonic stacking of clauses with well-defined connections)—the sense is never discretely given in any phrase, but rather jumps back and forth like patterns "flashing across a screen" between various, loosely interlocking grammatical constructions along "*renga*-like" associative progressions.[22]

Besides referring to the title of the fourth chapter of *Genji monogatari* (entitled "Yūgao," or "Evening Faces") and to the victim of Rokujō's first possession, the dilapidated carriage at the ruins of Yūgao's dwelling metonymically links up with the chain of Genji's consorts attacked by Rokujō's possessive jealousy during the course of *Genji monogatari* (including Yūgao, Aoi, Murasaki, and the Third Princess).[23] Moreover, the image of the "dilapidated carriage" itself reinscribes the *kuruma arasoi*, or "carriage quarrel," between Aoi and Rokujō at the lustration ceremony of the Aoi Festival (from which Aoi derives her name) in chapter 9 of *Genji monogatari*.

In *Genji monogatari*, the scene of the *kuruma arasoi*, or carriage quarrel, is as follows. Soon after arriving at the festival, the carriages of Aoi and Rokujō accidentally intersect and are forced to compete against one another for the best position from which to view the lustration procession. Rokujō's carriage is jostled about by Aoi's servants, shoved behind the carriages of lesser attendants, and then finally—quite literally—broken down and defeated, with its support stand (for the carriage shafts and yoke) smashed to pieces and the carriage itself propped up on the hubs of other carriages (*GM* 2: 16–17). Rokujō suffers such humiliation at the hands of Aoi's attendants that the dilapidated carriage effectively functions as a trope for her own wounded dignity and damaged pride. Indeed, the dilapidated carriage has even been viewed as the aching heart of Rokujō, which Genji damaged by breaking whatever lover's promises he had made to her.[24] Rokujō's own carriage is effectively torn, broken down, violated, and defeated (all connotations of *yareguruma*) at the Aoi Festival's lustration ceremony procession not only by Aoi's carriage and attendants (who occupy a position of comparatively greater symbolic capital because Aoi is Genji's principal wife), but also by Genji himself, who, despite being warned by his father, the Kiritsubo sovereign, not to incur Rokujō's resentment (*GM* 2: 12), nevertheless passes by the Lady from the Sixth Ward without even acknowledging her presence.

As a result of this unfortunate encounter at the Aoi Festival, it has become impossible for Rokujō either to drive out the *yareguruma* through the gate of the burning house, or to dispel her jealous attachment to Genji and bitter resentment of Genji's other lovers. Moreover, as will soon be evident, since Teruhi is ultimately unsuccessful in bringing about the expulsion of Rokujō's spirit and must appeal to the stronger powers of a *yamabushi* (mountain ascetic) priest for assistance, the line *yaru kata naki* also suggests that there is no way, at least at this stage, to drive out the tenacious spirit of Rokujō from the body of Aoi.

Finally, it is interesting to note that, in addition to producing meaning-effects such as "to break down" and "to drive away," *yaru* can also refer to the act of dispatching poetic missives. What does the logic of the poetic dispatch have to do with Rokujō's inability to drive through the gate of the burning house and drive away her karmic attachment? Before attempting to answer this question, let us briefly recall the form and function of poetic exchanges during the Heian period.

During the early and middle Heian period, when court culture was flourishing, women at court were compelled by court etiquette to lead such cloistered lives, hidden away behind screens, curtains, and ladies-in-waiting, that the exchange of poetic missives became the most important channel for the processing, storage, and transmission of messages between aristocratic women and men in the Heian capital.[25] The success or failure of a series of poetic exchanges often determined the course of one's relationship to a person of the opposite sex. The outcome of such an exchange was influenced not only by the "meaning" of *what* was written but also by the contingencies of *how* it was written: that is, by the handwriting style of the poet, the thickness, size, design, and color of the paper used, the sprig of seasonal blossoms to which the poem was attached, even the attire of the messenger who delivered the poetic missive. All of these contingent factors figured into the poetic exchange, not as transparently meaningful empirical facts but as discursively constituted semiotic differences.

Of all the elements that influenced the outcome of a poetic exchange, the single most important factor was probably the handwriting style of the poet. Though spoken language was generally mistrusted because of its unavoidable ambiguity, the Heian cult of calligraphy celebrated the handwritten materiality of poetry as a reliable indicator of sex, age, status, and taste: words, it was thought, may lie, but handwriting does not.

The character of Rokujō is well known in *Genji monogatari* for her unusually assertive behavior in the arena of poetic exchanges. She distinguishes herself not only by the number of Genji's lovers she possesses (four), but also by the number of *waka* poetry exchanges she initiates with Genji (an unparalleled seven out of nine). She is also known for the distinctive calligraphic style in which she inscribes her poetic missives, a style that Genji regards as unsurpassed in elegance and sophistication.[26] It is against the backdrop of such poetic assertiveness and distinction that Rokujō's frustration is exacerbated all the more in *Aoi no Ue* when she is unable to *yaru* (drive out, dispatch). In other words, Rokujō's inability to drive through the gates of the burning house is juxtaposed with her inability to dispatch poetic missives that actually *reach* Genji's emotions, her inability to communicate her bitterness and pain in a way that would elicit sympathy from Genji and compel him to stop neglecting her.

Rokujō continues her lament from the *issei* in the *shidai* and *sashi* sections that follow, the former sung in the *hiranori* style of a congruent (*hyōshi au*) song with twelve syllables of text matched to sixteen half-beats of music, and the latter sung in the *sashinori* style of a noncongruent song centered on the higher register with minimal inflection, making it one of "the most readily intelligible *shōdan* in noh":[27]

> Ukiyo wa ushi no oguruma no
> Ukiyo wa ushi no oguruma no
> Meguru ya mukui naruran.
> > (Yokomichi and Omote, 40: 125)

> This wretched floating world, like an ox-drawn carriage,
> this wretched floating world, like an ox-drawn carriage—
> is it not the always returning wheel of karmic retribution?

> Oyoso rinne wa kuruma no wa no gotoku
> Rokushu shishō wo ideyarazu
> Ningen no fujō bashō hōmatsu no yo no narai
> Kinō no hana kyō no yume to
> Odorokanu koso oroka nare
> Mi no uki ni hito no urami no nao soite
> Wasure mo yaranu wa ga omoi
> Semete ya shibashi nagusamu to
> Azusa no yumi ni onryō no
> Kore made arawareidetaru nari.
> > (Yokomichi and Omote, 40: 125–26)

> Reincarnation forever rolls on like the wheels of a carriage,
> unable to pass through the six realms and four modes of birth,
> the impermanence of human beings is like the banana plant
> or foam on water: it is the way of the world
> that yesterday's flowers are today's dreams—
> how foolish it is not to wake up!
> Harboring resentment towards others simply increases the
> misery of my floating life:

my troubled thoughts, which I can never forget,
if only I could pacify them for a while.
A vengeful spirit, summoned forth by the catalpa bow
is revealed here now.

In the *shidai* and *sashi*, Rokujō's repetition of "carriage" and "wheel" tropes metonymically returns us yet again to the emotionally charged incident at the Aoi Festival. Before examining the *shidai* and *sashi* in greater detail, let us consider the larger institutional framework out of which this collision of jealousy and aggression emerged: namely, the sociocultural context of the Aoi Festival.

Of Karma and Carriages:
Possessive Rivalry Between Rokujō and Aoi

Ever since it was first performed in the sixth century, the Aoi Festival (*Aoi no matsuri*), also known as the Kamo Festival (*Kamo no matsuri*), has been widely regarded as the most magnificent ceremonial procession on the court calendar, and certainly one of the most important Shinto celebrations of the year. The Aoi Festival, named after the ivylike, heart-shaped *aoi* (*Asarum caulescens*, or "heartleaf") that served as the decorative emblem of the festival, was traditionally performed in the middle of the fourth month (the first month of summer on the lunar calendar) at the Upper and Lower sanctuaries of the Kamo Shrine in Kyoto.[28] The Kamo Shrine has long been revered as one of the three great Shinto shrines of Japan (along with the Ise and Iwashimizu Hachiman shrines).

First established in the sixth century by Emperor Yōmei (540–87) in order to bring about an end to the drought and famine ravaging capital and countryside alike, the Aoi Festival, in its function as a *goryōe* festival to placate malevolent spirits, was considered a ceremonial event of great magnitude, even during the Muromachi period, because of the institutional need to ritually secure divine protection against all the natural disorders that plagued medieval Japan. In the first hundred years alone of the Ashikaga shogunate, the capital of Kyoto suffered at least fourteen major earthquakes, eleven plagues, five typhoons, five famine-producing droughts, four fires, and three floods.[29] Given the incredible frequency of such natural calamities, it is no wonder that residents of the Ashikaga capital continued to participate in various ceremonies of ritual purification and exorcism.

In addition to its religious significance, the Aoi Festival also functioned as a highly charged social space to which persons of all ranks went to see and be seen. The social importance of seeing and being seen at the Aoi Festival was closely linked to a fascination with the courtly splendors of *eiga*: a term that refers to the magnificent display and ritualized spectacle associated with court ceremonies, religious processions, and state functions. High-ranking courtiers, government officials, and ladies-in-waiting could be seen viewing the Aoi Festival procession from within private carriages or from atop specially constructed viewing stands. Commoners could be seen watching the festival from the street side or on nearby rooftops. Everyone jockeyed for the best possible position to insure that their view of the processional splendors was unobstructed. It is out of this socioreligious framework of the Aoi Festival that the *kuruma arasoi* between Aoi and Rokujō unfolds.

Rokujō's obsession with carriage and wheel imagery (the latter being an associative trope, or *engo*, for the former) in the *shidai* and *sashi* of *Aoi no Ue* points to the excruciating frustration and unbearable humiliation she experienced at the Aoi Festival.[30] Punning on the homophonic play of *uki*, which means both "wretched" (derived from *ushi*) and "floating" (from *uku*), Rokujō links "this wretched floating world" both to the "ox-drawn carriage" (*ushi no oguruma*) that carries the Kamo Shrine's high priestess to the Aoi Festival's lustration ceremony along the Kamo River, and to the "ox-drawn carriage" in the burning-house parable of the *Lotus Sutra*. Continuing this chain of carriage and wheel tropes, Rokujō compares her life to "the always returning wheel of karmic retribution" (*mukui*) and the cycle of transmigration that "forever rolls on like the wheels of a carriage" (*oyoso rinne wa kuruma no wa no gotoku*).

The turning wheels of Rokujō's karmic carriage exemplify the return of what is due (*mukui*), whether in the form of reward or retribution (*inga ōhō*).[31] Whence this return of karma comes is more difficult to say. Rokujō's karma never stops returning, and yet she is never able to return to the precise origins of her karma, since the accumulated karma of her existence is so deep and entangled as to be unfathomable. She cannot, as long as she remains in this world of desire, fully extricate herself from the delusory phantasms and attachments produced across the web of karmic returns. In the eternal return of karma, returns referring to returns, it is not possible to grasp the precise origins of return, only the returning trace of returns along the wheel of becoming. Karma is the concept that names the return of returns without giving access to the origin of returns. The origin is always elsewhere, always other: somewhere in the past of a former life that is absent but not altogether dead. Though the origins of karmic (dis)possession marking the *kuruma arasoi* in *Aoi no Ue* are beyond Rokujō's (and our) grasp, that does not mean that the remaining traces of (dis)possession are totally indecipherable. Indeed, such vestigial karmic traces are neither totally decipherable nor totally indecipherable, but somewhere in between.

Traditionally conceived, karma (*sukuse, en, gō, inga*) is a popular articulation of the Buddhist doctrine of "dependent origination" (*engi*), which refers to the intersection of interdependent causal series giving rise to the multiplicity of beings and actions in the phenomenal world.[32] Karma describes a person's lot in this life as bound by the contingent interplay between his own actions—whether physical, mental, or verbal—and the actions of others, in this and earlier lives. Considered one of the basic teachings of the Buddha and a key component of the Law of Buddha (*nori, minori,* or *buppō*), karma is often poetically figured in terms of ties, bindings, and knots, such as in the formulation *sukuse musubi,* or "bindings from a previous existence."

Insofar as they are often unforeseen, karmic bindings produce reversals (*gyakuen*) that, like contingent events,[33] appear to emerge out of nowhere in their occurrence. The weight of karma bears down on one's present actions, shackling one's conduct with the weight of historical baggage: one inherits karma with its binding ties and vestigial emotional attachments, whether one wants to or not. Consequently, the aim of religious austerities and meditative techniques practiced during the medieval period was to liberate oneself from the binding shackles of one's karmic inheritance.

One of the most common tropes during the medieval period for the karmic cycle of births and rebirths was the Buddhist taxonomy called *rokudō,* or "six paths."[34] In the *sashi* section Rokujō deplores the fact that she is "unable to pass through the six realms [*rokushu*] and four modes of birth [*shishō*]."[35] In addition to punning on Rokujō's name, *rokushu* is a Buddhist term that is synonymous with *rokudō*: the six lower destinations, realms, or states of reincarnation across which beings are distributed according to their individual accumulation of karma. The Buddhist discourse of *rokudō* posits a teleological taxonomy of ascending and descending levels of transmigration, assigned as reward or punishment for past actions. Karma determines "the direction of travel, the rate of travel, and the specifics of one's next birth"[36] across the cosmology of six paths. Insofar as one's karma is always in the process of becoming, one is always on the way to being reborn into another existence, another being. In ascending order, the six paths are: sufferers in hell (*jigoku*), hungry ghosts (*gaki*), animals (*chikushō*), warriors (*shura*), humans (*ningen*), and heavenly beings (*tenjō*).

During the tumultuous medieval period, didactic Buddhist paintings of the six paths (called *rokudōe*), depicting in graphic detail the hierarchically differentiated horrors of hell on up to the delights of paradise, were extremely popular among the masses. Such paintings and principles provided a metaphysical yardstick with which to measure and classify the medieval believer's soteriological status, and, in some cases, perhaps also the motivation to pursue a religious path toward the transcendence of the six karmic paths.

In addition to the six lower paths, there are also four higher paths: disciples of Buddha (*shōmon*), self-enlightened Buddhist sages (*engaku*), bodhisattva spirits (*bosatsu*) who stay on earth to help others attain enlightenment, and enlightened Buddhas (*butsu*). Together the six lower paths and the four higher paths are known as *jikkai*, or "ten realms." The top three paths on the way to buddhahood (namely, the way of *shōmon, engaku*, and *bosatsu*) have been traditionally identified with the "three vehicles (or carriages)" (*sanjō*) of the burning-house parable in the *Lotus Sutra*, and thus regarded as provisional or expedient (*hōben*) teachings and paths on the way to the One Vehicle (*ichijō*) of the One Buddha. In order to achieve enlightenment, one must transcend both the six lower paths (*rokudō*) and the three higher paths (*sanjō*) on the way to buddhahood.

By means of an intertextual reinscription of a couplet from the *Yuimagyō Sutra*—"This body, like foam on the water, is impermanent; this body, like a banana plant, is without center"[37]—Rokujō links her inability to transcend the karmic cosmology of the six paths to the radical contingency of human existence: "The impermanence [*fujō*] of human beings is like the banana plant or foam on water: it is the way of the world." The noun *fujō* plays upon the homophonic convergence of two different strands of meaning: (1) impermanence, uncertainty, undecidability, indefiniteness; and (2) pollution, stain, defilement. According to this view, the impermanence and undecidability of contingent phenomena are of a piece with the polluted world of delusion: karmic attachment to this world of delusion *is* attachment to contingency. The Buddhist name for the generalized contingency of life in this transient, phenomenal world, and the suffering produced by attachment to it, is *mujō*. From the perspective of *mujō*, it is the permanence of impermanence, the constancy of inconstancy, and the necessity of contingency that bind the jealous spirit of Rokujō to this floating world of delusion. Only by exorcising her delusory attachment to contingency will Rokujō begin to move toward a transcendence of her karmic inheritance and attainment of enlightenment.

Rokujō contemplates the karmic ties that bind when she remarks:

> Harboring resentment toward others [*hito no urami*]
> simply increases [*soite*] the misery of my floating life:
> my troubled thoughts, which I can never forget,
> if only I could pacify [*nagusamu*] them for a while.

Though the *hito*, "person(s)," of *hito no urami* remains nameless, it most likely refers to Rokujō's bitter resentment toward rivals such as Aoi, as well as to her sad regret that things could not be worked out between Genji and herself. The verb *soite* seems to reinforce the latter: in addition to meaning "to add to" or "to increase," *sou* can also mean "to get married," "to become husband and wife."[38] Instead of Rokujō displacing Aoi as Genji's principal wife, Rokujō's resentment of Aoi only succeeds in marrying greater misery to her already floating life. The conjugal connotations of *soite* accentuate the pain, bitterness, and uncertainty of Rokujō's position as one of Genji's paramours. Overwhelmed by *urami* (resentment), Rokujō is unable to bring her "troubled thoughts" under control, since she is neither able to overcome her attachments nor appease her restless spirit. Pacifying Rokujō's troubled spirit and determining more precisely the origins of her *urami* is the task of Teruhi the Shamaness.

In the sections immediately following the *shidai* and *sashi*, Rokujō provides us with a few more hints concerning the genealogy of her *urami*. The first song, called a *sageuta*, is sung in metered, congruent style, centered on the middle and lower registers. The second song, called an *ageuta*, is also sung in metered, congruent style, but centers on the upper register and ends in the lower register.

> Ara hazukashi ya ima tote mo
> Shinobiguruma no wa ga sugata.
>> (Yokomichi and Omote, 40: 126)

> How shameful even now:
> my appearance in a secret carriage.

> Tsuki wo ba nagame akasu to mo
> Tsuki wo ba nagame akasu to mo
> Tsuki ni wa mieji kagerō no
> Azusa no yumi no urahazu ni
> Tachiyori uki wo kataran
> Tachiyori uki wo kataran.
>> (Yokomichi and Omote, 40: 126)

> Though I gaze at the moon until daybreak,
> though I gaze at the moon until daybreak,
> I will not appear in the moon's light, a mayfly
>> flickering in the dark
> at the upper notch of the catalpa bow,
> I rise and approach so that I might tell the story
>> of my aimless misery,
> I rise and approach so that I might tell the story
>> of my aimless misery.

Though gazing at the moon (a conventional poetic image for enlightenment and Buddhist salvation), Rokujō's spirit, which "flickers" "in the dark" like an ephemeral "mayfly" (all meaning-effects produced by *kagerō*),[39] refuses to appear in the moon's light because she is not ready to relinquish her attachment to this world of desire. But despite her resistance, Rokujō cannot help but appear at the upper notch of the catalpa bow, where the shamaness plucks the bowstring that summons forth her possessing spirit.

In medieval Japan, plucking the string of a catalpa bow was also used as an apotropaic device (referred to as *tsuruuchi*, *meigen*, or *yuminarashi*) to drive away malign spirits and demons during periods of illness and confinement.[40] It was believed that the noise alone was enough to frighten away such spirits. However, in the present scene from *Aoi no Ue*, it is clearly the attractive, rather than the apotropaic, technique being exercised by Teruhi's bow-plucking.

Soon after the *sageuta* and *ageuta* songs, Teruhi describes—first from her own perspective and then from the perspective of Rokujō—the aftermath of the *kuruma arasoi*. Judging from what can be gleaned from Zeami's account in *Sarugaku dangi* of Dōami's performance of *Aoi no Ue*, this scene was probably dramatized on stage complete with carriage and maidservant. The following section is a lyric chant (*yowagin*) sung in the noncongruent style:

> Fushigi ya na tare to mo mienu jōrō no
> Yabureguruma ni mesaretaru ni
> Aonyōbō to oboshiki hito no
> Ushi mo naki kuruma no nagae ni toritsuki
> Samezame to nakitamō itawashisa yo.
> (Yokomichi and Omote, 40: 126)

> How uncanny! Who it is I know not:
>   an upper-ranking lady
> riding in a dilapidated carriage
> while someone—a young maidservant I think—
> clutches the shafts of an ox-less carriage,
> crying bitterly—how painful it all is!

Teruhi's description of the upper-ranking lady (*jōrō*),[41] riding in a dilapidated carriage, brings to the fore the immediate cause of Rokujō's ire. Though attending the Aoi Festival in a "secret carriage" (*shinobiguruma*)[42] so as not to be recognized, Rokujō's concealed identity was forcibly disclosed by the men attending Aoi's carriage, who violently jostled Rokujō's carriage into a humiliating position behind the carriages of lower-ranking women. Even now Rokujō cannot conceal (*shinobi*) her remembrance (*shinobi*) of this painful incident, nor the embarrassment it caused. What makes this contingent collision of carriages more politically charged than a mere traffic jam is that it takes place in such a highly charged social space: not only was Rokujō outmaneuvered by one of her fiercest rivals for the attention of Genji; this happened to her in front of all her peers. According to *Genji monogatari*, as Genji's carriage passed by this scene of disarray, his attendants all recognized Rokujō's carriage and the humiliating predicament it was in, but not wishing to get involved, they looked the other way, literally "putting on a face of nonrecognition" (*shi-*

razu kao wo tsukuru), "making a face that does not know" (*GM* 2: 17). More-over, to make matters even worse, as Genji's carriage passed by, Rokujō per-ceived that both Genji and his attendants honored Aoi with their solemn and respectful acknowledgment of her presence (and status as Genji's principal wife), but completely ignored Rokujō. Mortified by such circumstances, Ro-kujō whispers to herself the following *waka* in *Genji monogatari*:

Kage wo nomi
Mitarashigawa no
Tsurenaki ni
Mi no uki hodo zo
Itodo shiraruru.
(*GM* 2: 18)

Only a reflection
of the lustration river,
his coldness is matched
by the degree of
my own aimless misery!

Rokujō's shame and humiliation are especially acute because it was believed that by disgracing oneself, one also disgraced one's entire lineage—past, pre-sent, and future. In other words, one's sense of shame (*haji*) corresponded to the status of one's genealogical line: "the better the lineage, the greater potential for fall in status and the greater fear of ridicule (*hitowarae*) and social criticism."[43]

Shame and humiliation are very powerful motivations for Rokujō's pos-session of Aoi, but they are not the only ones. Other traces of (dis)possession, both in *Genji monogatari* and in *Aoi no Ue*, still need to be addressed. For ex-ample, we know from *Genji monogatari* that, as the daughter of a powerful minister, Rokujō was among those who might have been selected to become empress, since imperial consorts (*nyōgo*) were chosen from among "the daugh-ters of those aristocrats occupying the four ministerial posts": *sadaijin* (min-ister of the left), *udaijin* (minister of the right), *naidaijin* (minister of the in-terior), and *daijō daijin* (prime minister).[44] In fact, before becoming Genji's paramour, Rokujō was the principal wife (*kita no kata*) of the former crown prince (*zenbō*), who was next in line to the throne.[45] However, he died under mysterious circumstances and left her widowed at the age of twenty. Had her husband lived and ascended to the throne, Rokujō would have become em-press. Though the details of the former crown prince's death are nowhere ex-plicitly stated in *Genji monogatari* or *Aoi no Ue*, many commentators have in-terpreted the oblique references to Rokujō's dead husband in *Genji* as traces of dispossession suggesting that he was deposed by opposing political factions. Those traces of dispossession include the following highly relevant details, summarized by Norma Field:

(1) it is unusual for both the positions of crown prince and empress to be vacant at the opening of the tale (the two normally go hand-in-hand); (2) the *Genji* itself incorporates the historical reality of deposed crown princes in the person of the Eighth Prince of the Uji chapters; and (3) most pertinently, the appearance of the spirits of both the Rokujō Lady and her father at Aoi's bedside carries a strong hint of grievance.[46]

Moreover, Genji's father, the Kiritsubo sovereign, reproves Genji for neglecting Rokujō, reminding him of her importance to the deceased crown prince. The Kiritsubo sovereign offers Genji the following advice on how to treat a high-ranking woman such as Rokujō, advice that is especially poignant given what takes place soon thereafter at the *kuruma arasoi*:

> Hito no tame hajigamashiki koto naku, izure wo mo nadaraka ni motenashite, onna no urami na oi so. (*GM* 2: 12)

> Let there be no instances in which she is publicly humiliated; conduct yourself in a gentle manner toward everyone; do not shoulder female resentment.

Though Genji does not heed his father's advice, the Kiritsubo sovereign's prescription nevertheless serves as a prescient warning of the jealous rage stirred within Rokujō at the Aoi Festival lustration ceremony procession, when she (and, indirectly, her entire lineage) is publicly humiliated both by the carriage struggle with Aoi and by the cruel indifference of Genji (cf. *GM* 2: 20–21).

Perhaps the most striking piece of evidence supporting the interpretation that Rokujō's husband was a deposed crown prince (*haitaishi*) is the fact that, although the dead spirit (*shiryō*) of the former crown prince is never explicitly suspected of having exacted vengeance for political injustices suffered while he was alive, the ghost of Rokujō's father (at one time a powerful minister) *is* suspected of such vengeance in relation to the possession of Aoi.[47]

In *Genji monogatari*, as soon as it became clear that Aoi was possessed by a malevolent spirit, prayers were ordered and several spirits were identified and expelled. But one particularly vindictive spirit, which possessed Aoi with obsessive fervor, refused to be transferred to a medium: "Not submitting to such eminent Shūgendō exorcists made the spirit seem extraordinarily tenacious and vengeful" (*imijiki genzamonodomo ni mo shitagawazu, shūneki keshiki oboroke no mono ni arazu to mietari*) (*GM* 2: 26). Rumors eventually reached Rokujō to the effect that "either she herself was the living spirit [attacking Aoi] or that it was the dead spirit of her father, the minister" (*kono onikisudama, kochichiotodo no onrō nado iu mono ari to kikitamau*) (*GM* 2: 29).

The suggestion that Rokujō might have acted in concert with the malevolent spirit of her dead father (perhaps to avenge the injustices suffered by Rokujō's husband, the former crown prince) bears some resemblance to the tale of possession involving Major Counselor Fujiwara no Motokata and his daughter Sukehime. Motokata's and Sukehime's dead spirits were reported to have possessed Emperor Reizei because he occupied the position that they thought rightfully belonged to Sukehime's son Prince Hirohira. The fact that this father-daughter possession of Reizei was roughly contemporaneous with Murasaki Shikibu's composition of *Genji*, and that Reizei even appears as a character in Murasaki's tale, suggests that the incident could have served as intertextual material that was reinscribed in the form of the vengeful spirits of Rokujō and her father.[48] In any case, the designation of Rokujō's daughter Akikonomu as the high priestess of Ise Shrine, after the Kiritsubo sovereign abdicates and the new sovereign, Suzaku ("Shujaku" in *Aoi no Ue*), ascends to the throne (*GM* 2: 12–13), probably serves as partial recompense for the political injustices suffered by Rokujō and her family.

Exercises in Possession, Exorcising Dispossession

One of the most chilling accounts of Rokujō's possession of Aoi in *Genji monogatari* describes Rokujō's realization that the uncanny dreams that have been coming to her night after night are, in fact, first-hand experiences of the act of possession, viewed from the perspective of the possessor:

> While thinking about such things, might not her spirit detach itself from her in that way? At times she wondered. Although completely exhausting the possibilities of sorrow over the past years, she never felt this confused. . . . Ever since the occasion of that trifling, haphazard incident [at the Aoi Festival], when she [Aoi] ignored her and treated her as if she did not even exist, ever since the lustration ceremony, her thoughts, being not easily quieted, floated to this one matter, and whenever she fell asleep, she dreamed of going to the exceedingly beautiful residence of someone she thought was that lady [Aoi] and of jerking her this way and that. Bearing no resemblance to [how Rokujō behaved in] reality, her ferociously violent, single-minded heart came forth, and she had the repeated experience of seeing herself [in her dreams] as she struck and pulled and did other such things to the lady. Oh, how awful! Occasionally, when she felt dazed and confused, she wondered if it was indeed true that she discarded her body and wandered forth. (*GM* 2: 29–30)

Though Rokujō is horrified to contemplate how her peers at court will judge her "wretched, floating fate" (*sukuse no uki koto*) (*GM* 2: 30–31), which alienates her spirit from her body and compels her unconsciously to perform such supernatural assaults, nevertheless her spirit's hold on Aoi does not let up, but if anything, tightens. In response to the increased tenacity of Rokujō's malevolent spirit, which soon forces Aoi into premature labor, the exorcists increase their efforts at placation and expulsion. Interestingly, the more persistently Rokujō's spirit clings to Aoi, the more the smell of burnt poppy seeds, the sort used in rites of exorcism, clings to her own clothes and robes: "Uncannily, she continued to think that these feelings belonged to a different self; moreover, the smell of burnt poppy seeds permeated her robes to such an extent that even when she tried washing her hair or changing her clothes the same odor strangely remained" (GM 2: 35–36). Such telltale signs simply confirm Ro-kujō's worst suspicions about her own involvement in Aoi's possession.

In the midst of this great intensity of prayer and possession, Rokujō's spirit speaks through Aoi, summoning Genji into the room. As soon as Genji enters and appears beside Aoi's sickbed, Rokujō's spirit utters the following *waka*:

> Nageki wabi
> Sora ni midaruru
> Wa ga tama wo
> Musubitodome yo
> Shitagai no tsuma.
> (GM 2: 33–34; cf. 2: 24–25)
>
> Long depressed and lonely,
> in the sky wanders
> my soul confused:
> tie down
> your wife's hem!

Genji is initially startled since neither the voice nor the demeanor belong to Aoi, but he soon realizes—to his utter horror—that Rokujō's spirit is speaking through Aoi, using Aoi's body as a mouthpiece for her own grievances and demands. Rokujō's *waka* refers to the widely held belief that the spirit of a living person (*ikiryō*) could exit the mouth and wander around without the person realizing it. The only way to prevent a person's spirit from wandering forth (and possessing the body of another) was by tying a fold (*shitagai no tsuma*) in the skirt underneath the person's robe.[49]

Rokujō's *waka* is rendered all the more poignant by its pun on *tsuma*, meaning either "lower inside corner" or "wife."[50] By means of this pun, Ro-kujō exhorts Genji to bring her disconnected (*midaruru*) spirit back to its proper body, to bind it within the confines of its own corporeal domain. This scene from *Genji monogatari* of Rokujō's spirit seeking anchor after having gone adrift is intertextually reinscribed in the aurally climactic *kudokiguri* and *kudoki* sections of *Aoi no Ue*, which follow Teruhi's description of "an upper-ranking lady riding in a dilapidated carriage." The *kudokiguri shōdan* is a noncongruent, mostly uninflected song centered on the higher register. The *kudoki shōdan*, on the other hand, though also a noncongruent song with little inflection, is centered on the lower register, thus lending itself to elegiac articulations of sorrow and regret.[51]

Sore shaba denkō no sakai ni wa
Uramubeki hito mo naku
Kanashimubeki mi mo arazaru ni
Itsu sate ukaresometsuran.
    (Yokomichi and Omote, 40: 126–27)

In this contingent realm of delusion, as evanescent
    as a flash of lightning,
there is no one I should resent,
nor should my existence be filled with sorrow.
When, I wonder, did my spirit begin to go adrift?

Tadaima azusa no yumi no oto ni
Hikarete arawareidetaru wo ba
Ikanaru mono to ka oboshimesu
Kore wa Rokujō no Miyasudokoro no onryō nari
Ware yo ni arishi inishie wa
Unshō no hana no en
Haru no ashita no gyoyū ni nare
Sentō no momiji no aki no yo wa
Tsuki ni tawamure iroka ni somi
Hanayaka narishi mi naredomo
Otoroenureba asagao no
Hikage matsu ma no arisama nari
Tada itsu to naki wa ga kokoro
Monouki nobe no sawarabi no
Moeide someshi omoi no tsuyu
Kakaru urami wo harasan tote
Kore made arawareidetaru nari.
      (Yokomichi and Omote, 40: 127)

By the sound of the catalpa bow
I am drawn, appearing before you here and now:
Do you know who I am?
Here before you is the vengeful spirit of Rokujō no Miyasudokoro.
In bygone times, when I was still acquainted with the world
of imperial flower-viewing banquets above the clouds
and spring morning music concerts
on autumn nights filled with crimson leaves at the immortal's cave,
taking delight in the moon, imbued with seasonal colors and scents.
Though once flourishing like a flower, I have withered away:
a morning glory awaiting the sun's rays.
I know not when my bitter heart,
like fern shoots in a field of difficulties,
started sprouting forth. So that I might dispel such thoughts of dew
    ablaze with resentment,
I have appeared before you here and now.

The identification of the possessive spirit was considered one of the most important steps taken by an exorcist toward driving it away, insofar as it was believed that disclosing the proper name of a person or deity—that is, gaining knowledge of the *kotodama*, or "word spirit," signified by the name—gave one power over the bearer of the name.[52] Although Teruhi is ultimately unable to expel the vengeful spirit of Rokujō, by compelling Rokujō to reveal herself, Teruhi is at least able to weaken her malignant power enough so that she can be fully exorcised later in the play.

Even as Rokujō asserts the force of her perspective in the *kudoki*, both through the dramatic disclosure of her name and through the assertion of the personal pronoun *ware* ("I") in the line immediately following that disclosure, it is obvious that Rokujō's self-disclosure was compelled by another: namely, Teruhi's plucking of the catalpa bow. The entire *kudoki* laments the decline of Rokujō's status and beauty: "In bygone times, when I was still acquainted with the world of imperial flower-viewing banquets above the clouds" (*unshō no hana no en*) at the sovereign's palace. The homophonic polysemy produced by *en* in *hana no en*[53] intertwines at least three different semantic clusters: (1) banquet, entertainment, drinking party; (2) blood relations, marriage bonds, karmic ties, traces, connections; and (3) rapturous beauty, charm, allure.[54] Such polysemy insures that the force of Rokujō's lament is not simply aesthetic, since it places the aesthetic in the realm of the sociopolitical. In other words, Rokujō seems to say: "In bygone times, when I was still bound by marriage and karma to the charming (and powerful) world of the crown prince. . . . "

Though once flourishing like a flower, Rokujō has withered away physically, socially, and politically: *otoroenureba* (when/since/as I have fallen on hard times, declined, decayed, wasted away) combines all of these senses. She is in the unenviable position of an *asagao*[55] (morning glory), who has been hidden away or discarded by society (*hikage*) and must await the sun's rays (*hikage*) to open up her bitter heart. The duplicity of *hikage*[56] underscores the plight of Rokujō, who feels that she has been discarded not only by Hikaru ("Shining") Genji but also by the court as a whole since her husband, the former crown prince, died.

As she considers her own plight, Rokujō's "thoughts of dew ablaze with resentment" begin to proliferate. Assuming the role of mouthpiece for Rokujō, the chorus discloses her troubled thoughts in a congruent, metered song centered on the upper register and ending in the lower register (*ageuta shōdan*):

> Warehito no tame tsurakereba
> Warehito no tame tsurakereba
> Kanarazu mi ni mo mukuu nari
> Nani wo nageku zo kuzu no ha no

Urami wa sara ni tsukisumaji
Urami wa sara ni tsukisumaji.
　　(Yokomichi and Omote, 40: 127)

When you are cruel toward others,
when you are cruel toward others,
it will inevitably return to you.
Why do I grieve? Turning over the arrowroot leaf,
I see that my resentment will never be exhausted,
my resentment will never be exhausted.

Through the mouthpiece of the chorus, which assumes multiple perspectives during the course of the play without ever taking on its own individual persona or character, Rokujō fatalistically resigns herself to the eternal karmic return of her own inexhaustible resentment. If one looks (*mi*) at the underside (*ura*) of Rokujō's resentment (*urami*), as she does, one discovers the intertextual reinscription of two famous *waka*: one from the eighth imperial poetry anthology, *Shinkokinshū* (New collection of ancient and modern poems), compiled by Fujiwara no Teika and others under the aegis of Emperor Gotoba (r. 1183–98) in 1201, and another from the first imperial poetry anthology, *Kokinshū* (Collection of ancient and modern poems), compiled by Ki no Tsurayuki and others under the aegis of Emperor Daigo (r. 897–930) in 905. The two poetic intertexts are as follows:

Nagekajina
Omoeba hito ni
Tsurakarishi
Kono yo nagara no
Mukui narikeri.

I will not lament
recollecting the pain
I have caused others:
while in this world
there is retribution.[57]

Akikaze no
Fukiuragaesu
Kuzu no ha no
Uramite mo nao
Urameshiki ka na.

As the autumn wind
turns over
the arrowroot leaves,
I see the other side: the more I resent,
the more resentful I become.[58]

Playing off these poetic intertexts of retribution and resentment heightens the intensity of Rokujō's own returning cruelty and inexhaustible resentment. The poetic recollection of resentment incites Rokujō to strike out at the mute signifier of Aoi's empty *kosode* kimono in the following exchange (*kakeai*) between Rokujō and Teruhi:

ROKUJŌ
  Ara urameshi ya ima wa utade wa kanaisōrōmaji.

TERUHI
  Ara asamashi ya Rokujō no Miyasudokoro hodo no onmi nite
  Uwanari uchi no onfurumai ikade saru koto sōrōbeki tada
      oboshimeshitomarisōrae.

ROKUJŌ
  Iya ika ni iu to mo ima wa utade wa kanōmaji tote
  Makura ni tachiyori chōdo uteba

TERUHI
  Kono ue wa tote tachiyorite
  warawa mo ato nite ku wo misuru.

ROKUJŌ
  Ima no urami wa arishi mukui
  Shinni no homura wa mi wo kogasu.
       (Yokomichi and Omote, 40: 127–28)

ROKUJŌ
  Oh, how detestable!
  Even now I cannot refrain from striking her.

TERUHI
  How shameful! For one in Lady Rokujō's position
  to engage in the practice of secondary wife beating—how
      can such conduct be tolerated? Stop such thoughts
      at once!

ROKUJŌ
  Well, no matter what you say, I am unable to resist striking her now.
  Rising, she approaches her pillow, and just as she strikes . . .

TERUHI
  More than this I cannot allow. She approaches, saying:
  "I will inflict pain upon you at the foot of her bed."[59]

ROKUJŌ
  Today's bitterness is a vengeful return of the past:
  the flames of wrath envelop me.[60]

This scene of jealous rage and violence on stage refers to the Muromachi practice called *uwanari uchi*, or "secondary wife beating," which describes the violence committed by a man's original legal wife (*konami*) who had lost her husband's favor and support against a supplanting secondary wife or wives (*uwanari*).[61] *Uwanari uchi* was also performed sporadically during the Heian period (794–1185), but it was not until Muromachi that it became a full-blown social practice. A dramatization of *uwanari uchi* also occurs in Zeami's *Kanawa* (Iron crown), in which a jealous wife, who has been cast aside by her philandering husband in favor of another woman, seeks to avenge her humiliation by transforming herself into a demon and attacking a pair of dolls, which serve as substitutes for the husband and his new lover. In the end, her supernatural fury is subdued through the efforts of a sage named Abe no Seimei.

Generally speaking, the abandoned first wife would assemble her female friends and relatives within a month after her husband had adopted another wife; together, the first wife and her female army would besiege the new wife's house, attacking the new wife with bamboo sticks and poles, as well as smashing her belongings. The violence usually escalated when the new wife's own female friends, relatives, and servants entered the fray, each side exchanging blows with the other. Finally, mediators from both sides intervened to resolve the conflict. Throughout both the melée and its resolution, the husband maintained a safe distance on the sidelines, refusing to become involved. This desperate fight, initiated by his first wife, is waged both to recover the husband's support and to punish the perceived cause of its withdrawal.

In special cases, *uwanari uchi* could also refer to an abandoned or neglected secondary wife, who, out of jealousy, attacked the principal wife because she received greater support and affection from their shared husband. Although Rokujō was not an official secondary wife, the case of Rokujō's possession and beating of Aoi seems to be an example of the latter type of *uwanari uchi*. The Rokujō case does not match the paradigmatic form of *uwanari uchi*, since it is Aoi who is Genji's principal legal wife, or *kita no kata*, whereas Rokujō is merely one of his paramours. Even if one construes the *uwanari uchi* practice as simply a quarrel between an earlier wife and a later wife, irrespective of who is regarded as principal and who as secondary, the practice still does not apply exactly to the power dynamics binding Genji, Rokujō, and Aoi, since it is clear that Aoi is both an earlier wife and also Genji's principal wife. Whereas Genji and Aoi married when he was twelve and she sixteen, Genji did not adopt Rokujō as a lover until he was sixteen and she twenty-four. Therefore, neither is Rokujō an earlier or principal wife, nor is Aoi a later or secondary wife. Nevertheless, *Aoi no Ue* presents Rokujō's beating of Aoi as a special example of "secondary wife beating," which follows the Muromachi social practice in spirit if not in letter. As Genji's patronage and affection for Rokujō are displaced by the attention and support he gives to the pregnant Aoi, Rokujō's resentment erupts in the form of spiritual attacks on Aoi.

From another perspective, it is worth noting that, as *Aoi no Ue* is staged, Rokujō does not beat Aoi herself, but rather an empty, folded kimono lying at the front of the stage. Given Aoi's status as a substitutive signifier, Rokujō's staged beating of the empty kimono representing Aoi bears a strong resemblance to social practices in both the Heian past and the Edo future.

During the Heian period, substitutive dolls and talismans, called *hitogata*, *katashiro*, and *nademono*, were employed as forms of sympathetic magic during Shinto purification rites (*harae*): after rubbing the substitutive images against one's body, or breathing upon them, to bring about a transference of pollution and defilement (*kegare*), they were sent floating down a river or stream in order to restore the sociopolitical harmony that had been momentarily disrupted by the transgressive chaos of pollution.[62] In addition to their use in purification rites, such substitutive images could also be used to cast a curse upon one's enemies: in this case, one would first bury the image, and then recite magical spells and incantations. As Ivan Morris notes, if "carried out effectively, this could result in illness or even death for the victim, and it was of course one of the few methods of redress available against more powerful members of the hierarchy."[63]

Readers of the early Edo writer Ihara Saikaku (1642–93) will perhaps see in the figure of the violently jealous Rokujō, striking the empty kimono of Aoi, a Muromachi antecedent of the seventeenth-century practice of *rinkikō*, or "jealousy meeting," so vividly described in Saikaku's *Kōshoku ichidai onna* (Life of an amorous woman; 1686):

> Some three dozen women, including kitchen maids and serving girls, answered the summons and seated themselves without ceremony in a great circle. . . . The lady-in-waiting Yoshioka addressed us severally in these terms: "Each of you may speak without reserve and confess your troubles openly. If you thwart the love of other women by pouring forth your hate, if you revile men with your bitter jealousy, if you tell of loves that went awry—all this will be to the greater relish of the lady whom we serve." . . . The Lady Yoshioka extracted a female doll, which was the very image of a living person. . . . Thereat the women began to speak in turn of what lay on their minds. . . . "I was born in the town of Tochi in Yamato, and duly pledged my troth in marriage. But that rascally husband of mine went to the city of Nara and met the daughter of a priest at the Kasuga Shrine. . . . One day I followed him secretly. My heart was pounding as I eavesdropped by her house. I saw the girl open the side door to let my husband in. . . . Then, without the slightest sign of shame, she drew her body close to him. 'Oh no,' said I at this, 'that man is mine!' And opening my tooth-blackened mouth, I fastened my teeth on her."

So saying, the Lady Iwahashi fastened herself onto the beautiful doll that stood before us. Boundlessly terrifying it was, and I can remember her appearance at that moment as though she were before me now.

This was the beginning of the Jealousy Meeting. Next another lady-in-waiting squirmed her way forward, quite beside herself with spiteful rage. How wretched a thing is a woman's heart that it can express itself like this![64]

By enabling women to ritually discharge the festering jealousy and resentment harbored towards unfaithful husbands and their mistresses, the "jealousy meeting" redirected potentially violent feelings onto the substitutive figures of life-sized scapegoat dolls, and thereby contained the chaotic flames of jealousy that threatened to tear apart the polygynous social order.[65] During the Edo period, the "jealousy meeting" was the only institutionally authorized channel for women to articulate their grievances against their philandering husbands in particular, and against the polygynous system more generally; to do so in any other way was strongly prohibited by conventional social mores, and was even considered legal grounds for divorce.

Female jealousy had been legally codified long before as grounds for divorce in section 28 of the Law of Households under the Yōrō legal code of 718 (put into effect in 757), the supreme administrative and penal governing code in Japan until the mid nineteenth century: "The seven grounds for divorce of a wife by her husband are: (1) if she is childless (i.e., without a male child); (2) if she commits adultery; (3) if she disobeys her parents-in-law; (4) if she talks too much; (5) if she steals; (6) if she is jealous; and (7) if she has a bad disease."[66] Husbands could appeal to section 28 in order to divorce their wives and dispossess them of social and economic power, or, at the very least, to keep their wives under their control with the threat of such dispossession.

Though similarities between the Heian- and Edo-period practices suggest a distant historical affiliation, there is no evidence to prove that substitutive dolls were ever employed during the Heian period in the sort of institutionalized collective discharge of jealousy dramatized by Edo-period "jealousy meetings." Nor can I prove that Rokujō's beating of the folded kimono signifying Aoi on the Muromachi stage actually reiterates the Heian past or anticipates the Edo future. Nevertheless, the three-way comparison remains a provocative one, if only because Rokujō vents her jealousy on the empty kimono much in the same way that a Heian woman might have unleashed her frustration against the substitutive image of her rival by burying and cursing it, or an Edo woman, participating in a "jealousy meeting," might have discharged her rage against the life-sized scapegoat doll substituting for her husband's mistress by kicking and screaming at it. In each case, blame was displaced from the philandering husband onto the "other woman," since it was assumed that jealousy was ultimately the woman's fault.

In the next chapter, I examine how the staging of female jealousy and its exorcism in *Aoi no Ue* is linked to the loss of female power and property in the medieval period. *Aoi no Ue* is read as a striking revision of the sexual politics in *Genji monogatari* and against the sociohistorical backdrop of important changes in female inheritance rights that took place during the Kamakura and Muromachi periods.

CHAPTER 3

A Woman (Dis)possessed on the Muromachi Stage: Lady Rokujō in Aoi no Ue

The Question of Rokujō's Jealousy

Not surprisingly, Rokujō herself has often been interpreted as the archetypal embodiment of "feminine jealousy's destructive power."[1] But Rokujō is more than just the archetypal personification of female jealousy. Indeed, I would argue that Rokujō is not so much a jealous monster in the Shakespearean mode—"a monster / Begot upon itself, born on itself" (*Othello* 3.4.161–62)—as she is a malevolent spirit avenging the sociopolitical injustices she has suffered at the hands of Aoi, Genji, and opposing political factions at court. Rokujō's jealousy is not born of itself, nor is it produced *ex nihilo*; rather it is born out of the frustrations and resentment that are inevitably produced by a polygynous society: Rokujō desires both to avenge and to repossess that of which she has been dispossessed.

Jacques Derrida has written provocatively in *Glas* that "jealousy is always excessive because it is busy with a past that will never have been present and so can never be presented nor allow any hope for presentation." "One is never jealous in front of a present scene—even the worst imaginable—nor a future one. . . . [O]ne is only jealous of a *seing* [signature] or, what comes down here to the same, of an *already*."[2] According to Derrida, insofar as jealousy emerges from the otherness called the unconscious, "jealousy always has to do with some trace, never with perception"[3] of a present scene. While I would agree that jealousy is motivated by traces of events that are never totally recoverable in their contingent singularity, since, like any signifier or signature, such traces are divided from their origins of production as soon as they are inscribed, recalled, or cited, nevertheless, I would contend that, like the traces of karma, which are neither totally decipherable nor totally indecipherable but somewhere in between the two, the remaining traces of jealous (dis)possession *are* interpretable, even if they are never totally retrievable or unequivocally meaningful.

I read Rokujō's possession of Aoi as a possession out of dispossession, which is linked to Rokujō's displacement from her position at court after the death of her husband, the former crown prince. Such traces of (dis)possession, particularly those relating to Rokujō's deceased husband and father, though still legible in *Genji monogatari*, are almost totally illegible by the time of the Muromachi staging of *Aoi no Ue*, since no mention, either explicit or implicit, is made of Rokujō's husband or father in the noh performance. One of the few traces of (dis)possession that does remain legible in *Aoi no Ue*, and that is probably related to larger sociopolitical changes occurring in the Muromachi discourse network around the time that *Aoi no Ue* was performed, is the linkage between Rokujō's jealous possession of Aoi and the latter's pregnancy.

I have already noted that Rokujō possesses because she herself has been dispossessed by Aoi. But what is it precisely that Aoi has taken away from Rokujō? What is it that incites such violent jealousy? Rokujō provides a few hints in the following *dan'uta* section of *Aoi no Ue*, an evocative lyric chant (*yowagin*) sung in congruent style mostly through the mouthpiece of the chorus:

CHORUS
Urameshi no kokoro ya
Ara urameshi no kokoro ya
Hito no urami no fukaku shite
Uki ne ni nakasetamō tomo
Ikite kono yo ni mashimasaba
Mizu kuraki
Sawabe no hotaru no kage yori mo
Hikaru kimi to zo chigiran.

ROKUJŌ
Warawa wa yomogiu no

CHORUS
Moto arazarishi mi to narite
Hazue no tsuyu to kie mo seba
Sore sae koto ni urameshi ya
Yume ni da ni
Kaeranu mono wo wa ga chigiri
Mukashigatari ni narinureba
Nao mo omoi wa masukagami
Sono omokage mo hazukashi ya

Makura ni tateru yareguruma
Uchinosekakureyukō yo
Uchinosekakureyukō yo.

(Yokomichi and Omote, 40: 128)

CHORUS
How hateful is your heart,
oh, how hateful is your heart.
My resentment is deep-seated.
Even if I make you wail in misery,
while you are alive in this world,
you shall remain tied in bonds of marriage
to one more radiant than the image of fireflies
flashing over a dark marsh.

ROKUJŌ
Beneath the wormwood, I . . .

CHORUS
will not be the one I was before.
To disappear like dew on a leaf tip—
how bitter it all is!
Even in dreams,
our vow will not return,
having become a tale of bygone days;
and yet my attachment grows all the more:
in the clear mirror,
how shameful is the visage!
Standing by her pillow, into my dilapidated carriage
I shall conceal her and ride away,
I shall conceal her and ride away!

Rokujō's most bitter complaint is that Aoi "shall remain tied in bonds of marriage to one more radiant than the image of fireflies flashing over a dark
marsh" (*mizu kuraki, sawabe no hotaru no kage yori mo, hikaru kimi to zo chigiran*).
The "radiant one" (*hikaru kimi*), whose visage (*kage*) is like "fireflies flashing
over a dark marsh," is, of course, Hikaru Genji. Rokujō fears that Aoi's pregnancy will strengthen her bonds of marriage to Genji, and that Rokujō herself will, as a result, be completely dispossessed of Genji's support. Thus, in attacking Aoi, Rokujō's jealous spirit effectively attacks the progeny of Genji,
who will ensure Aoi's continued social and economic well-being. Indeed, it
might be said that in the famous scene of the "carriage quarrel" (*kuruma arasoi*), which is described in detail in *Genji monogatari* and alluded to more than
once in *Aoi no Ue*, one witnesses the struggle between two rivals, not only for
a better carriage position at the Aoi Festival, but also for the privilege of carrying Genji's child: that is, for the privilege of serving as the "carriage" or "ve-

hicle" of Genji's socioeconomic progeny, with all of the patriarchal connotations associated with that function.

Furthermore, insofar as Aoi eventually gives birth to Yūgiri, Genji's eldest son and principal heir, who later rises up through the court ranks and attains the powerful political position of chancellor, Rokujō has much to gain by spiritually possessing the pregnant body of Aoi and attempting to force it into miscarriage. In *Genji monogatari*, the fact that Aoi is carrying Genji's child transforms her in his eyes into "someone he cannot abandon" (*yamugoto naki kata*) (*GM* 2: 25); as Aoi's sickness worsens, he is especially pained and saddened because of the suffering she experiences during her pregnancy. Rokujō is well aware that Aoi's status as vehicle of Genji's progeny insures that she (and her child) will continue to receive his support, while Rokujō herself will continue to be neglected (*GM* 2: 28). This issue of pregnancy in relation to Rokujō's possession of Aoi may be explored further by examining the genealogy of female inheritance rights in medieval Japan. It is to this topic that I now turn.

Rights of Inheritance and Rights of Women

The linkages binding Rokujō's possession of Aoi to Aoi's pregnancy are underscored by a contingent reversal of the relationship of forces defining female inheritance rights on the stage of the Muromachi assemblage. Before analyzing this reversal, let us first consider the historical series of events leading up to it, from Heian to late Kamakura (1185–1333).

In the Heian period, women were almost completely excluded from the patriarchal court bureaucracy, and thus were unable to acquire—except through inheritance—the *shiki*, or titled properties, that were awarded to every government official according to his rank and post.[4] From the Heian period onward, the inheritance of *shiki* became practically synonymous with the acquisition of house and family guardianship: that is, the right to serve as head of one's family or clan. Not surprisingly, such guardianship was usually inherited by the eldest son.[5]

Though Heian aristocratic women rarely took control of their family's most valuable property, since such control was generally bequeathed to the principal male heir, nevertheless, the partible principle of inheritance rights, which had been employed since the eighth century, insured that mothers, daughters, and sisters gained some share of the family estate, whether in the form of land, residences, and/or movable property.[6]

In principle, since inheritance was lineal rather than lateral, an aristocratic woman could even inherit the family's main property holdings, if no suitable male heir was available. In fact, Heian women were more likely to inherit land from their parents than were their parents' male siblings or cousins: "Heian Japanese adhered to the sound principle that preference in inheritance be given to close women before distant males."[7] But in such cases, female heirs were bound to bequeath such important family property either to the first available male heir who would preserve the integrity of the family's lineage, or (in special cases) to an adopted kinsman who showed great promise as a prospective family head.[8] The relatively high status of Heian aristocratic women was the result of such basic female inheritance rights in combination with various uxorilocal (*shōseikon, tsumadoikon,* and *mukotorikon*) marriage practices.[9] The wife-visiting focus of such marriage practices, although not a sign of ascendant female power or matriarchal authority, as some commentators have made it out to be, did attest to the strength of a woman's family backing.[10]

With minor changes and variations, the two main principles of Heian inheritance rights—"lineal primogeniture in the matter of house succession, and divided inheritance in the matter of property"[11]—would remain in force until the end of the Kamakura period. After the political decline of the court aristocracy and the rise of the Kamakura *bakufu* (shogunate) in the late twelfth century, the *sōryō* (eldest son), or primogeniture, system of family guardianship and management became dominant. The eldest son now inherited not only possession of the family's most important land holdings but also administrative control over the family's entire estate, even those holdings legally possessed by his siblings.

Under the patriarchal *sōryō* system, women could, in special circumstances, inherit the most important family holdings (especially *shiki*) as temporary estate managers (called *jitō*) appointed by the shogunate, but *only* if there were no male offspring, or if the male offspring were too young to exercise control. Indeed, some women in the Kamakura period not only inherited *shiki*, they also, on occasion, bequeathed them to their own daughters, if a suitable male heir was not available. Still, it is clear that in the Kamakura period, just as in the Heian period, "males were the preferred vehicle for property exchanges"[12] that were critical to the preservation of the family line. In addition, the newly prevailing virilocal (*yometorikon*) marriage practices, which meant that the husband now effectively adopted the wife into his own family, ensured that the woman's interests were subordinated to those of her husband's family line.[13] During the Kamakura period, it became increasingly important to maintain the integrity and cohesion of the family line and its holdings for military purposes, so that the family would be in a stronger economic and political position if internecine war were to break out, as it often did.[14]

In the late Kamakura period the shogunate attempted to preserve the integrity of the family line from outside interference by issuing various prohibitions restricting inheritance to consanguineous kin, as opposed to adopted kin. By 1286 these restrictions were tightened even further to include only consanguineous *male* kin—to the utter exclusion of female kin—in response to recent conflicts with Mongol forces under Kublai Khan in the Battle of Bunei (1274) and the Battle of Kōan (1281). In an attempt to further expand his already burgeoning Yüan empire, Kublai had sought repeatedly through diplomatic channels to persuade the Japanese to establish voluntarily a tributary relationship with the khan, which would recognize the khan's supreme authority and Japan's subordinate status. After the Kamakura government refused to respond to any of the khan's diplomatic overtures, the khan sent an expeditionary force of some forty thousand men in 1274 (and reportedly as many as one hundred thousand in 1281) to invade the southern Japanese island of Kyushu and force it into subjugation. Though the khan's forces initially overwhelmed Japanese warriors with superior military tactics and technology, driving them into retreat at almost every battle or skirmish, the khan's army was miraculously driven away in both 1274 and 1281 by violent typhoons at Kyushu's northern Hakata Bay, in which large numbers of the khan's ships and men were destroyed. Japanese have long referred to these typhoons as *kamikaze*, or "divine winds," in the belief that the gods had sent them to rescue their country from the Mongol invaders, but the *kamikaze* were nothing more than particularly dramatic examples of how unexpected contingencies can influence the profusion of events that is history.

In response to this series of conflicts with the Mongols, which was the only significant military threat posed by a foreign power to Japan's national security during its long premodern history, restrictions were issued in 1286 that eliminated female inheritance rights altogether in order to maintain "a continuous anti-Mongol guard effort"[15] in Kyushu. It was feared that unless the Kamakura *bakufu* stepped in to prevent powerful families and clans from being fragmented into smaller secondary families through the dispersion of the family estate, Japan's national security would continue to be vulnerable to attacks from foreign powers such as the Mongols. Though the dramatic reversal in inheritance rights for women was initially intended only for those families residing in Kyushu, it eventually spread to other areas of the country as well, both as a way of maintaining the power of the main house over the smaller branch houses and also to enable the *bakufu* to exert influence over the family as a whole by approving or rejecting the proposed *sōryō* (eldest son and house chieftain).[16]

By the early Muromachi period, the Kamakura primogeniture (*sōryō*) system was completely denuded of its partible principle, and, as a result, inheritance practice was transformed into a *unigeniture* (or "one-heir") system, so that *all* family holdings were bequeathed in a single inheritance to the eldest son, who was to be authorized by the Ashikaga *bakufu* in his position of house leadership (*katoku*). "Under the Ashikaga, the position of house head had become, to a degree, appointive,"[17] something that would have been almost unthinkable during most of the Kamakura period.

The final excision of the partible principle dealt a serious blow to the inheritance rights and powers of Muromachi women, one that would adversely affect the status of Japanese women throughout the rest of the medieval and early modern periods of Japanese history.[18] Though junior male siblings were also adversely affected by the patriarchal system of unigeniture, and just as feudalistically bound to the patrimonial power of their elder brothers, women had the most to lose, since their status was rendered even more insecure. In the Muromachi period, women were no longer in a position either to inherit or to accumulate property as they had in the not-so-distant Kamakura and Heian past.

In the historical flow of becoming, the Mongol invasions unexpectedly served as the contingent spur that hastened the transformation of inheritance rights in the late Kamakura and early Muromachi periods. Though this reversal of inheritance rights and practices is not *explicitly* codified in *Aoi no Ue*, nevertheless, the very fact that the scene of Rokujō's possession of Aoi, indirectly linked to the birth of Genji's eldest son, was performed on a Muromachi stage, authorized by the patronage of the Ashikaga *bakufu*, in whose power it was to select and appoint *sōryō*, suggests that the record of contingent power struggles inscribed within *Aoi no Ue* was also linked to—and, therefore, inscribed by—the struggles being waged across the Muromachi discourse network. That the Muromachi discourse network effectively served as the theater for the staging of Rokujō's contingent (dis)possession simply heightens the dramatic poignancy and contemporaneous relevance of her plight, especially since women in Muromachi and later periods "had lost inheritance rights and were only esteemed for their motherhood": that is, for their ability to bear the heir that would "carry on the family line with its attendant property and authority,"[19] serving as the vehicle (or "carriage") of family continuity.

Hidden Complicities: Rewriting Genji's Involvement

"Beneath the wormwood, I . . . / Will not be the one I was before" (*Warawa wa yomogiu no / moto arazarishi mi to narite*). This poignant realization—begun by Rokujō and completed by the chorus in the *dan'uta* section (a lyric chant in the congruent style) of *Aoi no Ue*—underscores Rokujō's acute sense of loss by reinscribing a poetic intertext from chapter 15 of *Genji monogatari*, "Yomogiu" (Wormwood):

> Tazunete mo
> Ware koso towame
> Michi mo naku
> Fukaki yomogi no
> Moto no kokoro wo.
>
> (*GM* 2: 338)
>
> I will pay a visit
> even if I must search
> without path
> beneath the dense wormwood
> where feelings are as before.

In the *dan'uta* section of *Aoi no Ue*, the chorus completes the thoughts of Rokujō, speaking as her mouthpiece, and yet the chorus is not simply identical with Rokujō, since it can also serve as a mouthpiece for other characters. Though the chorus does not have a personality or character of its own, even as the mouthpiece of Rokujō, its performative separation on stage introduces an ineradicable element of otherness and exteriority into the subjectivity of Rokujō. In effect, the performative distancing of the chorus stages the very self-alienation exemplified by the separation of Rokujō's spirit from her body.

Genji wrote the above poem upon seeing the dilapidated old mansion belonging to Suetsumuhana, one of his most neglected (and—due to her prominent red nose—mocked) lovers. Like Suetsumuhana, Rokujō, too, was neglected by Genji, and her socioeconomic standing declined as a result. But unlike Suetsumuhana, who faithfully awaited Genji's return even as her position grew increasingly desperate, Rokujō's feelings did not remain the same, but instead grew more and more bitter as she became more and more attached to Genji. This bitterness is evoked in the following *dan'uta* passage from *Aoi no Ue*:

> Even in dreams,
> our vow will not return,
> having become a tale of bygone days;
> and yet my attachment grows all the more . . .

Though the vow of love between Genji and Rokujō lost its promise—becoming a fleeting dream that could not be revived—Rokujō's attachment to this broken promise nonetheless became increasingly tenacious. Her despair that their vow would not be reaffirmed "even in dreams" reinscribes a conventional poetic conceit illustrated by numerous poems from the *Kokinshū*, such as the following:

> Yume ni dani
> Au koto kataku
> Nariyuku wa
> Ware ya i wo nenu
> Hito ya wasururu.

> Even in dreams,
> meeting you
> has become difficult.
> Is it because I am unable to sleep,
> or have you forgotten me?[20]

It was commonly believed that by concentrating on one's lover before falling asleep, one could compel the lover to appear in one's dreams. Moreover, if the lover appeared in one's dreams without such presleep conjuring, then one was probably the focus of the lover's thoughts.

Rokujō is convinced that the bond that once tied her to Genji has been irreparably broken, since he will not appear before her "even in dreams." That their vow has become a *mukashigatari*, or "tale of long ago," self-reflexively underscores not only the fictionality of their status as characters from *Genji monogatari* but also the potential for any vow, whether in a work of fiction or not, to *become fictional* once it has been retrospectively turned into a narrative of the past after the relationship has come to an end. Perhaps there is something intrinsic to the performance of every vow that lends it to such fictionalization even before the relationship has become a *mukashigatari*, insofar as the vow is always a performative projection held out toward the indefinite future and its "as if," never a constative description of an actual state of affairs.[21] At any rate, Genji's own pangs of guilt eventually compel him in *Genji monogatari* to renew his support (and, in effect, his vow) for Suetsumuhana; but it is clear from Rokujō's bitter complaints in *Aoi no Ue* that she expects no such compassion. Does Genji bear any responsibility for the plight of Rokujō, or for Rokujō's possession of Aoi? It is to this question and its strikingly different answers in *Genji monogatari* and *Aoi no Ue* that I now turn.

In *Genji monogatari* it is Genji alone who hears the voice of Rokujō's malevolent spirit and Genji alone who sees her demeanor reflected in the visage of the women she possesses (*GM* 2: 33–34). Though the exorcists, performing prayers and rituals in order to expel the various spirits possessing Aoi, are able to compel numerous spirits to identify themselves and their grievances, and though they suspect that the most tenacious *mono no ke* of all belongs to Rokujō, they are never able to identify Rokujō's spirit as such. Only Genji recognizes that the possessive spirit belongs to Rokujō, since only he is able to con-verse with her spirit through the objects of her possession. Both while she is alive and after she is dead, Rokujō's spirit bitterly reproaches Genji for his ne-glect. In the following passage from *Genji monogatari*, Rokujō's dead spirit up-braids Genji through the mouthpiece of his most beloved consort, Murasaki: "At that time, when I was still living in this world, you thought me beneath another, contemptuously abandoning me" (*GM* 4: 227–28). The "other," for whom Genji abandoned Rokujō, is not specified in this passage, but is usually interpreted as being a reference to Aoi. Of course, it could just as well be a ref-erence to the myriad "others" whom Genji favored over Rokujō. The point, however, is that in *Genji monogatari* some linkage is at least intimated between the possession of Genji's lovers by Rokujō and Genji's own feelings of guilt over his neglect of Rokujō.

Two poems and their preceding headnote from Murasaki Shikibu's col-lection of poetry, though not directly tied to Genji's feelings of guilt, never-theless suggest a close parallel:

> On a painting is depicted the ugly figure of a woman possessed by a malevolent spirit. Behind her is painted the figure of a priest binding a man's former wife, who has turned into a demon. The man is reading a sutra in order to reproach and drive out the malevolent spirit. Looking upon this scene,

> Naki hito ni
> Kagoto wo kakete
> Wazurō mo
> Ono ga kokoro no
> Oni ni ya wa aranu.

> On one who is dead
> even suffering
> is blamed,
> but is it not the demon
> in his own heart?

Kaeshi (Reply):

> Kotowari ya
> Kimi ga kokoro no
> Yami nareba
> Oni no kage to wa
> Shiruku miyuramu.

> Indeed,
> out of your heart's
> darkness,
> the figure of the demon
> becomes clearly visible.[22]

Kokoro no oni, or "demon of the heart," is a phrase that occurs fifteen times in *Genji monogatari*.[23] This phrase, along with the above exchange from Murasaki Shikibu's poetry collection on the "heart's darkness" (*kokoro no yami*), aptly describes the pangs of guilt suffered by Genji upon witnessing the possessions of Aoi and his other lovers by Rokujō.[24] Though Genji actively represses such feelings of guilt, nevertheless they return to haunt him in the figure of Rokujō's malevolent spirit. In effect, Rokujō's *mono no ke* emerges both from the unconscious of her repressed jealousy and from the unconscious of Genji's repressed guilt.

Though Genji only passively bears responsibility for his neglect of Rokujō in the first thirteen chapters of *Genji monogatari*, in chapter 14, called "Miotsukushi" (Channel buoys), Genji actively begins to assume responsibility for his neglect by honoring Rokujō's deathbed request to look after her daughter Akikonomu. By providing support to Akikonomu—effectively adopting her as his own daughter—Genji not only appeases the vengeful spirit of Rokujō but also reinforces his own power at court through the manipulation of marriage alliances: Genji manages to position Akikonomu within the imperial harem of consorts, and eventually brings about her marriage to Emperor Reizei.[25] Such maneuvering ultimately puts Genji in a position of great influence vis-à-vis the new sovereign and empress, which is comparable to that of the famous Fujiwara regents (*sesshō*) and chancellors (*kanpaku*), who raised marriage politicking to a fine art by strategically forming alliances through marriage with members of the imperial family. By manipulating such conjugal ties, Genji greatly increases his own power, prestige, and influence at court. Once Akikonomu is installed as Reizei's principal wife, Genji becomes foster father to the empress and chancellor to the emperor.

In sharp contrast to *Genji monogatari*'s depiction of Genji's guilt and share of responsibility for Rokujō's possessive wanderings, *Aoi no Ue* almost completely omits Genji's involvement. In fact, the only reference to Genji in *Aoi no Ue* is the oblique allusion in the *dan'uta* section quoted above to "one more radiant than the image of fireflies flashing over a dark marsh." Genji never appears on the stage of *Aoi no Ue* as a character in the drama of Rokujō's possession of Aoi. Indeed, *Aoi no Ue* distinguishes itself as more than just a derivative representation of scenes from *Genji monogatari* by actively rewriting Rokujō's scene of possession so that Genji himself plays no role at all, neither bearing nor assuming any responsibility for what unfolds on the Muromachi stage. The absence of Genji in *Aoi no Ue*, along with the omission of his guilt, effectively mitigates the responsibility of a husband to both his principal and secondary wives (as well as to his numerous paramours), and thereby shifts the blame for Rokujō's possession of Aoi from the man's neglect to the woman's jealousy.

Aoi no Ue's rewriting of *Genji monogatari* is not merely a shift in emphasis; it is, more importantly, an active reconfiguration of power relations between men and women staged before the same Muromachi audience that
had witnessed the utter disinheritance of women. Unlike *Genji monogatari*,
which was composed by the "woman's hand" (*onnade*) and subjectivity of
Murasaki Shikibu, *Aoi no Ue* was written and rewritten exclusively by male
playwrights. In analyzing *Aoi no Ue*'s rewriting of *Genji monogatari*, it is important to recognize this implicit revision of gendered subject positions: instead of a female author enunciating feminine subject positions, *Aoi no Ue*
presents us with male playwrights enunciating feminine subject positions.
Moreover, the fact that all roles in noh, whether masculine or feminine, were
traditionally performed by male actors must also inform the staging of female jealousy in *Aoi no Ue*. As with other theatrical traditions (Greek tragedy,
Elizabethan drama) in which women were excluded from the creative process of theatrical image-making, women in noh plays such as *Aoi no Ue* op-
erate as mute signifiers and symbolic objects "manipulated and controlled ar-
tistically by male playwrights and male actors."[26] What *Aoi no Ue* stages, with
its ventriloquism of female jealousy and the possession of the female body by
male playwrights and actors, is nothing less than the exculpation of masculine responsibility in an era when women were more oppressed by men than
ever before. The force and effects of this exculpation are most clearly delineated by the revisionist ending of *Aoi no Ue*.

The Plot to Demonize Rokujō

At the end of the first act, Rokujō pulls her kimono up over her head
and withdraws to the rear of the stage. There, with the help of a stage assis-
tant, the *shite* removes the golden-eyed *deigan* mask and dons the golden-
horned *hannya*[27] mask of a vengeful female demon in a jealous rage. With its
protruding horns, disorderly hair, bulging golden eyes, and jutting teeth, the
mask is truly a horrifying sight. In modern performances, the *shite* also reveals a previously concealed *surihaku* upper kimono with a triangular pattern
printed across it, suggesting the scales of a serpent.

As the *shite* changes costume at the rear of the stage, the imperial retainer
sends a messenger to request the services of a holy man from Yokawa, a site
on Mount Hiei (northeast of Kyoto) famous for its innumerable Buddhist
temples belonging to the Tendai sect of esoteric Buddhism. The malevolent
spirit of Rokujō has proven to be too strong even for Teruhi's powers, and so
a male exorcist is summoned to Aoi's sickbed. The messenger arrives at the

holy man's abode and enters just as the holy man is reciting esoteric prayers
in the noncongruent style:

> Kushiki no mado no mae
> Jūjō no yuka no hotori ni yuga no hossui wo tatae
> Sanmitsu no tsuki wo sumasu tokoro ni.
>   (Yokomichi and Omote, 40: 128–29)

> Before the window of the nine forms of consciousness,
> around the seat of the ten vehicles, I am filled with the holy waters of yoga,
> which clarify the moon of the three secret practices.

The quick accumulation of Buddhist references right at the outset—"nine
forms of consciousness" (*kushiki*),[28] "seat of ten vehicles" (*jūjō no yuka*),[29]
"yoga" (*yuga*),[30] "holy waters" (*hossui*),[31] and "moon of three secret practices"
(*sanmitsu no tsuki*)[32]—leaves no doubt that we are dealing with a Buddhist
sage of esoteric stripe. The holy man initially resists breaking off his performance of special rites, but as soon as he discovers that it is the powerful Minister of the Left who has summoned him to exorcise the malevolent spirit
possessing Aoi, he reconsiders, and, in a condensation of time typical of *mugen*
noh, arrives at the minister's mansion with the very next step. The holy man
is ushered in to Aoi's bedside, and there he begins at once to perform the rites
of exorcism, singing a noncongruent strong chant (*tsuyogin*) with a forceful
melodic style and "a powerful vibrato":[33]

> Gyōja wa kaji ni mairan to
> En no Gyōja no ato wo tsugi
> Taikon ryōbu no mine wo wake
> Shippō no tsuyu wo haraishi suzukake ni
> Fujō wo hedatsuru ninniku no kesa
> Akagi no juzu no irataka wo
> Sarari sarari to oshimonde
> Hito inori koso inottare
> Namaku samanda basarada.
>   (Yokomichi and Omote, 40: 129)

> The ascetic priest comes to perform special prayers:
> he follows in the steps of En no Gyōja,
> scaling the peaks of the Womb and Diamond realms.
> In a hempen cloak, he brushes off the dew of seven jewels.[34]
> A robe of forbearance shields him from defilement.
> The redwood beads of the rosary
> rustle as I rub them
> and recite a single prayer:
> *namaku samanda basarada.*

By performing special prayers to expel the malevolent spirit of Rokujō, the holy man of Yokawa "follows in the steps of En no Gyōja." En no Gyōja (En the Ascetic), otherwise known as En no Ozunu (born ca. 634), is the legendary miracle worker, mountain ascetic (*yamabushi*), and founder of the Shugendō sect of syncretic mountain Buddhism on Mount Omine in Yamato province (present-day Nara prefecture). He taught his followers (called *shūgenja*) that, by performing ascetic practices, rites, and austerities in the mountains, they could attain mystic powers (*kenryoku* or *iryoku*), which would enable them to subdue demons, placate malign spirits, heal illnesses, and divine the future. Mountains were the privileged realm of En no Gyōja and later *yamabushi* pilgrims both because they were worshipped syncretically (*honji suijaku*), as natural manifestations of Shinto gods emanating from Buddhas and bodhisattvas, and because they were thought to reflect the cosmological patterns iconographically inscribed on esoteric Buddhist mandalas, such as the Womb and Diamond Realm mandalas.

Throughout the medieval period, *yamabushi* often performed exorcisms in conjunction with female shamans like Teruhi, with the former serving as the diagnostician of possession and the latter serving as the medium of possession.[35] By performing esoteric rituals involving divine offerings, magical incantations, and manual signs invoking Buddhist powers, professional exorcists such as the holy man from Yokawa transferred malign spirits to a spiritual medium or shamaness (*yorimashi*, *yoribito*, *miko*, or *reibai*). The shamaness served as a vessel through which the malign spirit articulated its identity and demands, effectively offering herself up for (dis)possession by the spirit in order to enable the possessed person to repossess his or her own body and spirit. Once the spirit had been transferred to the shamaness, the exorcist compelled it to identify itself and its motives, and then drove it away. Some scholars think that *yamabushi* priests and shamanesses eventually "became the predecessors of professional reciters, ballad singers and actor-dancers like those in the Noh theater."[36]

In *Genji monogatari*, Aoi is treated neither by Teruhi the Shamaness nor by the holy man from Yokawa, but rather is tended to by a number of exorcists referred to as *genza* (*GM* 2: 25–26). *Genza* is a Heian designation for *shūgenja*, or followers of the Shūgendō sect founded by En no Gyōja. *Genza*, like *yamabushi*, were ascetics who practiced various mystic rites in the mountains in order to overpower evil forces and attachments. But it should be added that, although the two figures have much in common, it would be anachronistic to equate them, since the term *yamabushi* had not yet come into usage as a term designating *shūgenja* during the period in which *Genji monogatari* was written (ca. 1002–6).

In *Aoi no Ue*, the *yamabushi* from Yokawa not only follows, inherits, and succeeds the legacy of En no Gyōja, he also transmits the special rites and prayers spoken by En no Gyōja, grafting the vestigial traces and marks (*ato*) of En no Gyōja onto a new context (all are connotations associated with the verb *tsugu*).[37] The citationality of the holy man's performance is marked syntactically by the particle *to*, which functions in *Gyōja wa kaji ni mairan to* ("the ascetic comes to perform special prayers") as a quotative particle whose modifying verb (e.g., "say," "think," "intend," "hear") has been omitted: "They say / I think / I heard that the ascetic comes to perform special prayers." By citing the magical incantations (*kaji*) conventionally associated with En no Gyōja, the holy man of Yokawa simultaneously invokes his exorcistic power and spiritual authority.[38] In effect, the holy man of Yokawa is himself a quotation of En no Gyōja—a quotation that repeats En no Gyōja without being identical to En no Gyōja—just as every follower who inherits and recites his master's teachings is a general repetition of the same that is nonetheless singularly different.

Let us follow more closely the movement of the holy man's citations. "Scaling the peaks of *taikon ryōbu*" refers to the two most important cosmological mandalas in esoteric Buddhism, the Womb and Diamond Realm mandalas, which provide iconographic figurations of the Buddhist universe centered on the cosmic Buddha Dainichi Nyorai (Great Sun Buddha), with various lesser Buddhas, bodhisattvas, and other deities hierarchically classified around the periphery according to rank. The Womb (or Matrix-Store) Realm Mandala (*Taizōkai mandara*) symbolizes the phenomenal, conditioned multiplicity of the Buddhist universe, with more than four hundred deities iconographically classified into twelve concentric squares radiating out from the noumenal unity at the center of the mandala, where Dainichi Nyorai is depicted at the heart of an eight-petaled lotus. Conversely, the Diamond Realm Mandala (*Kongōkai mandara*) symbolizes the noumenal, unconditioned unity of Dainichi Nyorai at the center of the Buddhist universe, infusing the phenomenal multiplicity on the periphery of the mandala, where more than fourteen hundred deities are iconographically classified into nine squares.

It was believed by practitioners of esoteric Buddhism that one could attain enlightenment in *this* world—"attaining buddhahood in this very body" (*sokushin jōbutsu*)—by meditating on the intertwining aspects of the two mandalas, particularly the way in which they evoke the chiasmic unity of phenomenal duality and noumenal nonduality: that is, the duality of nonduality and the nonduality of duality. Taken together, the two mandalas illustrate both the dualistic, phenomenal aspect of the Buddhist universe, with its proliferation of divisions, levels, and classifications, and also the nondualistic, noumenal aspect of the Buddhist universe, with its unification of dualistic phenomena at the center.

According to the syncretic doctrine of the Shingon sect of esoteric Buddhism, the two mandalas could also be interpreted as the "original [Buddhist]
essence" (*honji*) out of which the "manifest [Shintoist] traces" (*suijaku*) of the
Inner and Outer sanctuaries of the Ise Shrine emerged.[39] Just as *yamabushi*
scale the peaks of Mount Omine, performing ascetic rites and austerities
(*shugyō*) along the way in order to attain enlightenment and acquire superhuman powers, so too the holy man from Yokawa interpretively scales the
peaks of the two mandalas, playing on the multiple senses of *waku* (to scale,
interpret, differentiate).

"In a hempen cloak, he brushes off the dew of seven jewels. A robe of
forbearance shields him from defilement." This is a reference to the seven jewels (*shippō*) or treasures of paradise, listed in the *Lotus Sutra* as gold, silver, crys-
tal, clam shell, agate, carnelian, and cat's-eye gem.[40] Although the sparkling
dew may resemble the seven jewels of paradise, the mountain ascetic brushes
off the dew from the seven jewels because the resemblance is merely an illusion and the dew merely dew. In order to purify himself, the *yamabushi* must
dispel all attachment, including attachment to "the dew of seven jewels."

The "robe of forbearance" (*ninniku no kesa*) comes from the tenth chapter of the fourth fascicle of the *Lotus Sutra*, where the preacher of the *Lotus
Sutra* is described as cloaked in "the thought of tender forbearance and the
bearing of insult with equanimity."[41] Later, *ninniku no koromo* came to be
used as a generic term for Buddhist robes.[42] In *Aoi no Ue*, the "robe of forbearance" shields the holy man not only from defilement but also from attachment to the uncertainty and undecidability of contingency, punning on
the homophonic equivocality of *fujō*, as in the *sashi* above: on the one hand,
fujō signifies defilement, pollution, stain; on the other, it suggests impermanence, undecidability, and indefiniteness. In short, the stain of contingent attachment is viewed as something that must be transcended on the way toward buddhahood.

Finally, while rubbing the redwood beads of his rosary, the holy man
from Yokawa quotes the prayer "Namaku samanda basarada." This untrans-
latable pseudo-Sanskrit *dharani*, or magical incantation, is known as the Heart
Spell ("Shinshu") of Fudō Myōō (Immovable Wisdom King), and appears in
both the *Fudōkyo Sutra* and the *Dainichikyō Sutra*.[43] In addition to the Heart
Spell, there exist two other spells of Fudō: the Fireworld Spell ("Kakaiju")
and the Saving Compassion Spell ("Jikuju"), the latter of which is recited by
the holy man of Yokawa a few moments later.

The Heart Spell's mixture of magical nonsense syllables and pseudo-
Sanskrit ("pseudo" because Sanskrit words are transliterated into Sino-
Japanese phonetics), which need not be understood by anyone in order to be

effective, appeals to the assistance of one of the most ferocious and popular
Shingon deities, Fudō Myōō, he who defends the Buddhist Law and fights
against the multifarious attachments that bind beings to this world of delusion. Fudō is typically depicted as a ferocious, blue, demonlike being with jutting fangs and bulging eyes, who carries a sword and rope with which he
cuts down and binds the flames of evil attachment. During the Kamakura
and Muromachi periods, Fudō was extremely popular among military aristocrats, who probably likened themselves to Fudō in their role as "guardians of
the state in the face of disorder."[44]

The holy man's string of *yamabushi* citations stirs up the malevolent spirit
of Rokujō, who returns to center stage with her outer-kimono pulled up
over her head to conceal her mask and horns, carrying a staff in her hand.
The function served by Rokujō's kimono hood is quite similar to an Edo
practice, still performed today, of a bride's donning a *tsunokakushi*, or "horn-
concealer," a bride-hood worn during a wedding ceremony to conceal the
bride's "horns of jealousy," and thereby "immunize [her] husband against the
effects of this morbid emotion."[45]

In the final climactic section of the play, Rokujō, after removing her
hood and revealing her demonic mask, engages the *yamabushi* in the following brief exchange (*kakeai shōdan*) of metered poetry sung in noncongruent,
recitative style (*sashinori*), and centered on the higher register with minimal
inflection:

ROKUJŌ
  Ika ni gyōja haya kaeritamae
  Kaerade fukaku shitamōna yo.

HOLY MAN
  Tatoi daiji no akuryō nari tomo
  Gyōja no hōriki tsukubeki ka to
  Kasanete juzu wo oshimonde . . .
      (Yokomichi and Omote, 40: 130)

ROKUJŌ
  Return at once ascetic:
  return or else you will be vanquished through your recklessness!

HOLY MAN
  However formidable the evil spirit may be,
  is it possible for the ascetic's dharmic powers to be exhausted?
  Rubbing together the beads of the rosary yet again . . .

The holy man then proceeds to recite, with the assistance of the chorus, a
string of incantations invoking the dharmic powers that will finally exorcise
Rokujō's spirit. The following *chūnoriji* section, a rather uncommon congruent

song with the dynamic rhythm of two syllables of text for every beat of music, is typically used at the end of warrior plays depicting the torments of hell:

HOLY MAN
   Tōbō ni Gōzanze Myōō
CHORUS
   Tōbō ni Gōzanze Myōō
HOLY MAN
   Nanbō ni Gundariyasha
CHORUS
   Saihō Daiitoku Myōō
HOLY MAN
   Hoppō Kongōyasha Myōō
CHORUS
   Chūō Daishō Fudō Myōō
   Namaku samanda basarada
   Senda makaroshana
   Sowataya un tarata kanman
   Chōgasessha tokudaichie
   Chigashinsha sokushinjōbutsu.
       (Yokomichi and Omote, 40: 130)

HOLY MAN
   In the east, Gōzanze Myōō
CHORUS
   In the east, Gōzanze Myōō
HOLY MAN
   In the south, Gundariyasha
CHORUS
   In the west, Daiitoku Myōō
HOLY MAN
   In the north, Kongōyasha Myōō
CHORUS
   In the center, the most wise Fudō Myōō:
   namaku samanda basarada
   senda makaroshana
   sowataya un tarata kanman.[46]
   Whoever hears my teaching acquires great wisdom;
   whoever knows my mind attains buddhahood in this very body.[47]

Though it is quite unusual to find a *chūnoriji* section at the end of a fourth-category play such as *Aoi no Ue*, the almost masculine fierceness of the malevolent spirit of Rokujō, so horrifyingly evoked by the *hannya* demon mask, probably warrants such an exception.

The deities invoked by the *yamabushi*'s incantations in the *chūnoriji* section are collectively known as "Godai Myōō," or "Five Great Wisdom Kings." Godai Myōō are iconographically represented on the Womb Realm Mandala, and are regarded as incarnations or messengers of the "five Buddhas" (*gobutsu*) and "five wisdoms" (*gochi nyorai*) depicted on the Diamond Realm Mandala.[48] The Five Great Wisdom Kings are invoked as fierce divinities of esoteric Buddhism, who protect beings from harm and facilitate release from this world of attachment on the way toward enlightenment.[49] Of special relevance to the dramatic context of *Aoi no Ue* is the fact that the ritual of the Five Great Wisdom Kings, called *godaison no mizuhō* or *godan no hō*, was commonly performed in order to insure a safe birth.[50]

In response to the holy man's invocation of Godai Myōō, Rokujō sings the following congruent chant in a forceful melodic style (*tsuyogin*):

Araara osoroshi no
Hannyagoe ya
Kore made zo onryō
Kono nochi mata mo kitarumaji.
   (Yokomichi and Omote, 40: 130)

Oh, how terrifying
is the voice of perfect wisdom.
From this point forward, in the form of a vengeful spirit,
never will I come back again.

Though Teruhi by herself was not powerful enough to exorcise Rokujō's spirit from Aoi, the holy man from Yokawa is able to accomplish the expulsion through the power of his incantatory citations.[51]

Finally, in a strongly rhythmic, uninflected congruent song (*kiri shōdan*), the chorus brings the play—and the scene of possession—to an end, vibrantly chanting Rokujō's thoughts as she performs her last dance:

Dokuju no koe wo kiku toki wa
Dokuju no koe wo kiku toki wa
Akki kokoro wo yawarage
Ninniku jihi no sugata nite
Bosatsu mo koko ni raikō su
Jōbutsu tokudatsu no
Mi to nariyuku zo arigataki
Mi to nariyuku zo arigataki.
   (Yokomichi and Omote, 40: 130)

When I/she hears the sound of sutra chanting,
when I/she hears the sound of sutra chanting,
it pacifies the heart of the evil demon.

In the form of forbearance and merciful compassion,
bodhisattvas descend to this place to welcome me/her.
Attaining buddhahood, release from all worldly attachments,
I/she becomes filled with gratitude,
I/she becomes filled with gratitude.

Since person is unmarked in Japanese verbs, the final choral song blurs the boundaries between the first and third person perspectives, as Rokujō's spirit attains release from the duality of earthly existence. Rokujō's vision of bodhisattvas descending to welcome her (called *raikō* or *raigō*) reiterates the vision first propagated by Genshin[52] (942–1017), the famous Tendai priest from Yokawa and precursor of Amidism (Jōdo, or Pure Land Buddhism). *Raikō* describes the descent of Amida Buddha, along with his retinue of bodhisattvas, saints, and musicians, to welcome the departing spirit into Amida's Pure Land paradise in the west. With her demon's heart pacified, Rokujō attains release from her worldly attachments, and is welcomed into buddhahood by Amida and his heavenly retinue.

It is interesting to note that this ending is almost exactly the same as what appears in the warrior play *Michimori* (written by Seiami and revised by Zeami), in which the ghosts of the warrior Taira no Michimori and his wife Kozaishō no Tsubone return to tell how they died during the Genpei War. In the first act, a traveling priest visits the historical battlefield of Naruto and, while chanting sutras for the souls of Taira warriors who perished there, is approached by an old man and woman, the disguised ghosts of Michimori and his wife. After telling how Kozaishō no Tsubone drowned herself upon hearing news of her husband's death, the old man and woman disappear. In the second act, the old man and woman reappear in their true form as ghosts, and Michimori dramatizes, through chant and dance, his death in battle. In the end, with the aid of the priest's prayers, the ghostly couple is able to attain release from this world, expressing gratitude for their salvation through the mouthpiece of the chorus in almost exactly the same words that are used to end *Aoi no Ue*.[53]

Unlike the exorcism performed in *Genji monogatari*, *Aoi no Ue*'s exorcism is ultimately successful: Rokujō is released from the chains of karmic repetition, and—by implication—Aoi recovers. The ending of *Aoi no Ue* drastically revises *Genji monogatari* not only by enabling Rokujō's vengeful spirit to attain deliverance (*jōbutsu tokudatsu*) from this karmic world of desire, delusion, and attachment so that she is finally able to enter Amida Buddha's Land of Bliss, but also by saving Aoi's life so that she will be able to deliver Yūgiri—the child and heir of Genji—and live on to raise him. In *Genji monogatari*, by contrast, the episode of Aoi's possession does not end so happily, since Aoi is killed by Rokujō's vengeful spirit soon after giving birth to Yūgiri, and Rokujō continues to haunt Genji and his lovers throughout much of the tale.

The significance of *Aoi no Ue*'s various rewritings of *Genji monogatari* should not be underestimated. In the end, it should come as no surprise, given the numerous traces of (dis)possession I have considered over the last two chapters, that the threat posed by jealous, vengeful women such as Rokujō is forcefully exorcised on the stage of Muromachi Japan by the "voice of perfect wisdom" (*hannyagoe*), as uttered by the male sage from Yokawa. Moreover, in order for this gender-charged exorcism to be carried out, Genji's own role in the drama of female jealousy *had to be erased*, along with many of the circumstances complicating Rokujō's (dis)possession in *Genji monogatari*. Without reducing the plot to demonize Rokujō to a full-blown conspiracy, I would argue that the staging of jealousy in *Aoi no Ue*—the staging of the (dis)possession of female jealousy on the Muromachi stage—was also an exorcism of the contingencies associated with the reversal of female inheritance rights, which played an important role in the further consolidation of Ashikaga shogunal authority and its differentiation from imperial authority.

In Part III of this study, "Performativities of Power," I explore the intersection of gender and military politics on the noh stage from a slightly different methodological angle and in relation to plays from altogether different genres. Whereas my reading of *Aoi no Ue* alternated between line-by-line and macro-level analyses with an emphasis on the former, in the next two chapters, the emphasis shifts to the macro-level. In Chapter 4, I consider the politics of subjection at work in the plays *Ominameshi* and *Yumi Yawata* in relation to intertextual reinscriptions of the Hachiman cult. In Chapter 5, I sort through the multiple histories of the woman warrior Tomoe and tease out the implications of her transition in Japanese cultural history from a woman warrior to an itinerant entertainer of diverse stripe.

PART THREE

Performativities of Power

Engendering Female Suicide on Otokoyama: Ominameshi *and the Politics of Subjection*

Most noh plays dealing with the topic of female suicide involve the modus operandi of death by drowning, but differ according to the motives attributed to such acts of self-destruction. Using motive as a criterion, extant female suicide plays can be divided roughly into two groups. The first group consists of plays such as *Motomezuka* (Sought-after burial mound) and *Ukifune* (Boat upon the waters), which deal with women who commit (or, in the case of Ukifune, attempt to commit) suicide because they are faced with the dilemma of having to choose between competing suitors. The second group is comprised of plays such as *Mitsuyama* (Three mountains) and *Uneme* (Lady-in-waiting), which depict women who commit suicide out of despair over the neglect or abandonment inflicted upon them by their husbands or lovers. Although examples of male suicide by drowning also exist (e.g., in *Koi no omoni* [Burden of love] and *Aya no tsuzumi* [Damask drum]), that particular mode of death is more often than not gender-marked as feminine.

Among the dozen or so plays in the noh repertoire dealing with female suicide, *Ominameshi* stands out from the rest not only because extant performance records indicate that it was more popular than any other play of that genre performed during the Muromachi and Azuchi-Momoyama periods,[1] but also because it is the only female suicide play in the current repertoire in which the primary role of *shite* is given not to the suicide herself, but rather to her widowed husband.[2]

Yet another striking aspect of *Ominameshi* is the peculiar way in which its narrative of female suicide is both inscribed and displaced by politically charged tropes linked to Iwashimizu Hachiman Shrine on Otokoyama.[3] In what follows, with a glance toward Judith Butler's work, I explore the multiple forms of "subjection" intimated in the interstices of *Ominameshi*: namely, (1) religio-political subjection, or the domination of individuals, groups, and/or territories within a network of religiously marked class and power relations; (2) narrative subjection, or the regulation of modes of articulation, naming, and inscription; and (3) psychic-corporeal subjection, or the production and domestication of gender- and class-marked subjectivities.[4]

In this chapter, I analyze three Hachiman intertexts enframing the performance of *Ominameshi*—each one exemplifying a politics of subjection. The first intertext alludes to the institutional genealogy of Iwashimizu Hachiman Shrine. The second intertext reinscribes the Otokoyama of the god play *Yumi Yawata* with its appropriation of imperial symbolic capital in the service of shogunal politics. Finally, the third intertext juxtaposes the woman's suicide with the Hōjōe, or Life-Releasing Ritual, performed at both Usa and Iwashimizu Hachiman shrines. I argue that what *Ominameshi* offers through such intertextual juxtapositions is a performative analogue between the Hachiman-inflected religio-politics of subjection and the gender politics of subjection dramatized by the narrative of female suicide. Before proceeding to an analysis of the Hachiman intertexts, a brief overview of *Ominameshi* is probably in order.

Ominameshi is structured as a relatively conventional fourth-category, double-entry *mugen* noh. On his way to visit the capital in early autumn, the *waki*—an itinerant priest from Matsura in Kyushu—stops at Otokoyama. While gazing at the pale yellow *ominameshi*[5] flowers blooming in great profusion, the priest considers plucking one to take home as a souvenir. But just as he reaches out to pick one with his hand, the *shite*—an old man—enters and stops him. The two discuss the propriety of picking the flower, trading poetic citations by Sugawara no Michizane and Henjō. The old man then guides the priest to Iwashimizu Hachiman Shrine, where he recounts its history and an exchange concerning the etymology of the word *ominameshi* ensues. In the context of this discussion, the old man shows the priest the grave sites of Ono no Yorikaze and his wife, who are entombed at the foot of Otokoyama. Finally, the old man requests that the priest pray for their restless spirits, and disappears like a dream behind the shadow of a tree.

In the play's second act, the priest performs sutra-chanting to mourn their deaths. The *nochijite* and *tsure* make their entrance as the ghosts of Yorikaze and his wife, respectively, and proceed to tell the story of the wife's suicide, committed in response to her husband's infidelity. Yorikaze also describes the strange appearance of a single *ominameshi* flower upon his wife's burial mound. Yorikaze recounts how, after the burial of his wife, in a fit of depression and self-recrimination, he threw himself into the river in order to follow his wife to the world of the dead. Since then, Yorikaze's restless spirit has suffered innumerable tortures in the hell for adulterers. In the play's final scene, Yorikaze desperately prays for the transformation of the *ominameshi* into a lotus flower pedestal, upon which he hopes to float away from such hellish tortures to rebirth in Amida's Pure Land. Let us turn now to an analysis of the three Hachiman intertexts enframing the story.

Genealogies of Otokoyama

In an *ageuta shōdan* (metered, congruent song centered on the upper register and ending in the lower register) sung by the chorus just before the *shite* discloses the site of the two tombs and their link to the history of the *ominameshi* flower, the foundation myth of Iwashimizu Hachiman Shrine is intimated in the following gender-specific terms:

> Hisakata no
> Tsuki no katsura no Otokoyama
> Tsuki no katsura no Otokoyama
> Sayakeki kage wa tokorokara
> Kōyō mo terisoite
> Hi mo kagerō no Iwashimizu
> Koke no koromo mo taenare ya
> Mitsu no tamoto ni kage utsuru
> Shirushi no hako wo osamu naru
> Nori no jingūji
> Arigatakarishi reichi ka na.

> In the clear light of the celestial orb,
>   lunar *katsura* trees and the Man in the Moon shine brightly
>   over Man Mountain,
>   lunar *katsura* trees and the Man in the Moon shine brightly
>   over Man Mountain,
>   this clean, manly image is the spirit of the place,
>   along with the colors of autumn shining in the moon's light,
>   Iwashimizu Shrine, where pure water shimmers in the sunlight,
>   where the priest's fine robe of moss
>   has hallowed images traced onto its three sleeves,
>   where the sacred box containing the imperial seal is stored,
>   where Kami and Buddhas, shrines and temples, coexist according
>   to the Buddhist dharma,
>   how blessed is this sacred place![6]

As is made abundantly evident here and elsewhere in *Ominameshi*, Iwashimizu Hachiman Shrine is gender-marked as masculine. The "clean, manly image [which] is the spirit of the place" (*sayakeki kage wa tokorokara*) juxtaposes the terrestrial masculinity of Otokoyama with the celestial masculinity of Katsura no Otoko (man in the moon). To complicate matters further, this terrestrial-celestial gender politics is intertwined with the religious politics associated with Iwashimizu Hachiman Shrine's foundation myth.

The entire song, especially the description of the "the priest's fine robe of moss" with "hallowed images traced onto its three sleeves" (*mitsu no tamoto ni kage utsuru*), invokes the narrative of the founding of Iwashimizu Hachiman Shrine on Otokoyama in the year 859 (Jōgan 1) by Gyōkyō Oshō, head priest of Daianji Temple in Nara. After receiving special oracular instructions during a pilgrimage to Usa Hachiman Shrine in Kyushu, Gyōkyō returned to the capital to establish a new shrine-temple complex for Hachiman on Otokoyama.[7] The legitimacy of this mandate was reportedly demonstrated by the fact that Hachiman Daibosatsu became manifest and traced the images of the "three revered ones" (*sanzon*)—namely, Amida Buddha and his two attendant bodhisattvas, Kannon and Seishi—onto the sleeves of Gyōkyō. Given such an illustrious genealogy, it is no surprise that, upon seeing Iwashimizu Hachiman Shrine for the very first time, the *waki* feels compelled to remark upon the foundational connection between this shrine complex and Usa Hachiman Shrine back in Kyūshū, with which it is identified.[8] But concealed behind such an identification is the fact that Iwashimizu eventually attained administrative power over Usa.[9]

An even more significant political subtext to the founding of Iwashimizu Hachiman Shrine is the fact that its construction was authorized by the powerful *sekkan* politician Fujiwara no Yoshifusa (804–72) soon after the accession of his grandson, Emperor Seiwa (850–80), in 858 (Tenan 2). The reign of Seiwa, Japan's first child-emperor, was administered by his maternal grandfather Yoshifusa in the role of *sesshō*, or regent. Later, during the reign of Emperor Kōkō (830–87), Yoshifusa introduced a differentiation between the regent, who advised an emperor before coming of age, and the chancellor (or *kanpaku*), who advised him as an adult. This subjection of imperial power by the northern branch (*hokke*) of the Fujiwara clan after the enthronement of Seiwa thus marked the birth of *sekkan* (regent-chancellor) politics.

Viewed against the backdrop of this dispossession of imperial power by the Fujiwara clan, the founding of Iwashimizu Hachiman Shrine as a *gokoku*,[10] or "state-protecting," institution suggests that it not only served as "the special guardian of imperial legitimacy," as Christine Guth Kanda has noted,[11] but also as a silent monument to Fujiwara politics and the *sekkan* reterritorialization of Heian power relations.

Almost six hundred years later, under the protective eye of Hachiman, another subjection of imperial prerogatives and symbolic capital—this time for shogunal purposes—was undertaken by the distant descendants of Emperor Seiwa via the Seiwa branch of the Minamoto lineage: namely, the Ashikaga rulers Yoshimitsu and Yoshinori. This genealogical tie brings us to the second intertext linking *Ominameshi* to Iwashimizu Hachiman Shrine, this one viewed through the performative lens of the *waki* noh *Yumi Yawata*.

Shogunal Politics in Yumi Yawata

The only other play in the noh repertoire that comes close to invoking the topograph "Otokoyama" as often as *Ominameshi* is the god play *Yumi Yawata*, considered by Zeami to be a model play of its genre.[12] These two plays contain more inscriptions of Otokoyama (and its synonym Yawatayama) than any other plays in the repertoire, with *Ominameshi* containing eleven references total and *Yumi Yawata* seven.[13] Given the complementarity of their settings, it comes as no surprise that the two plays were often performed together on the same program. According to extant performance records covering the years 1429 to 1602, *Yumi Yawata* was performed on the same program as *Ominameshi* approximately 21 percent of the time.[14] Taking into consideration both the significant statistical and tropological associations between the two plays, it seems highly likely that the ideological connotations associated with the topograph Otokoyama in *Yumi Yawata* would have resonated intertextually with the Otokoyama of *Ominameshi*.

Although *Yumi Yawata* has often been read as a straightforward "paean to imperial rule and to the peace that it has brought to the land,"[15] its politics are greatly complicated by the circumstances surrounding its production. In the context of his discussion of the "straightforward style" (*sugu narutei*) of congratulatory noh plays (*shūgen nō*), Zeami singles out *Yumi Yawata* for praise in *Sarugaku dangi* and adds a tantalizing note regarding its inception: "Since it is a noh play that I wrote in honor of the inaugural celebration for the reign of the present shogun, there are no special secrets to performing it" (*tōgodai no hajime no tame ni kakitaru nō nareba, hiji mo nashi*).[16] The exact date of the play and the shogun for whom it was intended remain uncertain; however, circumstantial evidence seems to favor Yoshinori. Insofar as Yoshinori was the shogun at the time *Sarugaku dangi* was written—that is, in the eleventh month of 1430 (Eikyō 2/11)—it seems highly likely that "the reign of the present shogun" (*tōgodai*) refers to Yoshinori. Moreover, the fact that Yoshinori was selected as shogun by a lottery drawn at Iwashimizu Hachiman Shrine in 1428 (Shōchō 1) lends further credence to the view that *Yumi Yawata* was written in honor of Yoshinori's ascension.[17]

Following the practice of their ancestors the Seiwa Genji, the Ashikaga clan regarded Hachiman as the *ujigami*, or "tutelary deity," of their lineage.[18] Thus, it is not surprising that the Ashikaga rulers made countless visits to Iwashimizu Hachiman Shrine, both to pay respects and to pray for continued protection. Yoshimitsu is on record as having visited the shrine twenty times and Yoshimochi thirty times.[19] But in light of the unique role played by Hachiman in selecting Ashikaga Yoshinori as the next shogun following the death of his brother Yoshimochi—effectively legitimizing the reign of Yoshinori by means of divine favor in the context of a lottery drawing—it must be said that Yoshinori's regime had a special association with Hachiman.

In view of the special nature of Yoshinori's association with Hachiman and the context of shogunal investiture enframing the production and inaugural performance of *Yumi Yawata*, one might expect shogunal ideology to enter the play in some fashion, but scholars have traditionally insisted upon reading *Yumi Yawata* as proimperial and antishogunal in its rhetoric. Take, for example, the following *sashi shōdan*[20] sung by the *shite*, the god of Kawara disguised as an old man:

> May the emperor's reign [*kimi ga yo*] endure
> For a thousand years,
> For thousands of years,
> Till small pebbles become a large boulder
> Covered with moss.
> May it endure forever
> Like the color of the pine needles
> On Eternity Mountain.
> The azure sky is calm,
> The emperor secure [*kimi ansen ni*],
> The people are kind-hearted,
> Passes have not been closed.
> From the beginning, ours has been a land
> Where the gods protect the emperor [*kimi wo mamori no shinkoku ni*].
> The vow of this god in particular
> Illumines the night
> Like the light of the moon.
> The waters of Iwashimizu flow ceaselessly,
> And as long as the stream runs on
> Living beings are released.
> How glorious is the god's compassion!
> Truly this is an auspicious time.[21]

With an eye toward passages such as this (and others in which the reign of legendary Emperor Ōjin is glorified), Ross Bender writes: "Although the play was written in Muromachi times . . . its view of Hachiman denies the contemporary association of the god with the ruling military house. It rather dramatizes an earlier conception of the deity, portraying a Hachiman who is intimately linked with the imperial institution."[22] And Bender is not alone in this view: Watsuji Tetsurō states even more strongly his view that "it must be said that it is quite evident that, within the setting of this play, the rule of the military houses, the shogun, and the daimyos are completely nonexistent."[23] Such comments are typical in their underestimation of *Yumi Yawata*'s ideological equivocality. Neither Bender nor Watsuji considers the circumstances surrounding the play's production, such as the fact that it was expressly written, according to Zeami, "in honor of the inaugural celebration for the reign of the present shogun."[24] *Yumi Yawata* may not be the most dramatic play in the repertoire, but I would contend that it is more complex than many commentators have allowed.

The crux of the matter is how to translate and interpret the ideologically charged terms *kimi ga yo* (or *miyo*) and *kimi*, which are repeated throughout the play and translated above as "emperor's reign" and "emperor," respectively. There is no denying that this is the most common interpretation of these terms, but as Wakita Haruko has argued, the Muromachi usage of such designations was far from unambiguous. More specifically, Wakita suggests that the usage of *kimi* in *waki* noh was not limited to the emperor, but was also used to refer to the shogun.[25] Moreover, as Zeami's own usage in *Sarugaku dangi* of *godai* (an alternative reading of the same characters composing *miyo*) attests, a similar ambiguity applied to honorific designations referring to the reigns of both emperors and shogun.

Another argument put forward in defense of the proimperial interpretation of *Yumi Yawata* is that the play's reference to the *seki no to*,[26] or "toll barrier gates," in the line "passes have not been closed" symbolizes "a time before military rule was established."[27] But the opening of the toll barrier gates does not in itself imply either imperial or shogunal rule so much as it suggests a country that is not at war. Since the authority to establish and administer toll barriers had been transferred from the emperor to the shogun around the turn of the fifteenth century,[28] such a trope could just as easily be construed as describing peace during the new shogun's reign. Indeed, when one takes into consideration the shogunal context of its production, as well as the undecidability of its most crucial ideological signifiers, it seems just as plausible to read *Yumi Yawata* as a celebration of shogunal rule and a prayer for continued peace as it does to read it as "a paean to imperial rule and to the peace that it has brought to the land."[29]

What *Yumi Yawata* stages is not merely a blurring of boundaries between the figure of the emperor and that of the shogun, but a performative appropriation of imperial prerogatives and symbolic capital on the stage of the inaugural celebration for the new shogun. Just as the northern branch of the Fujiwara clan had subjected imperial power to nonimperial purposes, so, too, Ashikaga rulers, such as Yoshimitsu and Yoshinori, subjected imperial prerogatives and symbolic capital to shogunal purposes. This is not to reduce *Yumi Yawata* to a passive reflection or transparent representation of the historical context out of which it emerged, but rather to explore the complex interchange between the historicity of a noh performance text and the textuality of its history. Rather than simply mirroring the sociopolitical context in which it was produced, *Yumi Yawata* performatively contributed to the subjection of imperial symbolic capital aspired to by Yoshinori.[30] To ignore this constitutive reciprocity by reducing the performance text to a mere product of historical influence or the ideological reflection of economic infrastructure would be to efface the text's active, productive force in the theater of the Ashikaga shogunal imaginary.

Taking Ashikaga Yoshimitsu as precedent, the shogun became resubjectivized yet again under Yoshinori's regime in the figure of the *Nihon kokuō*, or "king of Japan."[31] By officially legitimizing the shogun with this title, the Tally Trade Agreement with the Ming dynasty both usurped the emperor's control over foreign affairs and repositioned the shogun as monarch. As John Whitney Hall has remarked: "Whether or not Yoshimitsu intended to displace the emperor, he and his successors as shogun did preside over the demise of the tradition of imperial rule as it had been up to that point."[32]

As a footnote to this discussion, it should be added that whatever symbolic capital and divine tutelage *Yumi Yawata* may have contributed to Yoshinori's shogunal image-making was not enough to protect him from his political enemies. It is surely one of the great historical ironies of Yoshinori's regime and his association with noh that both his ascension to shogun and the closure of his reign were enframed by noh performances. Yoshinori was assassinated in 1441 (Kakitsu 1/6/24) while viewing a performance of *U no ha* by his favorite noh actor, Onnami (Kanze Motoshige, 1398–1467), at the residence of Akamatsu Mitsusuke (1381–1441). This unfortunate association between *U no ha* and Yoshinori's death eventually led to its being banned from the noh canon at the insistence of Tokugawa Tsunayoshi (1646–1709). After all, it is one thing for a play to be associated with the inauguration of a shogun, but quite another for it to be linked, if only metonymically, to his assassination.[33]

Hōjōe and the Subjection of the Hayato

The third and last Hachiman intertext I shall consider juxtaposes the woman's suicide in *Ominameshi* with the Hōjōe, or Life-Releasing Ritual, performed at both the Usa and the Iwashimizu Hachiman shrines. The first inscription of the Hōjōe appears in act 1, where the *shite* and *waki* celebrate the auspicious syncretism associated with that ceremony of liberation:

> Wakō no chiri mo nigorie
> Kasui ni ukamu urokuzu wa
> Geni mo ikeru wo hanatsu ka to fukaki chikai mo arata nite
> Megumi zo shigeki Otokoyama
> Sakayuku michi no arigatasa yo.[34]

> Even as the dust mingles with the divine light of Buddhas
>   and bodhisattvas,
> in the flow of the muddied inlet, fish float to the surface
>   of the water
> —certainly, to liberate living beings such as these
> shows that the profound vow of Buddhas and Kami has become
>   miraculously manifest.
> Such benevolence!
> Flourishing as I climb up luxuriant Man Mountain—
>   how blessed!

Another inscription appears in the second act of the play in one of the very few passages actually sung by the *tsure* herself:

> Onnagokoro no hakanasa wa
> Miyako wo hitori akugareidete
> Nao mo urami no omoi fukaki
> Hōjōgawa ni mi wo naguru.[35]

> The fragility of a woman's heart:
> it is because I left the capital yearning for one man alone
> that my resentful thoughts are even more profound
> as I hurl myself into the depths of the Life-Releasing River.

For the wife of Yorikaze to commit suicide by throwing herself into the Hōjōgawa, the river into which one released life, is not only ironic, it may also have been subversive. Such an act of suicide would have polluted the Hōjōgawa's pure waters of liberation, suggesting a darker subtext haunting the Hōjōe ritual with connotations of subjection and death as opposed to emancipation and life. Moreover, as various *engi* (foundation narratives) dealing with the genealogy of the Hōjōe attest, the ritual appeasement of victims of political subjection was central to its performative function.

According to accounts in *Hachiman Usagū Hōjōe engi* (History of the founding of Usa Hachiman Shrine's Life-Releasing Ritual) and *Rokugō kaizan Nimmon daibosatsu hongi* (Biographical history of the Great Bodhisattva Nimmon, founder of the Rokugō cult center),[36] the establishment of the Hōjōe derives from political incidents that occurred in southern Kyushu in the early eighth century. In the year 719 (Yōrō 3),[37] the Hayato people of Ōsumi and Hyūga provinces launched an organized rebellion against the hegemony of the centralized Yamato government. Acts of rebellion by the Hayato had occurred previously, but 719 marked the first time that an all-out assault was waged with the intent of conquering Japan.

Fighting escalated in 720 when the governor of Ōsumi province was assassinated. In response to these events, the Yamato court issued an imperial petition requesting assistance from the Hachiman cult at Usa Hachiman Shrine. Hachiman responded with an oracle that ordered the subjugation of the Hayato and offered to lead the government's army in that endeavor. After two years of fighting, the Hayato rebels were finally suppressed.

Although the *Rokugō kaizan Nimmon daibosatsu hongi* states that "following the subjugation of the Hayato rebels, peace and tranquillity were restored to the people and to the empire,"[38] other sources indicate that a plague broke out in the region, which was attributed to the malevolent spirits of fallen Hayato.[39] In order to appease the Hayato and provide ideological closure to the violence authorized by the Bodhisattva Hachiman, the following oracular command was issued in the year 724 (Jinki 1)[40] to establish the Hōjōe: "I, the god, as the retribution for killing many of the Hayato, decree that on separate years we will do a *Hōjō-e*."[41] Greatly complicating the performative force of that appeasement is a statement included in *Hachiman Usagū Hōjōe engi*, in which the subjugation of the Hayato is legitimized by means of Buddhist rhetorical sophistry:

> The rite began with the Great Bodhisattva Hachiman. Even though he kills, because he has an enlightened status and does good there is a lot of merit in his killing. The internal proof is that there is no hiding the bright light, and the rays cross each other. As a result of this rite at Usa, they began to perform the *Hōjō-e* in all the provinces.[42]

One notices that in the metaphorics of Hachiman's meritorious killing, which shines forth with the bright light of his divinity, the trope of the *wakō no chiri*, or dust that mingles with the divine light of Buddhas and bodhisattvas, is translated into murder ideologically justified for religio-political purposes. Such a politically charged subtext for the Hōjōe casts into a radically different light the ritual release of birds and fish performed on the fifteenth day of the eighth month each year to celebrate Buddhist compassion for all sentient beings and honor the prohibition against taking life.

As Jane Marie Law has suggested in a provocative article on the ideological history of the Hōjōe: "At the heart of this rite is a deep concern over the violence within the Hachiman cult and the need to make amends and appease the victims. It also demonstrates how a public rite and spectacle ultimately legitimates the violence of dominant authority, even when claiming to appease the victims of the original event itself."[43]

In sum, the ideological logic of the Hōjōe in its religio-political context of performance is twofold: the subjection of military enemies is both legitimized in the name of Hachiman and domesticated through the appeasement of Hachiman's victims. Even as living beings are saved in the ritual performance of the Hōjōe, such a liberation takes place on the basis of a previous subjection of living beings. In effect, the Hōjōe's ritual liberation appeases by means of substitution, metaphorically transforming the victims of military violence into the bodies of fish and birds that are then released into nearby rivers and fields.[44] In time, other victims of political subjection and military violence besides the Hayato—ranging from the victims of Empress Jingū's legendary subjugation of Korea to the defeated Mongol forces who invaded Japan in the late thirteenth century[45]—also came to be included among the appeased, but the Hayato remain the paramount political subtext.

Subjecting Ominameshi

Perhaps the most difficult question facing any micropolitical reading of *Ominameshi* is what the ideologically charged tropes of Iwashimizu Hachiman Shrine and its related intertexts have to do with the narrative of female suicide. All of the Hachiman intertexts considered—the genealogy of Iwashimizu Hachiman Shrine, the shogunal politics inscribing Otokoyama in *Yumi Yawata*, and the political subtexts of the Hōjōe—share a politics of subjection. I would contend that what *Ominameshi* offers through such juxtapositions is a performative analogue between the religio-politics of subjection and the gender politics of subjection.

The wife of Yorikaze, whose name is unknown to us, drowns herself because of her husband's infidelity. Wracked with guilt and grief, Yorikaze then takes his own life, hoping to join his wife in the next world, but instead is cast into the hell for adulterers. At first glance, it might seem as if the only one who is subjected in *Ominameshi* is Yorikaze. In the climactic scene of the play, sung in the heightened emotional style of the *noriji shōdan*, the phallocratic implications of Otokoyama are disclosed in phantasmagoric detail as Yorikaze articulates through the mouthpiece of the chorus a nightmarish vision involving the violence of penetration:

Jain no akki wa
Mi wo semete
Jain no akki wa
Mi wo semete
Sono nenriki no
Michi mo sagashiki
Tsurugi no yama no
Ue ni koishiki
Hito wa mietari
Ureshi ya tote
Yukinoboreba
Tsurugi wa mi wo tōshi
Banjaku wa hone wo kudaku
Ko wa so mo ika ni
Osoroshi ya
Tsurugi no eda no
Tawamu made.[46]

Cursed devils of sexual infidelity
incite me, then reproach me, torturing my body,
cursed devils of sexual infidelity
incite me, then reproach me, torturing my body,
blind will power
impelled by desire along the path of peril,
on top of Sword Mountain
my beloved has appeared.
How gratifying!
But as I climb,
double-edged swords penetrate my body,
enormous rocks crush my bones.
How terrifying it all is!
Sword-branches
bend down under the weight of my sin.

According to the imaginary geography of the play, the stage of Otokoyama has now been transformed into its dark underside: Sword Mountain. As the poetics of Otokoyama is translated into the eroticized horrors of Sword Mountain, Yorikaze the philanderer experiences firsthand the pain of subjection. The fact that it is Yorikaze who is tortured on Sword Mountain rather than his self-destructive wife stands in sharp contrast to another play in the noh repertoire concerning female suicide: *Motomezuka*.

In *Motomezuka*, the young maiden from Unai, who commits suicide when faced with the competing claims of overzealous suitors, suffers tortures similar to those of Yorikaze. For her indirect involvement in the deaths of her two suitors, she, too, suffers on Sword Mountain, in terms probably borrowed from Genshin's elaborate description in *Ōjōyōshū* (Essentials of salvation) of the numerous divisions and subdivisions of the Buddhist network of hells. That it is the man who is punished for the woman's suicide in *Ominameshi* rather than the other way around, as in *Motomezuka*, might strike some viewers and readers as a form of poetic justice. After all, compared to the philandering ways of a Genji, who pursues and abandons multiple lovers with only the occasional twinge of conscience, Yorikaze pays dearly for his sexual infidelity. But from another perspective, although Yorikaze is punished for precipitating the suicide of his beloved, the narrative of Yorikaze's suffering displaces the story of his wife, which all but disappears.

Much more than simply a play about a neglected wife who commits suicide and her adulterous husband who sees the error of his ways, the story of the *ominameshi* is displaced not by the other woman (as is the case in female-suicide plays such as *Mitsuyama*), but rather by her own husband. The fact that Yorikaze chose to commit suicide by drowning underscores the depth of his grief and the extent of his identification with his wife's suffering, and yet his suicide and subsequent torture in the hell for adulterers results in the up-staging of her story.

Just as the Hayato are not permitted to tell their own story, but function only as mute signifiers of political subjection and objects of appeasement in the performance of the Hōjōe, so, too, the woman in *Ominameshi* is not allowed to tell her own story, since it has been displaced by the narrative constructed for her by her husband, Yorikaze. In other words, the religio-political subjections implied by the Hachiman intertexts are paralleled by the narratival and psychic-corporeal subjection of Yorikaze's nameless wife. Even as Yorikaze, disguised as an old man in the first half, preached against plucking the *ominameshi*, against taking the life of any being, whether sentient or nonsentient, he has already taken the life out of the *ominameshi*'s story by appropriating her narratival voice for himself and subordinating her subjectivity to his own. The woman behind the *ominameshi* is quite literally reduced to a mere botanical trope.

Translating the plight of Yorikaze's wife into the botanical *ominameshi* is clearly a reinscription of the Buddhist doctrine of *sōmoku jōbutsu* (plants and trees attain buddhahood) and the debate over whether or not nonsentient beings are capable of attaining or have already attained buddhahood.[47] But it is also symptomatic of Buddhist patriarchal discourse, which objectifies the female body—in this case, literally turning the female body into a botanical "thing," an *ominameshi*—as a rhetorical strategy in the service of Buddhist soteriology—in this case, the salvation of the *ominameshi*'s husband, Yorikaze. At the end of the play, the gender politics of subjection come to the fore as the *ominameshi* is translated into yet another sort of flower—a lotus flower—the vehicle by which Yorikaze hopes to gain entrance into Pure Land paradise:

> Ominameshi
> Tsuyu no utena ya hana no en ni
> Ukamete tabitamae
> Tsumi wo ukamete tabitamae.[48]

> Damsel Flower,
> upon your dewy calyx tied to the lotus flower pedestal,
> I beseech you: let me flo(at up to Pure Land paradise,
> send my sins to the surface and deliver me from them!

It is no accident that *Yorikaze* and *Otokoyama* are alternate titles for the play, since it is the proper name of Yorikaze that provides the measure of subjectivity, just as Otokoyama provides the gender-marked, religio-political space in which both the woman's subjection and the man's subjectivity emerge. That it is the man's story as much as (if not more than) the woman's that is being told here is also suggested by the traditional classification of the play as a fourth-category "male attachment piece" (*shūshin otokomono*).

Told from the perspective of the man whose infidelity precipitated the woman's tragic end, the staging of female suicide on Otokoyama is upstaged by the man's own suicide, thus making the subject of *Ominameshi* that of subjection itself. Although female suicide sometimes functioned in the medieval cultural imaginary as an act of resistance against the unchecked circulation of masculine desire and the patriarchal exchange of female bodies, in *Ominameshi* such an act of resistance is co-opted by the very fact that it is Yorikaze who tells the story of his wife's suicide, it is Yorikaze whose narrative of his wife's suicide ends up displacing her own. In the end, the woman's suicide becomes simply another emotionally charged moment in the karmic history of the man. This may very well be an allusion to the medieval commonplace that "worldly desires and enlightenment are one and the same" (*bonnō soku bodai*), but to leave it at that would be to underestimate the politics of subjection infusing Yorikaze's exploitation of the female body in the service of his own enlightenment. That Hachiman discourse played a constitutive role in the theatrical framing of such exploitation sheds new light on the performativity of power and desire in the Muromachi period. The next chapter offers another perspective on the medieval staging of gender by analyzing performance texts featuring the woman warrior Tomoe.

CHAPTER 5

From Woman Warrior to Peripatetic
Entertainer: The Multiple Histories of Tomoe

Among the many memorable female characters in *Heike monogatari* (Tale of the Heike) perhaps the most provocative is the one whose name has become synonymous with the image of the woman warrior in Japanese cultural history: Tomoe Gozen. Tomoe is renowned not only for her beauty and unparalleled physical strength, but also for her skills and accomplishments as an archer and mounted warrior, who "was prepared to confront both demons and gods, a warrior equal to a thousand men" (*oni ni mo kami ni mo aō do iu ichinin tōzen no tsuwamono nari*).[1]

While most *Heike monogatari* recensions—whether produced for reading or recitation—concur in their depiction of Tomoe's martial accomplishments, there is profound disagreement over what became of Tomoe after the death of her lord and lover, Kiso no Yoshinaka (1154–84). During the Kamakura and Muromachi periods, the name Tomoe came to be associated with various types of female performer, ranging from *asobime* (waterfront entertainer) to *arukimiko* (traveling *miko*) to *bikuni* (itinerant nun).[2] The noh play *Tomoe*, first performed during the Sengoku period, offers yet another version of Tomoe's post-Genpei history, one that brings to the fore the gender politics infusing the figuration of Tomoe as both woman warrior and female entertainer.

In this chapter I analyze the multiple histories of Tomoe circulating in the medieval period. Taking into account the sociopolitical functions served by the dual operation of the proper name "Tomoe"—a signifier designating both the textual constructions of the woman warrior Tomoe and the performative channels through which such texts were transmitted—I explore the conditions under which that proper name became inscribed by issues of performativity, historicity, and citationality.

Reading the Traces of "Tomoe"

Although more than a little hyperbole embellishes the extant accounts of Tomoe's military exploits, there is little disagreement over the basic outline of Tomoe's involvement in the Genpei War.[3] Taking into account various manuscript lines produced either for reading or recitation, it is possible to reconstruct the highlights of Tomoe's brief military career with the army of Kiso no Yoshinaka: In the sixth month of 1181 (Jishō 5/6), Tomoe made her debut in the Battle of Yokotagawara, defeating seven mounted warriors. In the fifth month of 1183 (Juei 2/5), appointed as one of Yoshinaka's principal commanders, Tomoe led more than one thousand cavalrymen in a desperate fight that resulted in victory over the Taira at Tonamiyama. Finally, in the first month of 1184 (Juei 3/1), after distinguishing herself in battle at Uchide no Hama against six thousand horsemen and managing to survive after Yoshinaka's army had been reduced from three hundred mounted warriors to five, Tomoe made her last appearance on the battlefield as a woman warrior at Awazu, where she vanquished one more mighty opponent before forever discarding her armor. The following description of her last fight is from the ninth chapter of the Kakuichi manuscript line of *Heike monogatari*:

> As before, Tomoe was not about to flee, but after she had been told repeatedly [by Lord Kiso], she pulled back and thought, "Oh, what I wouldn't give for a fine enemy, that I might fight my last battle before [Lord Kiso's] gaze." While she watched and waited for an opportunity, Onda no Hachirō Moroshige, known in Musashi province for his awesome strength, came forth along with about thirty mounted warriors. Tomoe galloped into close proximity, forcefully rode up next to Onda no Hachirō, grabbed hold of him with all her strength, pulled him down from his horse, pressed him against the pommel of her own saddle, and without allowing him to move even the slightest, twisted and cut off his head, and then discarded it. After that, she pulled off and discarded her equipment, and fled toward the eastern provinces. (*HM*, 30: 196)

Much greater uncertainty exists concerning Tomoe's personal and genealogical history: where she was born, where she died, who her parents were, whether or not she had children, and so on. It has been speculated that in the earliest stages of the development of the "Kiso no saigo" (Death of Kiso) episode as oral literature, the image of Tomoe was probably restricted to the fig-

ure of a *binjo*, or female servant, in the employ of Yoshinaka, but the roles of
Tomoe seem to have multiplied with each retelling of her history. Tomoe
comes to be described variously as a female warrior, servant, general, mistress,
wife, nun, *miko*, and *asobime*.[4] Indeed, Tomoe's biography is so enfolded in legend that it is impossible to say precisely where the historical reality ends and
the literary construct begins when confronted with the plethora of contradic-
tory accounts purporting to describe the details of her life.

Consider, for example, the details of Tomoe's birth and lineage. Tomoe's
age at the time of the battle at Awazu is reported as twenty-two years in the
Hyakunijūkubon manuscript line, twenty-eight years in *Genpei seisuiki* (Record of the rise and fall of the Minamoto and Taira), and thirty years in the
Enkeibon recension. In *Genpei seisuiki*, she is said to be the daughter of Nakahara Kanetō; the sister of Higuchi no Jirō Kanemitsu, Imai no Shirō Kanehira, and Ochiai no Gorō Kaneyuki; and the foster sister and lover of Kiso no
Yoshinaka. However, in *Genpei tōjōroku* (Chronicle of the Minamoto-Taira
conflict), Tomoe is represented as the mistress of Higuchi no Jirō Kanemitsu
rather than his sister. And yet elsewhere, she is described as the daughter of
this same Higuchi no Jirō Kanemitsu rather than his lover. Moreover, we are
told in *Genpei tōjōroku* that, after fleeing from Awazu, Tomoe was summoned
by Minamoto no Yoritomo (1147–99) to Kamakura, where she met and married Wada Yoshimori (also known as Wada Saemon, 1147–1213), one of Yoritomo's chief administrators and an accomplished warrior in his own right.
Their union supposedly produced one child, the legendary warrior Asahina
Saburō Yoshihide, said to have inherited his superhuman strength from his
mother's side.[5] But an account in *Azuma kagami* places into question the historical veracity of this story by suggesting that Asahina was already nine years
of age at the time of the Battle of Awazu,[6] making it unlikely that Tomoe
could have been his mother.

Not surprisingly, the place where Tomoe lived out her remaining years
and eventually died is also open to question. Tomoe reportedly spent her later
years both in the cities of Tomioka in Echigo province and Ishiguro in Etchū
province, was buried at no fewer than three different locations in Shinano
province, and was enshrined in the village of Kokubu in Ōmi province. In
short, the figure of Tomoe seems to be as divided and multiplied as her name
itself, which is written in seven different ways in manuscript lines ranging
from the Kakuichibon to the Hiramatsukebon, from the Nagatobon to the
Nantobon.[7] Tomikura Tokujirō views these apocryphal reports and graphic
variants as providing abundant evidence for the hypothesis that Tomoe trav-
eled widely throughout the eastern provinces.[8] But from a Derridean perspective, one might also view the vicissitudes of the proper name Tomoe in

the medieval period as demonstrating the infinite divisibility of a name and its bearer in a culture of performance.

According to Jacques Derrida, as soon as any mark is emitted, whether oral or written, whether a message, a proper name, or a signature, it no longer belongs to its author or bearer. The citationality of the mark cuts off both a mark and its producer from "all absolute responsibility" for the effects it produces in the course of its reiteration and reception, insofar as the singular historicity of every mark is—in the very moment of its production—cut off "from consciousness as the ultimate authority."[9] Every mark, in its self-division, opens itself up to the possibility of being countersigned by the mark of the other, splitting its idiom open for the other to sign into a new idiom, a new singularity (which, in turn, is open to the self-division, contamination, and alteration of yet other inscriptions performed in other contexts).[10] From this perspective, the question "Who was Tomoe?" seems impossible to answer, insofar as the proper name "Tomoe" was self-divided and multiplied as soon as it became an object of historiography and cultural production—that is, as soon as it was countersigned by others.

Gendered Transmissions

Perhaps the greatest scholarly dissension surrounds the so-called "battlefield withdrawal" (*senjō ridatsu*) scene and its influence on the formation of the Yoshinaka and Tomoe *setsuwa* (narratives). In the ninth chapter of the Kakuichi manuscript, we are told that, after being reduced from three hundred mounted warriors to only five, Yoshinaka's warriors either fled or stayed to fight to the death. As he prepares to meet his own death, Yoshinaka gives Tomoe the following instructions in the Kakuichi version: "Quickly," said Lord Kiso, "since you are a woman, go wherever you like" (*onore wa tōtō onna nareba izuchi e mo yuke*) (HM, 30: 195). The rationale Yoshinaka provides for this slight to Tomoe's gender is that since he wishes either to die in battle or to take his own life if he is mortally wounded, "it would be unbecoming if it were said that in his last battle, Lord Kiso brought a woman along (*Kisodono no saigo no ikusa ni onna wo guseraretarikeri nan do iwaren koto mo shikarubekarazu*) (HM, 30: 196). Why does Yoshinaka send Tomoe away from the battlefield? Is he embarrassed by Tomoe's presence? Or does he fear for her safety? Since Yoshinaka has obviously not just arrived at the realization that Tomoe is a woman, why does Tomoe's gender become such an issue for him at this late date? Does Yoshinaka fear that the woman warrior Tomoe, who is "equal to a thousand men," may die a more glorious death than himself? Or is it that he wishes to ensure that someone from his faction will survive to retell the story of his life and death from a sympathetic perspective?

It can hardly be said that Yoshinaka fears for Tomoe's safety, since he was perfectly willing to dispatch Tomoe into battle after battle as his foremost commander (*ippō no taishō*). There is no question that Tomoe had already proven her abilities and valor as a warrior:

> She was a splendid archer who could draw a strong bow exceedingly well; on horse or on foot, she was prepared to confront with sword in hand both demons and gods, a warrior equal to a thousand men. She rode unusually strong, untamed horses and went down steep mountain paths on horseback in full gallop. Whenever battle was announced, [Yoshinaka] had her wear armor made out of the best materials and carry a heavy long sword and strong bow. She was sent out first as his leading commander. (*HM*, 30: 193)

Why, then, this sudden reluctance by Yoshinaka to permit Tomoe to die a glorious death by his side? Whether this reluctance is motivated by Yoshinaka's profound concern for Tomoe's well-being,[11] or whether it expresses a fear of being upstaged by Tomoe in the final moments of his life, this puzzling scene is crucial for understanding the complex gender politics and tensions inscribing the figure of Tomoe.

That the death of a warrior was the defining moment in a warrior's life within the cultural imaginary of *Heike monogatari* is clearly evidenced by the fact that, although the term *saigo* does not appear in any major works of Heian literature, there are thirty-eight instances of the word in the Kakuichi version of *Heike monogatari* alone,[12] many of which can be found in episodes devoted to the deaths of famous warriors, such as Tadanori, Atsumori, Tomoakira, and so forth. Why, then, is Tomoe not allowed to die in a manner befitting a warrior?

The answer to this question is as divided and multiplied as other aspects of Tomoe's life, insofar as important differences exist between the Kakuichi version of the "battle withdrawal" scene and accounts in other manuscript lines. For example, the Hyakunijūkubon text of the Yasaka line contains the following detail omitted from the Kakuichi version of Yoshinaka's last instructions to Tomoe:

> Onna wo tsurete uchijini sasetari nando iwaren koto mo kuchioshikarubeshi. . . . Kore yori izuchi e mo ochiyuki, Yoshinaka ga gose wo mo toburainan ya.[13]

> Were it said that [Yoshinaka] died in battle with a woman as companion and so forth, it would undoubtedly be humiliating. . . . Would that you might flee from here to wherever you like, and pray for the repose of Yoshinaka in the next world!

Yet another variation appears in the thirty-fifth chapter of *Genpei seisuiki*, in a section entitled "Tomoe's Departure from the Capital to the Kantō District" (*Tomoe Kantō gekō no koto*). Yoshinaka's last words to Tomoe are reported as follows:

> Kozo no haru, ware, Shinano no kuni wo ideshi toki, saishi wo suteoki, mata futatabi mizu shite, nagakiwakare no michi ni iran koto koso kanashikere. Sareba nakaran ato made mo, kono koto wo shirasete, nochi no yo wo toburawaba ya to omoeba, saigo no tomo yori mo sarubeki zonzuru nari. Tōtō shinobiochite, Shinano e kudari, kono arisama wo hitobito ni katare. (Mizuhara, 4: 310–11)

> Last spring, when I left Shinano province, leaving behind my wife and child, without looking back a second time, entering a path that probably leads toward death filled me with sorrow. For that reason, since traces [of me] will probably cease to exist in this world, please make these circumstances known: if only you will pray for me in the next world, rather than become my companion in death —I believe it must be this way. Quickly conceal yourself and flee, go down to Shinano, and recite these circumstances to various people.

Although filled with feelings of regret, Tomoe followed Yoshinaka's orders. After pulling off her armor and discarding it, Tomoe "put on a ceremonial *kosode* robe and went down to Shinano, where she recited these matters" (*kosode shōzoku shite Shinano e kudari, nyōbō kintachi ni kaku to katari* [Mizuhara, 4: 311]) to Yoshinaka's legal wife and child.

What these variants add to the Kakuichi version is a more explicit delineation of Yoshinaka's motivation for sending Tomoe away from Awazu: fearful that all traces of his existence might vanish, Yoshinaka ordered Tomoe to hold memorial services for the repose of his departed spirit and charged her with the obligation of transmitting his story after his death. Just as the early recitation of *Gikeiki* (Story of Yoshitsune) has been linked to Minamoto no Yoshitsune's (1159–89) lover, the *shirabyōshi* ("white-beat" dancer) Shizuka Gozen, and the recitation of *Soga monogatari* (Tale of the Soga brothers) to Soga Sukenari's (1172–93) mistress, the *asobime* Tora Gozen, so, too, transmission of the Yoshinaka *setsuwa* has been attributed to Tomoe Gozen.[14] In addition to serving as one of the performative channels through which her lover's *setsuwa* was transmitted, Tomoe shares with these other female entertainers the *gozen* suffix.

Tomoe is never once addressed as "Tomoe Gozen" in any of the extant *Heike monogatari* variants, and yet this is how she is widely known today. How is the *gozen* epithet being used with respect to Tomoe? A quick review of its history of usage reveals the following differentiations:

1. An honorific term used in the presence of or in relation to members of the nobility (commonly used in *Heike monogatari* and *Towazugatari* [Lady Nijō's confessions])

2. An abbreviation for *gozenku*, an outrider in the service of the nobility (see *Kohon setsuwashū* [Collection of old *setsuwa* tales])

3. A second-person pronoun used to address one's own or another's legal wife (examples in *Uji shūi monogatari* [Tales gleaned from Uji] and *Gikeiki*)

4. An honorific pronoun used during the Edo period to refer to *daimyō*, samurai in the employ of the Tokugawa shogunate, and members of the nobility, as well as their legal wives (see *Kōshoku ichidai onna*)

5. An honorific suffix (sometimes abbreviated as *goze*) linked throughout the medieval and early modern periods to the names of *kami*, members of the nobility, *miko*, *shirabyōshi*, and other types of female entertainer. The latter usage is amply demonstrated in *Heike monogatari* and *Gikeiki* by the names of *shirabyōshi*, such as Giō Gozen, Hotoke Gozen, and Shizuka Gozen[15]

Mizuhara Hajime makes the point that, whenever it was that Tomoe started to be addressed as Tomoe Gozen, it must have been because of the perception that she was related to persons of rank—as the daughter of Nakahara Kanetō, brother of Imai Kanehira, and lover of Kiso Yoshinaka.[16] But if that were so, surely Tomoe's name would have appeared with the *gozen* suffix in one or more of the *Heike monogatari* recensions. Insofar as Tomoe only comes to be addressed as Tomoe Gozen much later (sometime in the late medieval to early modern period), after her biography has had a chance to acquire additional associations, it seems more plausible to assume that, rather than indicating noble lineage, or her relationship with Yoshinaka, Wada Yoshimori, or other men of power, the *gozen* suffix signifies Tomoe's legendary association with female performers.

Tomoe's role in the production and transmission of the Yoshinaka *setsuwa* is the subject of the only *shuramono* about a woman warrior that is still performed in the current noh repertoire: the *mugen* noh *Tomoe*.[17] *Tomoe* stands as an important document in the culturo-historical dissemination of Tomoe's biography. Although *Tomoe* is widely regarded as the only woman–warrior play from the second category, in fact that is only true with respect to the current repertoire. At least two other extant plays about Tomoe, *Kinu Kazuki Tomoe* (Veiled Tomoe) and *Katami Tomoe* (Bamboo-basket Tomoe) (also known as *Kinen Tomoe* [Keepsake Tomoe] and *Ōgi Tomoe* [Folding-fan Tomoe]), belong to the *shuramono* category, even if they are no longer performed.[18] Moreover, two noncanonical *genzai noh* dealing with Tomoe—that is, *Genzai Tomoe* (Present-day Tomoe) and *Konjō Tomoe* (Present-life Tomoe)—are also extant.[19] The remainder of this chapter will track Tomoe's transformation from woman warrior to peripatetic entertainer by focusing on the *mugen* noh *Tomoe* in comparison with these noncanonical variations.

Cross-Dressing History

Although the *maejite* of *Tomoe* is glossed in current editions as a "village woman" (*sato no onna*), in the earliest manuscripts she was depicted as a *kannagi* or *miko* in the service of a shrine dedicated to Kiso no Yoshinaka.[20] This representation of Tomoe in the guise of a *miko* appears in the very first few lines sung by the *shite*:

> Omoshiro ya Nio no uranami shizuka naru
> Awazu no Hara no matsukage ni
> Kami wo ioo ya matsurigoto
> Geni shinkan mo tanomoshi ya
> Kyō wa Awazu ga Hara no gojinji nite sōrō hodo ni
> Kannagidomo mo mairaba ya to omoisōrō
> Ara arigata ya sōrō
> Mukashi no koto no omoiideraretesōrō.[21]

> How charming! The waves on Lake Nio are calm;
> in the pine shade of Awazu Field,
> performing festive rites and rituals to honor the gods,
> how promising the divine response!
> Today, on the occasion of the festive ceremonies at Awazu,
> even we *miko* intend to go.
> Oh, how blessed, to be reminded of events from the past.[22]

The second to last line, "Even we *miko* intend to go" (*kannagidomo mo mairaba ya to omoisōrō*), taken from the *shimogakari* manuscript line, is almost identical to the Kanze and Hōshō schools' current *kamigakari* texts except for the inclusion of one additional word: *kannagidomo* (translated as "we *miko*"). Insofar as the earliest manuscript versions from both the *shimogakari* and *kamigakari* manuscript lines also include *kannagidomo*, Itō Masayoshi has argued against its omission from current performance texts, suggesting that the representation of Tomoe as a *miko* marks an important innovation that goes beyond both the *setsuwa* and *heikyoku* (recitation of *Heike monogatari*) traditions even as it amplifies certain elements from each.[23]

This depiction of Tomoe as a *miko* is further reinforced in the *mondō* (spoken dialogue) that follows, where the *shite* attempts to justify her strange behavior to a pair of wandering monks, who find her lachrymose demeanor quite odd during a shrine visit.[24] The *shite* proceeds to recite a foundation tale in the *honji suijaku* ("original essence, manifest traces") tradition, just the sort of legend an *arukimiko* or *bikuni* might tell. The *shite* relates the tale of the founding of Iwashimizu Hachiman Shrine on Otokoyama by Gyōkyō Oshō, which we encountered in our discussion of *Ominameshi* in the previous chapter. But unlike *Ominameshi*, in which the Hachiman foundation myth figures into the multilayered politics of subjection operating in that play, here it functions primarily to underscore Tomoe's status as a *miko*. After recounting this foundation narrative, the *shite* then informs the monks that the shrine at Awazu Field is the very site where Kiso no Yoshinaka is celebrated as a *kami*, and they all clasp their hands in prayer.

Although the depiction of Tomoe as a *miko* seems to be an invention of this Sengoku-period *yōkyoku*, such a representation is not unrelated to the account of Tomoe taking the tonsure in *Genpei seisuiki*:[25]

> Wada gassen no toki, Asahina utarete ato, Tomoe wa nakunaku Etchū ni koe, Ishiguro wa shitashikarikereba, koko ni shite shukke shite Tomoe no Ama tote, Butsu ni hana kō wo tatematsuri, shū oya Asahina ga gose toburaikeru ga kyū-jūichi made tamochite. (Mizuhara, 4: 311–12)

> At the time of the battle of Wada, after Asahina was killed, Tomoe crossed in tears to Etchū. Since Ishiguro was familiar to her, there she took the tonsure, and as Tomoe the Nun made offerings of flowers and incense to the Buddha, and prayed for the repose of her lord, her parents, and her son Asahina in the next world. She lived until the age of ninety-one.

Tokue Motomasa has investigated historical records from several provinces indicating the existence of a nun or nuns named Tomoe, but it remains unclear whether any of those nuns was actually Tomoe the woman warrior.[26] Moreover, Sunagawa Hiroshi[27] has discovered a connection between an itinerant *bikuni* entertainer named Tomoe and the "Eight Hundred *Bikuni*" from Wakasa province. Yet another representation of Tomoe the entertainer appears in the Bunrokubon manuscript of the Yasaka line. After the battle at Awazu and before marrying Wada Yoshimori, Tomoe is said to have served for a period of time as "an *asobime* at the residence of Hashimoto" (*Hashimoto no yado ni yū-kun to shite ita*).[28]

To this list one could add the figure of Tomoe appearing at the end of the *mugen* noh *Tomoe*, which resembles that of a *shirabyōshi*. In the second half of the play, after she has disclosed her identity, Tomoe recounts through the mouthpiece of the chorus how she pleaded with Yoshinaka to commit double suicide together with her:

> Kono matsu ga ne ni ontomo shi
> Haya onjigai sōrae
> Tomoe mo tomo to mōseba
> Sono toki Yoshinaka no ōse ni wa
> Nanji wa onna nari
> Shinobu tayori mo arubeshi.[29]

> Accompanying my lord to the base of this pine tree,
> I said humbly: "Quickly take your own life,

please, together with Tomoe."
Upon hearing this, Yoshinaka issued the following command:
"Given that you are a woman,
this ought to be an opportunity for you to go into hiding."

Here the alliteration of *tomo shi*, *Tomoe mo*, and *tomo to* phonetically links Tomoe and her desire to accompany her lord to the next world.[30]

Despite Tomoe's insistence, Yoshinaka refuses, issuing the following per-
emptory response: "Deliver this talisman and *kosode* robe to Kiso. If you dis-
obey my orders, our karmic bond of three lives as master and servant will
cease to exist" (*kore naru mamori kosode wo Kiso ni todoke yo kono mune wo so-
mukaba shūjū sanze no chigiri taehate*).[31] Interestingly, in two noncanonical *genzai* noh, *Genzai Tomoe* and *Konjō Tomoe*, Tomoe expresses the wish to "die in
battle on the same pillow, and accompany her Lord across *two lives*" (*onaji
makura ni uchijini shite, nise no ontomo mōsubeshi*),[32] rather than three. The latter reference to "two lives" has been taken by some scholars—including Haga
Yaichi—as suggesting that, from Tomoe's perspective, she and Yoshinaka were
more than simply lovers: they were husband and wife. According to the well-
known Buddhist maxim, social relationships could be differentiated according
to the longevity of their karmic bonds: "Parent and child, one life; husband and
wife, two lives; master and servant, three lives" (*oyako wa isse, fūfu wa nise, shūjū
wa sanze*). In short, the Tomoe of both *Genzai Tomoe* and *Konjō Tomoe* emphasizes her two-lifetime marital bond with Yoshinaka over her three-lifetime
feudalistic one.

In a significant departure from the *Heike monogatari* manuscript tradition,
the spirit of Tomoe recounts in the *mugen* noh *Tomoe* that, after Yoshinaka
had committed suicide (a much more honorable end than he experiences in
Heike monogatari), she returned to collect Yoshinaka's personal talisman and
kosode robe. Naturally, she is overcome with intense feelings of *ushiromedasa*:
regret that she did not insist on fulfilling her duty to die with Yoshinaka; humiliation that she was not permitted—as her brother Kanehira was—to die
a warrior's death at Awazu; and perhaps also resentment that Yoshinaka had
never before used her gender as an excuse to exclude her from battle. In the
midst of such emotional turbulence, Tomoe performs a *monogi*, or costume
change, on the stage as the chorus vocalizes the scene:

> Goyuigon no kanashisa ni
> Awazu no migiwa ni tachiyori
> Uwaobi kiri mono no gu
> Kokoroshizuka ni nugioki
> Nashiuchi eboshi onajiku
> Kashiko ni nugisute

Onkosode wo hikikazuki
Sono kiwa made no hakizoe no
Kodachi wo kinu ni hikikakushi.[33]

In her sadness over Yoshinaka's last words,
she stopped at the waterside in Awazu,
cut loose her outer *obi*,
and with quiet heart pulled off her armor and put it down.
Likewise the hat she wore under her helmet,
she took off and discarded.
Her lord's *kosode* robe she pulled over her head;
his short sword worn up to the time of death,
she withdrew and concealed in her robe.

Similar *monogi* occur at the end of noncanonical Tomoe plays, such as *Konjō Tomoe* and *Kinu Kazuki Tomoe*, but with the important exception that there is no suggestion that the robes donned by Tomoe in those plays (*natsuginu* [summer robe] in *Konjō Tomoe*, *usuginu* [light robe] in *Kinu Kazuki Tomoe*) originally belonged to Yoshinaka. Moreover, in the sword-fight play *Genzai Tomoe*, Yoshinaka entrusts to Tomoe various keepsakes (*katami*) without disclosing what those keepsakes are or suggesting that Tomoe do any more than return them to his home town, take the tonsure, and pray for the repose of his spirit.

The *monogi* of the *mugen* noh *Tomoe* intertextually reinscribes a similar scene from *Genpei seisuiki*:

Awazu no ikusa owarite ato, mono no gu nugisute, kosode shōzoku shite Shinano e kudari, nyōbō kindachi ni kaku to katari, tagai ni sode wo zo shibo[ru]. (Mizuhara, 4: 311)

After the battle at Awazu had come to an end, she pulled off her armor and discarded it, put on a ceremonial *kosode* robe and went down to Shinano; upon reciting these matters to Yoshinaka's legal wife and child, they wrung their sleeves together.

What distinguishes the *Genpei seisuiki* passage from the *monogi* at the end of *Tomoe* is that there is no suggestion in *Genpei seisuiki* that the robe belongs to anyone else but Tomoe; whereas, at the end of the noh play, we witness an act of cross-dressing as Tomoe dons Yoshinaka's robe and short sword.

It might be argued that the donning of Yoshinaka's robe is yet another reiteration of Tomoe's role as *miko* in the first half of the play, suggesting the conventional figure of possession through the donning of another's clothing, which is the climactic moment of many a play in the noh repertoire, such as *Matsukaze*, *Izutsu* (Well curb), *Sotoba Komachi* (Komachi at the stupa), and *Futari Shizuka* (Two Shizukas). Such scenes of possession hearken back to the shamanistic role of the *miko* as a medium of spiritual possession through which a spirit articulates its identity and demands. But Tomoe does not perform the sort of *utsurimai*, or possessed dance, one would expect in such circumstances. Instead, the play comes to a quiet end, with the final *shōdan* sung in the lyrical *yowagin* style to the ordinary beat of *hiranori* rhythm (a congruent song with twelve syllables of text matched to sixteen half-beats of music). Rather than behaving like one possessed, Tomoe, "together with only her falling tears" (*namida to Tomoe wa tada hitori*), requests that "prayers be said to console her deep attachment to feelings of regret" (*ushiromedasa no shūshin wo toitetabitamae*).[34]

I would like to suggest that, rather than reiterating the figure of the *miko*, this final act of cross-dressing likens Tomoe to the figure of the *shirabyōshi* without actually going so far as to turn her into one. Granted, the *shirabyōshi* costume had changed somewhat by the time the play was performed in the Sengoku period,[35] dispensing with the man's hat while retaining the man's *suikan* robe. But whatever costume changes had taken place did not alter the fact that *shirabyōshi* entertainers were regarded as cross-dressing performers within the medieval cultural imaginary, as is attested by the notable scene of *shirabyōshi* cross-dressing from the Muromachi text of *Gikeiki*, in which Shizuka Gozen creates a stir by attiring herself in a man's hunting costume (*karishōzoku*) at Yoshitsune's request.[36] Insofar as she wears stylized military attire and a man's *nashiuchi eboshi* (soft black cap worn under a warrior's helmet) on the noh stage,[37] perhaps Tomoe has already cross-dressed even before she dons Yoshinaka's *kosode* robe and short sword, but the donning of Yoshinaka's garb seems to underscore not only Tomoe's attachment to Yoshinaka, but also her likeness to *shirabyōshi* performers.[38]

What happens when the performance of feminine-to-masculine cross-dressing, such as displayed by Tomoe's appearance on the battlefield in the full armor of a male warrior, is reperformed in the form of masculine-to-feminine cross-dressing, such as exhibited by the male actor playing the role of Tomoe on the noh stage? Does this reconversion of Tomoe's cross-dressing, which turns her feminine-to-masculine act inside out, not reaffirm the predominance of masculinity in the medieval gender hierarchy? I would contend that such acts of feminine-to-masculine and masculine-to-feminine cross-dressing in the noh tradition are not "subversive," but in fact uphold the very gender categories blurred by performatively demonstrating on the noh stage that man is still the measure of all things.[39] To read cross-dressing as yet another stratagem serving the network of power relations in medieval Japan may seem too Foucauldian in its cynicism, but such a conclusion seems much closer to the historically specific effects of cross-dressing in the Kamakura and Muromachi periods than the all too modern assumption that gender-bending is subversive. I would say that no cultural artifact or practice is intrinsically "subversive" or "coopted," but that it is only the historically specific network of cultural production, circulation, and reception that characterizes it as such.

It seems unlikely that the figure of Tomoe actually pushed the medieval boundaries of gender, since on the battlefield Tomoe was rarely perceived as anything other than a *woman* warrior. Likewise on the noh stage, though the *waki* in *Tomoe* is initially dumbfounded by the *nochijite*'s appearance, he soon recognizes that the *nochijite* is a *woman* dressed in military garb:

> Fushigi ya na Awazu ga Hara no kusamakura wo
> Mireba aritsuru nyoshō naru ga
> Katchū wo taisuru fushigisa yo.[40]

> How strange! Looking upon the grassy pillow of Awazu Field,
> I see the woman who was here before,
> but wearing helmet and armor—how strange!

At no point during the play, even when she appears cross-dressed as Yoshinaka, is Tomoe permitted to behave like a conventional male warrior ghost in a *shuramono* play. The fact that Tomoe neither discloses the typical *ashura* "tale of repentance" (*sange monogatari*), nor reenacts through dance the scene of her death, is due entirely to Yoshinaka's refusal to allow her to die a warrior's death by his side because of her gender and insistence that she fulfill her obligation to her lord by telling and retelling the tale of Yoshinaka and thereby rescuing his proper name from infamy or oblivion. In short, the gender politics inscribing the figure of Tomoe on the noh stage has as much to do with what she *does not* say or do as it does with what she *does* say and do.

It remains an open question whether such acts of cross-dressing in noh, in addition to reinforcing the hierarchization of gender, also produced effects of homoerotic enticement similar to later performances of *onnagata* (female roles) in kabuki. There is no denying the homoerotic undertones of certain types of noh plays, particularly those involving scenes of cross-dressing, such as *Matsukaze* and *Izutsu*; those that foreground youthful male beauty, such as *Atsumori* and *Tsunemasa*; or even those that involve the licentious behavior of phallicized *tengu* goblins disguised as *yamabushi* priests, such as *Kurama tengu* (Goblin of Kurama) and *Kuruma zō* (Carriage priest). Indeed, given the more than patronly affections offered to the young Zeami by Yoshimitsu, it is hard to believe that other noh actors of distinguished abilities and physical beauty, whether performing in the capital or in the provinces, were not also objects of sexual interest.[41] But noh's complex mixture of religiosity, entertainment, gender, and sexuality means that all such effects need to be contextualized in relation to their historically specific discourse networks.

Whether as *arukimiko, bikuni, asobime,* or even *shirabyōshi,* such figurations depict a Tomoe who not only prays for the repose of Yoshinaka's spirit in the next world, but also recites the tale of Yoshinaka's death at Awazu and thereby ensures a place for both Yoshinaka and Tomoe in the archives of cultural memory. It is impossible to say whether Tomoe the entertainer was the same person as Tomoe the woman warrior, especially since it is well known that during the medieval period peripatetic entertainers, pretending to have been present at famous scenes of battle, made a living performing military tales and songs at former battle sites.[42] Indeed, Watanabe Shōgo has argued that most, if not all, the details of Tomoe's post-Genpei history—for instance, that she became a nun, moved to the village of Tomomatsu in Echigo province, and lived until the age of ninety-one—were fabricated by such peripatetic entertainers. Watanabe thinks the same goes for Shizuka Gozen and Tora Gozen. Such entertainers thrived throughout the medieval and early modern periods, drawing in the masses with the feigned authenticity of their supposed eyewitness accounts and giving historical legitimacy to claims that, in many cases, were either largely or totally fabricated.

It seems highly likely that the performers named "Tomoe" were just such pretenders, but even if that is so, the fact that such individuals adopted the name of the most famous woman warrior in Japanese history would have contributed not only to the dissemination of the Yoshinaka narrative, but also to the elevation of Tomoe's stature in the medieval cultural imaginary.

The Hegemon as Actor:
Staging Hideyoshi in Postmedieval Noh

Of all the rulers who patronized noh, the only one who surpassed even
Yoshimitsu in largesse was Toyotomi Hideyoshi,[1] one of the three major uni-
fiers of premodern Japan. Although some scholars consider the second most
important turning point in the patronage history of noh (the first being the
Imagumano performance in 1374 or 1375) to be the year 1609, when the
Tokugawa shogunate established official patronage for all four major noh
troupes of the Yamato *sarugaku* line, such a shogunal patronage policy would
probably never have been instituted had it not been for the unique precedent
set by Hideyoshi during the late Azuchi-Momoyama period. Hideyoshi's patronage and involvement with noh helped create a cultural space within which
noh drama would eventually be designated the official ceremonial music and
entertainment (*shikigaku*) of the Tokugawa shogunate.

Hideyoshi Performing "Hideyoshi"

Although Hideyoshi was never officially designated shogun, he was clearly
the *de facto* ruler of Japan between 1590 and 1598, governing with as much,
if not more, power than Ashikaga Yoshimitsu two hundred years earlier, but
lacking Yoshimitsu's cultural authority and legitimacy because of his obscure
family background. Although it is often said that Hideyoshi followed the
political example of Minamoto no Yoritomo,[2] the founder of the Kamakura
shogunate, it should also be recognized that in an effort to increase his sym-

bolic capital and legitimize the cultural authority of his regime, Hideyoshi seems to have emulated the example set by Yoshimitsu during the cultural efflorescence of the Kitayama epoch. Like Yoshimitsu, Hideyoshi actively acquired the distinguishing symbols of imperial rank and office, arranging for his own self-promotion to the offices of *kanpaku* (chancellor) in 1585, *daijō daijin* (prime minister) in 1587, and *taikō* (retired regent) in 1592.[3] Moreover, like Yoshimitsu, Hideyoshi patronized art and artists in order to increase his own culturo-political prestige: artistic pursuits such as *waka* poetry, tea ceremony, and noh drama were all means toward the "aristocratization" of Hideyoshi, as George Elison puts it,[4] means toward the transformation of Hideyoshi from an uncultured upstart into a highly refined hegemon. Hideyoshi's patronage of noh seems also to have led to an entirely new configuration of relations between politics and theatricality during the late Momoyama era.

Of all the rulers who patronized noh, Hideyoshi stands out not only because he was the first one to establish regular stipends for all four troupes of the Yamato *sarugaku* line,[5] but also because he was the only one to perform the role of himself on the noh stage. Hideyoshi's earliest recorded contact with the world of noh dates back to 1571, when—under the surname Kinoshita—he made inquiries to the Kanze *iemoto* (head of school) about taking up the study of noh song and dance. But Hideyoshi's preliminary contacts with noh did not develop into a full-fledged association until he was appointed *kanpaku* in the seventh month of 1585.[6] Two days after assuming his duties as *kanpaku*, Hideyoshi sponsored his first program of five noh plays at the imperial palace.[7] After regularly attending and sponsoring noh productions for the better part of a decade, Hideyoshi commenced formal study of noh song and dance at the Nagoya center of operations during the Korean campaign, making his stage debut in 1593.[8]

Perhaps because of the close association between the Konparu school of noh and the Yagyū school of martial arts, Hideyoshi studied under the direction of the Konparu teacher Kurematsu Shinkurō. During this period, Hideyoshi became so obsessed with noh that he even had a portable noh stage constructed so that he could take it with him whenever he went to battle "in order not to get out of practice."[9] If noh could serve as "a prayer for peace to reign over the entire country,"[10] as Zeami claimed, then it could also improve the morale of Hideyoshi's troops in Kyushu. Therefore, the ruler summoned all four troupes of the Yamato *sarugaku* line and had them perform for his soldiers at the Nagoya headquarters. Hideyoshi also encouraged the *daimyō* (regional military governors) to study noh in order to discipline their bodies and make their ignoble demeanor noble: that is, to aristocratize themselves as he had himself.[11]

Members of the military elite had been studying noh song and dance at the amateur level of *tesarugaku* since at least the middle of the fifteenth century, but Hideyoshi became the first and only ruler of Japan ever to perform in a noh play *as himself*. In the early 1590s Hideyoshi appeared in god plays such as *Takasago* and *Yumi Yawata*, warrior plays such as *Tamura* and *Yorimasa*, woman plays such as *Matsukaze, Izutsu,* and *Sekidera Komachi* (Komachi at Sekidera), mad person plays such as *Tōsen* (Chinese ship) and *Kantan*, and demon plays such as *Daie* (Great assembly) and others.[12] But Hideyoshi also commissioned the writing of ten special noh plays that celebrated his numerous accomplishments and virtues. Indeed, in the third year of Bunroku (1594), Hideyoshi may have starred as himself in at least five of the ten plays, performing the role of "Hideyoshi" in play after play at the Osaka Castle. These so-called "new noh plays" (*shinsaku nō*), or *Taikō nō* as they came to be called, were composed by an *otogishū* (storyteller) named Ōmura Yūko (1536?–96),[13] Hideyoshi's officially appointed chronicler and an accomplished poet in his own right. Konparu Anshō (1549–1621), a renowned actor six generations removed from Konparu Zenchiku, provided the music. The Taikō noh celebrated and memorialized Hideyoshi's power and family genealogy, as well as his political, military, and cultural achievements.

Five of the ten plays originally commissioned by Hideyoshi are still extant: the god play *Yoshino mōde* (Pilgrimage to Yoshino), the warrior plays *Shibata, Hōjō,* and *Akechi uchi* (Conquest of Akechi), and the woman play *Kōya sankei* (Pilgrimage to Kōya).[14] Taken together, the Taikō noh present a highly selective version of Hideyoshi's "greatest hits." As with *Tenshōki* (Record of Tenshō),[15] Hideyoshi's official chronicles, no mention is made of Hideyoshi's military failures in Korea or elsewhere. Indeed, in *Yoshino mōde*, playwright Ōmura Yūko engages in the most blatant historical revisionism by having the *waki*, an imperial retainer, describe the "brave deeds" (*buyūkō*) accomplished by Taikō Hideyoshi, who "subdues the three kingdoms of Korea, as well as granting petitions from China" (*Sankan wo tairage, amassae Morokoshi yori mo konkwan wo iruru ni yori*).[16] Of course, even to hint at Hideyoshi's failures in Korea would not only have been regarded as inauspicious, it also would have compromised the symbolic efficacy of Hideyoshi's self-staging. Let us look more closely at the plays themselves.

Although *Yoshino mōde* was written in the style of a commemoration of Hideyoshi's journey to the hills of Yoshino to view cherry blossoms around the end of the second month of 1594, in fact, it was commissioned *before* Hideyoshi made the trip. *Yoshino mōde* was first performed in Yoshino on the first day of the third month in front of the Yoshino Shrine.[17] It was as if Hideyoshi's flower-viewing excursion had already been scripted in advance. Insofar as the writing of the play preceded the actual trip, the performance text cannot be said to have simply *reflected* the historical event it supposedly commemorated.

In addition to turning the apparent mimeticism of the drama on its head, *Yoshino mōde* also foregrounds the theatricality operative in such a flower-viewing procession by drawing attention to the multiple levels of performer-spectator reflexivity at work. First, Hideyoshi commissioned the play to be written about his upcoming trip to Yoshino. Next, Hideyoshi made the trip, dressed in his usual costume of "false whiskers" (*tsukurihige*), "false eyebrows" (*mayu tsukarase*), and "blackened teeth" (*kaneguro*).[18] Indeed, Hideyoshi's entire entourage proceeded with such pageantry that crowds quickly assembled to observe. Once Hideyoshi and his entourage arrived in Yoshino, the most distinguished poets in Hideyoshi's retinue—including Satomura Jōha (1527–1602) and Ōmura Yūko—gathered to compose *waka* poetry. Finally, after paying respects to Zaō Gongen, chief *kami* of Yoshino Shrine, Hideyoshi ordered the performance of *Yoshino mōde* in front of Yoshino Shrine and compelled his entourage to observe again as "Hideyoshi" (the character in the play) took in the beauty of the cherry blossoms on the stage of Yoshino.

Members of the audience who observed the drama of Hideyoshi's *hanami* (cherry-blossom viewing) excursion as it was reperformed before Yoshino Shrine were thus placed in the interesting position of twice playing the role of audience to Hideyoshi's displays of cultural refinement. In the highly self-reflexive theatrical space of *Yoshino mōde*, the boundaries between performers and spectators became blurred as spectators turned into performers and performers turned into spectators. As with all of the "new noh plays" commissioned by Hideyoshi, such "commemorative" scenes were designed not merely to entertain Hideyoshi and his retinue, but more importantly, to compel his audience to witness twice over the edifying example of his life (once during the actual event and then again during the reperformance of that event on stage). In effect, Hideyoshi repeatedly staged and restaged his life.

In the initial production of *Yoshino mōde*, Hideyoshi played the role not of himself but rather of Zaō Gongen. In the syncretistic world of Momoyama Japan, Zaō Gongen was revered not only as the chief *kami* of Yoshino Shrine, but also as the fierce bodhisattva encountered by Shugendō founder En no Gyōja on Mount Kinpu in Yoshino after engaging in religious austerities for a thousand days. According to the cult of Zaō Gongen, his ferocity was an expedient device to frighten the unenlightened into embracing the teachings of the Buddha,[19] but as enacted by Hideyoshi, such intimidating displays more likely served the purpose of reminding the audience of Hideyoshi's unparalleled power. *Yoshino mōde* closes with Zaō Gongen vowing to protect Hideyoshi and his entourage on their way back to the capital (*miyako ni kwangyo no michi wo mamori*).[20] At the end of his life, Hideyoshi made arrangements to play the role of a god again in his next life by being awarded the posthumous title of Shin Hachiman,[21] the new Hachiman god of war. Although Hideyoshi's wish of apotheosis was granted soon after his death, it was a role he would only be allowed to play until 1619,[22] when the Shin Hachiman Shrine was destroyed, probably by Itakura Katsushige (1545–1624), then the shogunal deputy (*shoshidai*) of Kyoto. Despite his most fervent wishes, the run of Hideyoshi's performance as a god was less than eternal.

Kōya sankei, another play commissioned before Hideyoshi made the actual trip, picks up where *Yoshino mōde* left off, depicting Hideyoshi's journey from Yoshino to Mount Kōya to visit his mother's mortuary temple. According to performance records, *Kōya sankei* was first performed on Mount Kōya during Hideyoshi's visit. As with *Yoshino mōde*, the highly self-reflexive theatrical space of *Kōya sankei* blurs the boundaries between performers and spectators, theatrical fiction and historical fact. During the play, the character of Hideyoshi, performed on stage by a *kokata*, or child actor, encounters the spirit of his mother played by the *shite*. In the first half of the play, Hideyoshi's mother appears disguised as an old nun, but in the second half, she discloses her identity not only as the mother of Hideyoshi but also as a bodhisattva of song and dance. Hideyoshi's mother celebrates her present state of enlightenment, attributing her ascendance to bodhisattvahood to the prayers of her devoted son, that paragon of filial piety.

It is interesting to note that in the debut performances of both *Yoshino mōde* and *Kōya sankei* the character of Hideyoshi was represented on stage by means of a *kokata*, or child actor. Why wasn't Hideyoshi portrayed by one of the leading actors of the day? The use of such a device is instructive insofar as it was the accepted theatrical convention to employ unmasked *kokata* when depicting emperors or high-ranking political or military figures. This usage is thought to suggest the impossibility of adequately representing such figures of authority on stage. The convention of employing *kokata* in the representation of powerful figures has been followed in the stage portrayal of Emperor Keitai (450–531) in the play *Hanagatami* (Flower basket), Minister Fujiwara no Fusasaki (681–737) in *Ama* (Diver), Minamoto no Yoritomo in *Daibutsu kuyō* (Dedication ceremony for the Great Buddha), Minamoto no Yoshitsune in *Funa Benkei* (Benkei in the boat), *Ataka*, and so forth. But what sharply distinguishes the *kokata* portrayal of such renowned figures from that of Hideyoshi is that the former were long dead by the time they were dramatized on stage, whereas Hideyoshi was still alive. What starts out as a means of showing respect toward the power of the dead ends up in the hands of playwright Ōmura Yūko as a technique for increasing the symbolic capital of the living.[23]

Shibata, based on Ōmura Yūko's historical chronicle of the subjugation of Shibata Katsuie in *Shibata taijiki* (Record of the conquest of Shibata), eulogizes Hideyoshi's military victory over Shibata in the battle of Shizugatake in 1583. The ghost of Shibata appears on stage as *shite* to recount his army's march into Ōmi province, where they fought with great skill and valor. According to Shibata, as his army was on the verge of achieving victory, Hideyoshi rode up on his horse and single-handedly challenged tens of thousands of Shibata's men, many of whom fled the field in fear, unable to withstand the overwhelming force of Hideyoshi.[24]

Hōjō, based on Ōmura Yūko's historical account in *Tenshōki* of the siege of Odawara Castle, extols Hideyoshi's military prowess in his victory over Hōjō Ujimasa (1538–90) in 1590. Appearing on stage as the *shite*, the ghost of Hōjō Ujimasa recounts to the *waki*, a Gozan Zen priest, the events surrounding his death. Ujimasa describes how Hideyoshi's relentless siege of the castle at Odawara eventually forced both himself and his brother Hōjō Ujinao (1562–91) to commit suicide in defeat. But rather than having the ghost of Ujimasa vent his *ressentiment* at Hideyoshi, the play ends with Ujimasa's prayer for Hideyoshi's continued success.

The Taikō plays stretched the historicity of medieval noh theatricality by dealing with the very recent past or even the still current present, rather than the distant, remote past represented in the canonized classics by Zeami and others, which typically involved topics set in the Heian or Kamakura periods.[25] In the late sixteenth century, Christian missionaries also experimented with noh on contemporary topics as an ideological vehicle for the propagation of Christianity,[26] but "Kirishitan noh" never attained the level of self-reflexivity exemplified by Hideyoshi's Taikō noh: St. Francis Xavier never took the stage à la Hideyoshi.[27]

Hideyoshi's most outrageous break with theatrical tradition came with his performance of himself, Hashiba Chikuzen no Kami Hideyoshi, in *Akechi uchi*, a play that celebrates Hideyoshi's military victory over Akechi Mitsuhide (1528–82) in the Battle of Yamazaki in 1582.[28] Although Hideyoshi made plans to perform all five of the extant Taikō noh during the third month of 1594 at Osaka Castle,[29] *Akechi uchi* is the only documented example in which we know for certain that Hideyoshi actually performed the role of himself.

In *Akechi uchi* Hideyoshi plays the role of the loyal vassal who avenges the death of his lord, Oda Nobunaga, who had been treacherously attacked by one of his own generals, Akechi Mitsuhide, and forced to commit suicide at Honnōji Temple in Kyoto. Hideyoshi manages both to kill the traitor Mitsuhide and to fill the power vacuum left after Nobunaga's and Mitsuhide's deaths. By the end of the play, rather than coming off as a Machiavellian opportunist, the character "Hideyoshi" epitomizes the refined military leader who, by combining the arts of both the brush and the sword (*bunbu no michi*), is able to calm the four seas through the Mandate from Heaven (*tenmei*),[30] that ultimate seal of ideological legitimation deployed by so many politicians during the Sengoku and Tokugawa periods. This calming of the "four seas" (*shikai*) not only hearkens back to Hideyoshi's unification of the entire country after more than a century of civil war, but also looks ahead to Hideyoshi's imperialistic ambition to conquer China and expand the empire of Japan—goals that would elude even Hideyoshi.

Additional plays, such as *Toyokuni mōde* (Pilgrimage to Toyokuni) which elevates Hideyoshi to the level of a god worshipped both in Japan and China, were written and produced after Hideyoshi's death in order to contribute to his myth-making, but such dramatizations lack the self-reflexive theatricality that only Hideyoshi could bring to a performance of himself on the noh stage.

"Falseness with a good conscience; the delight in simulation exploding as a power that pushes aside one's so-called 'character,' flooding it and at times extinguishing it; the inner craving for a role and mask, for *appearance*"[31]—this statement by Friedrich Nietzsche on "the problem of the actor" sounds like an apt description of the actor-hegemon Hideyoshi. If Hideyoshi pushed the envelope of theatrical self-reflexivity far beyond that of any Japanese ruler before or after, perhaps it had something to do with the calculated role-playing he had engaged in throughout his career.[32]

Given the level of Hideyoshi's histrionics, which enabled him to cross class boundaries and attain the highest ranks and titles imaginable, it is certainly ironic that he chose toward the end of his life to prohibit others from making similar histrionic leaps across social divisions. Hideyoshi the actor, who played the role of the cultured military aristocrat so well that he eventually became one, refused to allow others to change their social standing. Farmers were not allowed to be anything else but farmers, warriors nothing else but warriors. Soon after Hideyoshi's death, such measures of class segregation would be applied to the world of noh acting as well: in an effort to standardize all aspects of the shogunate's official ceremonial music and entertainment, the Tokugawa government expressly prohibited the interclass mixing of aristocrats, warriors, priests, and townspeople that had come to characterize the performance of amateur noh, or *tesarugaku*.[33] Amateurs were now forbidden to play the role of actors. In turn, professional actors were also forbidden to take up the military arts, as so many had done during the Azuchi-Momoyama period, when a close association existed between the Konparu school of noh and the Yagyū school of martial arts. Such official admonitions may not have been followed in every case, but the very fact that they were issued correlates with the increasing ideological stratification of Tokugawa society.

Hideyoshi's theatrical self-glorification was obviously political propaganda of the most ambitious sort, but what makes the Taikō noh more interesting than merely propagandistic exercises in self-aggrandizement is that in drawing attention to the fact that the hegemon was actually an actor, Hideyoshi's performances also seem to have disclosed the very mechanisms of self-fabrication and image-making upon which they relied. *Yoshino mōde* and *Kōya sankei* brought Hideyoshi's pilgrimages to Yoshino and Kōya literally onto the noh stage, and thereby set in relief the theatricality of such pilgrimages. Likewise, *Shibata*, *Hōjō*, and *Akechi uchi* restaged Hideyoshi's military conquests over Shibata Katsuie, Hōjō Ujimasa, and Akechi Mitsuhide, respectively, drawing our attention to the mechanisms of theatricalization that enframed military leadership in the Sengoku theaters of war. By disclosing the self-reflexive staging of Hideyoshi's political power, both on stage and off, the Taikō noh unmasked the theatricality of politics operative in the Momoyama era.

Halfway around the world, in the theater of Elizabethan England, similar engagements with the theatricality of power were also being performed around the end of the sixteenth century in the plays of William Shakespeare. In Shakespeare's historical plays, such as *Richard II*, *Henry IV*, and *Henry V*, the complex interrelations between politics and theatrical forms of visibility are brought to the fore:

> O for a muse of fire, that would ascend
> The brightest heaven of invention,
> A kingdom for a stage, princes to act,
> And monarchs to behold the swelling scene

proclaims the chorus in the prologue to *Henry V*.[34] Such theatricalities of power were not merely the fanciful inventions of disempowered playwrights dreaming about the privileges of a future actor-king, but seem to have been part and parcel of the sovereign's own self-conception. Before a delegation of Lords and Commons in 1586, Queen Elizabeth I remarked: "We princes are set on stages in the sight and view of all the world."[35] Numerous Elizabethan playwrights explored the theatricality of politics and the politics of theatricality, but for all her pageantry and histrionics, not even Elizabeth ever *literally* took the stage as an actor playing the role of herself in a drama about herself. The Taikō noh plays written for Hideyoshi are, so far as I am aware, unique in the history of world drama by virtue of the unprecedented role played by Hideyoshi in his own self-staging, thus blurring the boundaries between theatricality and politics to a degree unimaginable even on the Shake-spearean stage.

One question that must be posed is whether, in so explicitly drawing at-tention to the theatrical mechanisms upon which his production of symbolic capital was based, Hideyoshi did not effectively *delegitimize* the cultural au-thority and prestige he worked so hard to foster. In other words, if Pierre Bourdieu is correct in arguing that the arbitrary constructedness of symbolic capital must be *misrecognized* in order for it to be effective and received as le-gitimate,[36] then how effective was Hideyoshi's self-staging in accruing sym-bolic capital? Did any spectators, upon witnessing Hideyoshi's unabashed self-glorification, respond to it as if it were a parody of self-legitimation? Given Hideyoshi's ruthless execution of his nephew and adopted son Toyotomi Hi-detsugu (1568–95), the tea master Sen no Rikyū (1522–91), and others, who in the audience would have dared to laugh at such an unwitting self-parody?[37] Although contemporaneous accounts seem to indicate that Hideyoshi's au-dience responded positively to his theatrical performances, Hideyoshi's em-ployment of special court critics to praise his accomplishments after every performance makes it difficult, if not impossible, to distinguish the genuine responses of Hideyoshi's audience from the strategic ones designed to please "the Bountiful Minister."[38] But if the caustic remarks of Kōfukuji monk Ta-mon'in Eishun (1517–96) in *Tamon'in nikki* (Diary of Tamon'in) are at all representative, not everyone approved of Hideyoshi's unabashed self-promotion and spectacles of self-aggrandizement. Tamon'in Eishun criticizes Hideyoshi's boundless self-glorification as an example of the "*bushi* madness" (*bukegurui*) that was "unheard of in previous ages."[39] The fact that Hideyoshi's spectacle of authority and prestige was largely fabricated by means of various genealogical and theatrical manipulations did not escape the notice of the most discerning of Hideyoshi's contemporaries, even if it was impossible for them to raise such objections in public.

Hideyoshi, the ultimate political impresario, sought to turn himself into myth. Indeed, this seems to have been his purpose from early on. In 1586, during a conversation with Portuguese Jesuit Luis Frois, Hideyoshi remarked that, having already subjugated all of Japan, he was less interested in acquir-ing additional kingdoms than he was in "immortalizing himself with the name and fame of his power."[40] Hideyoshi's wish was nothing less than that his "name be known throughout the three countries [of Japan, China, and India],"[41] as he asserted in a message to the Korean king in 1590. By bring-ing the ruler literally onto the postmedieval noh stage, the plays written for Hideyoshi not only raised self-aggrandizement to an art form but also trans-formed noh drama during the Momoyama era into an explicitly political spectacle, with special performances by Hideyoshi playing the role of himself in front of foreign diplomats,[42] powerful *daimyō*, the imperial family, and high-ranking court aristocrats, whose very attendance served to legitimize such aristocratic myth-making. Subsequent rulers such as Tokugawa Ieyasu (1542–1616) tried to emulate Hideyoshi's theatrical accomplishments by performing in more traditional noh plays, but no one ever equaled Hideyoshi's megalomaniacal fabrication and celebration of himself on the noh stage.

Appendices

Lady Aoi
(Translation of *Aoi no Ue*)[1]

Author: revised by Zeami
Category: fourth (female demon piece)
Schools: performed by all five schools
Place: before Lady Aoi's sickbed
Time: uncertain

Dramatis Personae

Shite: Vengeful Spirit of the Living Lady Rokujō
Tsure: Teruhi the Shamaness
Waki: Holy Man of Yokawa
Wakizure: Imperial Retainer
Aikyōgen: Messenger from the Minister of the Left

Act I

(*A stage-attendant places a kimono signifying
Lady Aoi on her sickbed at the front of the stage.*)

IMPERIAL RETAINER (nanori, *spoken*)

Here before you now is a retainer in the service of Emperor Shujaku. The malevolent spirit possessing the Minister of the Left's daughter Lady Aoi has recently proven to be excessively strong. So we have summoned venerable priests of great virtue to perform various secret rites and medical cures, but there have been no signs of improvement. I shall invite someone here called Teruhi the Shamaness, a well-known and highly skilled catalpa-bow diviner, and have her determine by plucking the string of a catalpa bow whether it is the spirit of someone living or dead.

(mondō, *spoken*)
  Is someone there? Summon forth Teruhi the Shamaness.

TERUHI (*unspecified, noncongruent*, yowagin)
  Heaven be pure, earth be pure,
  inside and outside be pure, six sense organs be pure.

(jōnoei, *noncongruent*, yowagin)
  One possessed
  now along the shore approaches
  on a dappled-gray horse,
  loosely shaking the reins.

LADY ROKUJŌ (issei, *noncongruent*, yowagin)
  Riding in three carriages on the path of the Law,
  might one pass through the gate of the burning house?
  At the ruins of Yūgao's dwelling, a dilapidated carriage:
  how sad that there is no way to drive it out!

(shidai, *congruent*, yowagin)
  This wretched floating world, like an ox-drawn carriage,
  this wretched floating world, like an ox-drawn carriage—
  is it not the always returning wheel of karmic retribution?

(sashi, *noncongruent*, yowagin)
  Reincarnation forever rolls on like the wheels of a carriage,
  unable to pass through the six realms and four modes of birth,
  the impermanence of human beings is like the banana plant
  or foam on water: it is the way of the world
  that yesterday's flowers are today's dreams—
  how foolish it is not to wake up!
  Harboring resentment towards others simply increases the misery
        of my floating life:
  my troubled thoughts, which I can never forget,
  if only I could pacify them for a while.
  A vengeful spirit, summoned forth by the catalpa bow
  is revealed here now.

(sagueta, *congruent*, yowagin)
  How shameful even now:
  my appearance in a secret carriage.

(agueta, *congruent*, yowagin)
  Though I gaze at the moon until daybreak,
  though I gaze at the moon until daybreak,
  I will not appear in the moon's light, a mayfly flickering in the dark
  at the upper notch of the catalpa bow,
  I rise and approach so that I might tell the story of my aimless misery,
  I rise and approach so that I might tell the story of my aimless misery.

(*unspecified*, *noncongruent*, yowagin)
    Whence comes the sound of the catalpa bow?
    Whence comes the sound of the catalpa bow?

(genoei, *noncongruent*, yowagin)
    Though at the door of the main room
    of the eastern cottage,
    since I am without form,
    no one questions me.

TERUHI (*unspecified*, *noncongruent*, yowagin)
    How uncanny! Who it is I know not: an upper-ranking lady
    riding in a dilapidated carriage
    while someone—a young maidservant I think—
    clutches the shafts of an oxless carriage,
    crying bitterly—how painful it all is!

(mondō, *spoken*)
    I wonder: is this the one?

IMPERIAL RETAINER
    I can probably guess who it is. Tell us your name without concealment.

LADY ROKUJŌ (kudokiguri, *noncongruent*, yowagin)
    In this contingent realm of delusion, as evanescent as a flash of lightning,
    there is no one I should resent,
    nor should my existence be filled with sorrow.
    When, I wonder, did my spirit begin to go adrift?

(kudoki, *noncongruent*, yowagin)
    By the sound of the catalpa bow
    I am drawn, appearing before you here and now:
    Do you know who I am?
    Here before you is the vengeful spirit of Rokujō no Miyasudokoro.
    In bygone times, when I was still acquainted with the world
    of imperial flower-viewing banquets above the clouds
    and spring morning music concerts
    on autumn nights filled with crimson leaves at the immortal's cave,
    taking delight in the moon, imbued with seasonal colors and scents.
    Though once flourishing like a flower, I have withered away:
    a morning glory awaiting the sun's rays.
    I know not when my bitter heart,
    like fern shoots in a field of difficulties,
    started sprouting forth. So that I might dispel such thoughts of dew
        ablaze with resentment,
    I have appeared before you here and now.

CHORUS (sagueta, *congruent*, yowagin)
    Do you not know that in this world
    compassion is not for the sake of others?

(agueta, *congruent*, yowagin)
> When you are cruel toward others,
> when you are cruel toward others,
> it will inevitably return to you.
> Why do I grieve? Turning over the arrowroot leaf,
> I see that my resentment will never be exhausted,
> my resentment will never be exhausted.

LADY ROKUJŌ (kakeai, *congruent*, yowagin)[2]
> Oh, how detestable!

(*spoken*)
> Even now I cannot refrain from striking her.

TERUHI (*noncongruent*, yowagin)
> How shameful! For one in Lady Rokujō's position
> to engage in the practice of secondary wife beating—

(*noncongruent*, tsuyogin)
> how can such conduct be tolerated?
> Stop such thoughts at once!

LADY ROKUJŌ (*spoken*)
> Well, no matter what you say, I am unable to resist striking her now. Rising, she
> approaches her pillow, and just as she strikes . . .

TERUHI (*noncongruent*, yowagin)
> More than this I cannot allow. She approaches, saying:
> "I will inflict pain upon you at the foot of her bed."

LADY ROKUJŌ
> Today's bitterness is a vengeful return of the past:
> the flames of wrath envelop me.

TERUHI
> Do you not realize this?

LADY ROKUJŌ (*noncongruent*, tsuyogin)
> You must realize . . .

CHORUS (dan'uta, *congruent*, yowagin)
> How hateful is your heart,
> oh, how hateful is your heart.
> My resentment is deep-seated.
> Even if I make you wail in misery,
> while you are alive in this world
> you shall remain tied in bonds of marriage
> to one more radiant than the image of fireflies
> flashing over a dark marsh.

LADY ROKUJŌ
> Beneath the wormwood, I . . .

CHORUS
will not be the one I was before.
To disappear like dew on a leaf tip—
how bitter it all is!
Even in dreams
our vow will not return,
having become a tale of bygone days;
and yet my attachment grows all the more:
in the clear mirror,
how shameful is the visage!
Standing by her pillow, into my dilapidated carriage
I shall conceal her and ride away,
I shall conceal her and ride away!

(*The* shite *pulls her kimono up over her head
and withdraws to the rear of the stage.*)

Act II

IMPERIAL RETAINER (mondō, *spoken*)
Is anyone there?

MESSENGER
I humbly appear here before you.

IMPERIAL RETAINER
Since the malevolent spirit possessing Lady Aoi has proven to be excessively strong, please summon the holy man of Yokawa.

MESSENGER
Very well, sir.

(*unspecified, spoken*)
This is exceedingly unexpected! It was my understanding that Lady Aoi was already on the way to recovering from spirit possession, but since the malevolent spirit is still out of control, I have been instructed to summon the holy man of Yokawa. I plan to go now. . . .

(mondō, *spoken*)[3]
Greetings, please show me into the house so that I may deliver a message.

HOLY MAN (*noncongruent*, tsuyogin)
Before the window of the nine forms of consciousness,
around the seat of the ten vehicles, I am filled with the holy waters of yoga,
which clarify the moon of the three secret practices.

(*spoken*)
Who is it that greets me, wishing to be admitted?

MESSENGER

I have come with a message: the malevolent spirit possessing Lady Aoi is so excessively strong that I have been instructed by the Minister to give you a message kindly requesting that you appear with great haste so that she may receive the power of your prayers.

HOLY MAN

At this time I am engaged in special rites and cannot go anywhere, but since it is a message from the Minister I will go immediately.

MESSENGER

We are greatly indebted to your kindness. Please go in this direction. The holy man has arrived. Please enter.

IMPERIAL RETAINER (mondō, *spoken*)

I am much obliged to you for coming right away.

HOLY MAN

I received your message. Where is the person who is suffering from illness? Well, then, I shall perform special prayers immediately.

IMPERIAL RETAINER

Kindly do so.

HOLY MAN (*unspecified, noncongruent*, tsuyogin)

The ascetic priest comes to perform special prayers:
he follows in the steps of En no Gyōja,
scaling the peaks of the Womb and Diamond realms.
In a hempen cloak, he brushes off the dew of seven jewels.

(*spoken*)

A robe of forbearance shields him from defilement. The redwood beads of the rosary rustle as I rub them and recite a single prayer: *namaku samanda basarada.*

(*After changing the* deigan *mask to a* hannya *mask,
Lady Rokujō returns to center stage with her head (and horns)
covered with an outer-kimono, carrying a staff in her hand.*)

LADY ROKUJŌ (kakeai, *noncongruent*, tsuyogin)[4]

Return at once ascetic:
return or else you will be vanquished through your recklessness!

HOLY MAN

However formidable the evil spirit may be,
is it possible for the ascetic's dharmic powers to be exhausted?
Rubbing together the beads of the rosary yet again,

(chūnoriji, *congruent*, tsuyogin)

In the east, Gōzanze Myōō,

CHORUS

In the east, Gōzanze Myōō,

HOLY MAN
  In the south, Gundariyasha,

CHORUS
  In the west, Daitoku Myōō,

HOLY MAN
  In the north, Kongōyasha Myōō,

CHORUS
  In the center, the most wise Fudō Myōō:
  namaku samanda basarada,
  senda makaroshana,
  sowataya un tarata kanman.
  Whoever hears my teaching acquires great wisdom;
  whoever knows my mind attains buddhahood in this very body.

LADY ROKUJŌ (*unspecified, congruent,* tsuyogin)
  Oh, how terrifying
  is the voice of perfect wisdom.
  From this point forward, in the form of a vengeful spirit,
  never will I come back again.

CHORUS (kiri, *congruent,* tsuyogin)
  When she hears the sound of sutra chanting,
  when she hears the sound of sutra chanting,
  it pacifies the heart of the evil demon.
  In the form of forbearance and merciful compassion,
  bodhisattvas descend to this place to welcome her.
  Attaining buddhahood, release from all worldly attachments,
  she becomes filled with gratitude,
  she becomes filled with gratitude.

Damsel Flower
(Translation of *Ominameshi*)[1]

Author: unknown (Kiami?)
Category: fourth (male attachment)
Schools: performed by all five schools
Place: Otokoyama in Yamashiro province
Time: autumn (eighth month)
Alternate Title: *Yorikaze, Otokoyama*[2]

Dramatis Personae

Maejite (*shite* in Act I): Old Man
Nochijite (*shite* in Act II): Ghost of Ono no Yorikaze
Nochitsure (*tsure* in Act II): Ghost of Yorikaze's Wife
Waki: Itinerant Priest from Matsura
Aikyōgen: Local Person

Act I

(nanoribue)

PRIEST (nanori, *spoken*)
Here before you is a monk who has come from Matsura in Kyushu. Since I still
have not seen the capital, I plan to make a trip there this fall.

(agueta, *congruent*, yowagin)
I left the village of Matsura,
I left the village of Matsura,
where I lived for many years,
the future I know not, haunted by
the unknown fires at Tsukushi Lagoon
so quickly receding behind me,

my journey's path stretches far off into the distance,
my journey's path stretches far off into the distance.

(tsukizerifu, *spoken*)

Having hastened, I have already arrived here at Yamazaki in Tsu province. I believe the hallowed shrine on the opposite shore, to which people pray, is called Iwashimizu Hachiman Shrine. Since it is identified with Usa Hachiman Shrine in my province, I wish to go there. Oh, how the damsel flowers of this field now bloom in profusion and begin to scatter! I intend to stop and gaze at them.

(sashi, *noncongruent*, yowagin)

And when one approaches the field at the foot of Man Mountain,
seeing the flowers of a thousand grasses
adorned in multifarious colors, holding droplets of dew,
even the sound of insects creates the impression of true elegance.
The field grasses bear flowers, as if displaying the finest Chinese brocades
    side by side;
the *katsura* grove brushes away the rain, as if keeping
rhythm with the music of the wind through the pines.

(*unspecified, spoken*)

The damsel flowers on this Man Mountain are well-known plants celebrated in ancient poetry. Since it would make a fine souvenir to bring home, I would like to pick just one. So saying, upon approaching the damsel flowers . . .

OLD MAN (mondō, *spoken*)

Excuse me, please do not pick those flowers! The flower's color is like steamed millet. It is commonly called "damsel," so that even when one hears the name in flirtation, they say it is a pledge to live together as husband and wife until one's hair turns gray.

(*noncongruent*, yowagin)

Especially here, with the name of Man Mountain
in mind, the blooming damsel flowers
are distinguished from numerous other flowers by their special relation
    to this place,
so why do you cruelly pluck them?
Oh, what a truly insensitive sightseer you are!

PRIEST (*spoken*)

Well, what sort of person are you that you feel such pity even for the damsel flowers that bloom and scatter?!?

OLD MAN

Expressing pity for the flowers is perfectly natural, as I am the flower guardian of this field.

PRIEST

Even if you are the flower guardian, please be so kind as to take a good look at me. As I myself am a priest, certainly you may grant me a single flower: consider it an offering to the Buddha.

OLD MAN

Indeed, since you yourself are a priest, one would expect you to want to make an offering to the Buddha, but please do so without plucking a flower from the sacred plum tree, as Sugawara no Michizane wrote. So, too, in the following ancient poem:

(*noncongruent*, yowagin)
"If one picks a flower,
the hand becomes stained
just standing there . . . "

(*spoken*)
When offering flowers and other such things to the Buddhas in the three worlds of past, present, and future—especially for a priest such as yourself—it is only right to feel even more compassion.

PRIEST

Citing another ancient poem in that connection, is that why the revered Archbishop Henjō composed poems such as the following?
"Only because I have fallen in love with your name
did I pluck you,
damsel flower."

OLD MAN

No, it is for that very reason that he deeply concealed the poem's final lines:
"Do not tell others
that I have altogether fallen away from my vows."
Concealed in a patterned robe from Shinobu, he must have made a vow with a damsel flower, since there is no doubt that he arranged his traveler's pillow of grass side by side with one. If you, good sir, cite that revered figure of speech, your own understanding as a priest must be in error.

PRIEST (*noncongruent*, yowagin)
When I hear you speak in this manner,
making fun of my inconstant heart
in love with flowery colors and fragrances and female charms,

(*spoken*)
no matter what I say, it will not change your mind, so I will just bid farewell and be on my way.

(*noncongruent*, yowagin)
I will continue on the road that brought me here.

OLD MAN (*spoken*)
Oh, how elegant it is here! Surely, sir, you know the ancient poem associated with this site.

CHORUS (uta, *congruent*, yowagin)
What a refined traveler!
This flower, the damsel flower with a husband,

since I admire the name of him who understands the connection,
I humbly give you permission:
please pick one flower.

(agueta, *congruent*, yowagin)
Damsel flowers stand there showing off their charms,
damsel flowers stand there showing off their charms—
does the attention make them feel uneasy?
Who might it have been who made the pledge to live
together as husband and wife until their hair turned gray
because the name of the flower was written as "damsel"?
Surely it is true,
surely it is true:
the case of the dream lived for fifty years in a world of refinement
on that ephemeral pillow in Kantan.

PRIEST (mondō, *spoken*)
Because I have been gazing earnestly at the damsel flowers of this field, I still
have not gone to Hachiman Shrine.

OLD MAN
What? Why have you still not proceeded to Hachiman Shrine? I myself am the
old man who climbs up the mountain. I should guide you to Yawata. Please
come.

PRIEST (sashi, *noncongruent*, yowagin)
Although you have no doubt heard of its reputation, what an exceedingly august and blessed sacred place it is!

OLD MAN
At the foot of the mountain, people's houses lie side by side.

OLD MAN and PRIEST
Even as the dust mingles with the divine light of Buddhas and bodhisattvas,
in the flow of the muddied inlet, fish float to the surface of the water—
certainly, to liberate living beings such as these shows that the profound vow
        of Buddhas and Kami has become miraculously manifest.
Such benevolence!
Flourishing as I climb up luxuriant Man Mountain—how blessed!

CHORUS (uta, *congruent*, yowagin)
Around the middle of the eighth month,
we bow our heads and worship at the traveler's place,
whither the gods progress and are temporarily enshrined.

(agueta, *congruent*, yowagin)
In the clear light of the celestial orb,
lunar *katsura* trees and the Man in the Moon shine brightly over
        Man Mountain,
lunar *katsura* trees and the Man in the Moon shine brightly over
        Man Mountain,

this clean, manly image is the spirit of the place,
along with the colors of autumn shining in the moon's light,
Iwashimizu Shrine, where pure water shimmers in the sunlight,
where the priest's fine robe of moss
has hallowed images traced onto its three sleeves,
where the sacred box containing the imperial seal is stored,
where Kami and Buddhas, shrines and temples, coexist according
    to the Buddhist dharma,
how blessed is this sacred place!

(uta, *congruent*, yowagin)
Pines rise high above the cliff,
mountains tower over, valleys surround below
with multifarious tree boughs,
when the dove crosses the summit in this direction and looks down,
even the three thousand worlds do not appear far away,
even the thousand villages are gathered together in the
brightness of the same moonlit evening,
at dawn gazing at the scarlet-jeweled fence and brocade curtains of state,
I bow down and pray in awe at such a blessed scene.

OLD MAN (mondō, *spoken*)
Here before you is Iwashimizu Hachiman Shrine. Please pray with reverence.
Since the day quickly draws to a close, I must humbly bid farewell.

PRIEST
Excuse me, what is the history of the association between the "damsel flower"
and this Man Mountain?

OLD MAN
What?!? Earlier when I cited the ancient poem about the damsel flower, I spoke
in jest: it was to no purpose. That it is called Man Mountain is surely because of
its history with the damsel flower. Moreover, at the foot of the mountain, I would
like to show you the tombs of a man and a woman. Please come this way. This is
the man's tomb, and that is the woman's tomb. The history of the damsel flower
is also connected to these two tombs, the man's and the woman's. The two buried
in the earth were husband and wife.

PRIEST
Well, from what province did this married couple harken? What was their family name?

OLD MAN
The woman was from the capital; and as for the man, here on Mount Yawata,

(*noncongruent*, yowagin)
he was called "Ono no Yorikaze."

CHORUS (uta, *congruent*, yowagin)
How abashed I am! I do not know whether I should
tell the story of these past events or not.

Since I do not speak of such matters, to whom will it occur
to pray even occasionally for the repose of their dead spirits?
As the wind blows, Yorikaze approaches under the late-night moon,
concealed in the shadows of the trees,
like a dream he disappears,
like a dream he disappears.

> (*A local man tells the priest the story of Yorikaze and the damsel flower,
> and recommends that he hold a service to mourn their departed spirits.*)

Act II

PRIEST (agueta, *congruent*, yowagin)
  I will lie down here for the night
  on a sheaf of grass near a tomb marked by stag's antlers,
  on a sheaf of grass near a tomb marked by stag's antlers,
  chanting sutra passages to pray
  for the restless spirits who have appeared out of the shadows.

(*sutra chant, noncongruent*, yowagin)
  Homage to the restless spirits! May you attain release from the karmic cycle of
  life and death and enter Nirvana.

(deha *entrance music*)

YORIKAZE (sashi, *noncongruent*, tsuyogin)
  How uncommon it is to see people pass through this vast
  plain! What else is there besides my old tomb?!?

YORIKAZE'S WIFE
  Impossible to stop the beasts of prey from attacking and
  greedily devouring the corpses.

YORIKAZE (issei, *noncongruent*, tsuyogin)
  How nostalgic I feel when I hear the autumn winds of old!

CHORUS
  Is it lavender—the color of resentment—on the back side of
  the arrowroot leaf?

YORIKAZE
  If you turn it over, let us go together as husband and wife,
  if we return, let it be together as coupled waves breaking upon the shore.

CHORUS (noriji, *congruent*, tsuyogin, ōnori *rhythm*)
  The bejeweled cord of life,
  the spirit of the damsel flower,
  which had vanished,
  has now reappeared
  together with her husband.
  How blessed is the Law of the Buddha!

PRIEST (kakeai, *noncongruent*, tsuyogin)
  Like shadows, the restless spirits appear. How strange!

YORIKAZE'S WIFE (*noncongruent*, yowagin)
  I am someone who used to live in the capital.
  I made a vow of marriage to that Yorikaze.

YORIKAZE (*spoken*)
  Because of a brief period when I could not visit you, did you really think that I
  had broken off relations altogether?

YORIKAZE'S WIFE (*noncongruent*, yowagin)
  The fragility of a woman's heart:
  it is because I left the capital yearning for one man alone
  that my resentful thoughts are even more profound
  as I hurl myself into the depths of the Life-Releasing River.

YORIKAZE (*spoken*)
  I, Yorikaze, heard this and was terribly frightened; when I went to see what had
  happened,

(*noncongruent*, yowagin)
  there was only her corpse, so fragile and transient, too late to save.

YORIKAZE'S WIFE (*noncongruent*, yowagin)
  Crying he took away my corpse, and buried it in the earth at the foot of this
  mountain.

YORIKAZE (*spoken*)
  From her burial mound, as if thinking in her heart of Yorikaze, a single damsel
  flower sprouted forth. Yorikaze thought to himself:

(*noncongruent*, yowagin)
  Now that my wife has turned into a damsel flower,
  I am even more nostalgic for her flowery colors and charms;
  both her sleeves of grass and my own sleeves
  begin to moisten with the dew of tears when I draw near.
  But this flower keeps giving me a look of resentment:
  whenever I, her husband, approach,
  she flutters and moves away;
  and then as soon as I withdraw,
  she returns to her earlier state.

CHORUS (uta, *congruent*, yowagin)
  In view of this place, Ki no Tsurayuki, too,
  wrote in beautiful calligraphic style of
  "recalling past days on Man Mountain,
  or lamenting the brief life of the damsel flower."
  A passage cherished by future generations!

(kuse, *congruent*, yowagin)
  At that time, Yorikaze
  understood her sadness:

"It was because of my own cruelty
that she disappeared like insignificant foam on the water.
She who died in vain
has me to blame most of all!
Not wishing to outlive her in this floating world of pain and sorrow,
I shall follow the same path to the world of the dead."

YORIKAZE

Following her, I throw myself into this river. . . .

CHORUS

Since the time they buried me in the earth together with her,
my grave facing hers,
it has been called Man Mountain.
The tombs I speak of are these here, and I am the husband
who has come as a ghostly apparition.
Please, sir, be so kind as to pray for the repose of my spirit.
Please, sir, be so kind as to pray for the repose of my spirit.

(issei, *noncongruent*, yowagin)
Oh, how I long for the land of the living!
(kakeri)

CHORUS (noriji, *congruent*, tsuyogin, ōnori *rhythm*)
Cursed devils of sexual infidelity
incite me, then reproach me, torturing my body,
cursed devils of sexual infidelity
incite me, then reproach me, torturing my body,
blind will power
impelled by desire along the path of peril,
on top of Sword Mountain
my beloved has appeared.
How gratifying!
But as I climb,
double-edged swords penetrate my body,
enormous rocks crush my bones.
How terrifying it all is!
Sword-branches
bend down under the weight of my sin.

(*congruent*, yowagin, ōnori *rhythm*)
What sin engendered this end?!?
An utterly foolish one.

CHORUS (uta, *congruent*, yowagin)
Even lamenting
the brevity of the flower's life is but a dream!
Damsel flower,
upon your dewy calyx tied to the lotus flower pedestal,
I beseech you: let me float up to Pure Land paradise,
send my sins to the surface and deliver me from them!

Conquest of Akechi
(Annotated Translation of *Akechi uchi*)[1]

Author: Ōmura Yūko
Category: second (warrior)
Place: Yamazaki Castle (south of the capital)
Time: summer (sixth month)

Dramatis Personae

Shite: Hashiba Hideyoshi, Lord of Chikuzen province
Waki: Akechi Mitsuhide
Tomo: Attendant to Hideyoshi

HIDEYOSHI (shidai, *congruent*, yowagin)
> The future rushes toward one as fast as a swift-moving horse viewed
> through a crevice,[2]
> the future rushes toward one as fast as a swift-moving horse viewed
> through a crevice,
> oh, how my heart gallops back to the capital amidst the clouds.

(nanori, *spoken*)
> Here before you is Hashiba[3] Hideyoshi, Lord of Chikuzen province,[4] who hum-
> bly received the orders of Lord Barbarian-Subduing Shogun Nobunaga for the
> subjugation of the western provinces.[5] From the spring of the tenth year of Ten-
> shō,[6] at the site near Bitchū province[7] where the enemy army has taken up po-
> sition, I have plotted against the traitorous heart of Akechi, Lord of Hyūga prov-
> ince. Since the circumstances surrounding the murder of the shogun[8] are being
> reported to those in command, I intend to move quickly and pluck off Mitsu-
> hide's head.

(sashi, *noncongruent*, yowagin)
> Around the beginning of the sixth month,
> while commanding a huge army,

the clouds and waters of my future pass by swiftly,
like the arrow of the quickly flowing year
I proceed, guided by my intrepid heart.
Returning to look for tracks over a great distance along the front
    of Bitchū and Bizen . . . [9]

(uta, *congruent*, yowagin)
The early morning sky at Akashi Bay,
the early morning sky at Akashi Bay,
the bay breeze of Suma rises up and drifts about,
from the clouds falls the flow of Nunobiki Waterfall in the distance,
passing by even the open sea at Ashiya,
hastening only through the Naniwa Inlet,
I have just arrived at Akuta River,
I have just arrived at Akuta River.

(*spoken*)
For some time I have arranged myriad troops at this site and cut our way into
the enemy's position; I intend to conquer that traitorous man and offer a memorial service for the shogun.[10] Anyone there?

ATTENDANT
At your service, sir.

HIDEYOSHI
Draw everyone near to hear the story.

CHORUS (kuri, *noncongruent*, yowagin)
Beginning with what is called the world of human beings,
whenever the bright light of the full moon shows,
the scattered, ephemeral clouds are jealous;
and whenever kings are brought to light,
again, they say that slandering retainers conceal this.

HIDEYOSHI (sashi, *noncongruent*, yowagin)
Well, speaking of the traces of Mitsuhide's actions,
on the outside he assumed the pose of meek forbearance.

CHORUS
But inside, in the inner recesses of his treasonous retainer's
unjust heart, was the plain spindletree bow.

HIDEYOSHI
Entrusting himself to him from the beginning,

CHORUS
Lord Nobunaga was vanquished helplessly and without
warning—how sad the bounds of his destiny!

(kuse, *congruent*, yowagin)
In the meantime, Hideyoshi
approached and attacked the castle at Takamatsu,[11]
which bears the same name, by means of inundation.

Sinking under the waves, hanging onto the pathos of ephemeral foam,
he seized the enemy with his daring spirit,
waiting for reinforcements from the rear.
Already in the midst of performing meritorious deeds,
from the moment he was secretly informed of the shogun's defeat,[12]
even Hideyoshi's spirit wore out,
so choked with tears was he.
His spirit weakened, thinking that he would probably not be able to
        carry it out,
at long last, he obtained battle position;
in order to calm the hearts of his allies,
he simply wrote a single poem:

HIDEYOSHI
"Since two rivers
have become one
and sunk low,

CHORUS
it is said that even the guardian of Takamatsu[13] has met a watery grave."
What happened differs not from the words recited. When
the lord of Takamatsu Castle committed *harakiri*[14] within,
Hideyoshi ordered the reinforcements to withdraw.
Combining the arts of the brush and the sword,
he pulled out his teary-eyed troops.
On the way back to the capital, marching day and night,[15]
with the determination to conquer the enemy,
there was probably not a single person left unmoved.

HIDEYOSHI
So it was when dear old Chinese King Kōu[16] was defeated.

CHORUS
When the Chinese ancestors hear of this,
they will check the current of the Ukō River,[17] cross over,
and conquer the enemy of our Lord Nobunaga.
To calm the four seas—is this not the Mandate from Heaven?
That was a battle fought more than seventy times,
but the warrior who intends to accomplish
the long-cherished ambition of fighting a battle one time only at this
        very moment
possesses a brave, fierce heart.

HIDEYOSHI
I will not tolerate a moment's delay.
When one looks at the sun's rays, they are waning.
The firmament of flags waving and fluttering amidst the clouds,
the waterless moon's Minase River,[18]
passing from Yamamoto to Yamazaki,

I set up shelter to the east,
proceeding to draw near to the enemy lines.

MITSUHIDE

Well, now, I myself am the one they call Akechi Mitsuhide, Lord of Hyūga
province.[19]

(*spoken*)

At one time I set my sights on the entire country; in order to make a name for
myself that would be remembered by future generations, I humbly attacked the
shogun. For that reason, Hashiba Hideyoshi, Lord of Chikuzen, is racing his
horse here; so I am determined to settle the contest over the course of a single
battle.

CHORUS

Without even exchanging words, from the attacking force,
without even exchanging words, from the attacking force,
there came forth an enormous battle cry.
They readied their swords and the killing started.

MITSUHIDE

At that time, I, Mitsuhide,
at that time, I, Mitsuhide,
since the vanguard quickly collapsed,
at first fled to Shōryū Temple[20] and shut myself up inside.
When the sun, too, had entered the long-jointed, violet bamboo night,
it became so utterly dark that the space between things
was no longer visible and I mixed in with large numbers of enemy troops.
Fleeing toward the Yodo and Toba districts of the capital with Hideyoshi
        in hot pursuit,
I wondered to myself "How far can I go?"
when he shattered my helmet at the middle of the forehead.
With my enemy thinking this was karma
turning on the wheels of a rickety carriage,
I approached him on white-crested waves and attacked,
then he returned the attack,
dealing severe blows repeatedly—
a hundred times, a thousand times—
striking with his long sword—
at this very moment my enmity came to be dispelled.
His name will be honored throughout the country
as one who showed his loyal service here,
the magnitude of his power truly awesome![21]

Reference Matter

Notes

Prologue: The History in Noh

1. See Gilles Deleuze, *Negotiations: 1972–1990*, trans. Martin Joughin (New York: Columbia University Press, 1995), 7–9, and Deleuze and Félix Guattari, *A Thousand Plateaus: Capitalism and Schizophrenia*, trans. Brian Massumi (Minneapolis: University of Minnesota Press, 1987), 22–23. Such a distinction offers not a metaphysical opposition, but rather two poles along a continuum of possible readings and lines of variation, which are often intertwined in the same act of criticism. To read a text as a "nonsignifying" assemblage is to suggest not that practices of signification are irrelevant to its operations, but rather that a given text is much more than a semiotic system. To read a text in terms of what it does, the semiotic system (or regime of signs) operative in that text must be situated in relation to the pragmatic system (or machinic assemblage) through which it enters into determinable relations of power with material and social flows. On assemblages and regimes of signs, see ibid., 22–23, 119–22, 141, 504.

2. By investigating the complex negotiations at play between theatricality and politics in the context of Elizabethan England, new-historicist scholars such as Stephen Greenblatt, Joel Fineman, and Louis Montrose have been trailblazers for this sort of analysis. Mixing Foucauldian poststructuralism with Bourdieuian sociology, such studies have brought to the fore the extent to which "theatricality is not set over against power but is one of power's essential modes." See Stephen Greenblatt, *Shakespearean Negotiations: The Circulation of Social Energy in Renaissance England* (Berkeley: University of California Press, 1988), 46. Also see Greenblatt, ed., *Representing the English Renaissance* (Berkeley: University of California Press, 1988); H. Aram Veeser, ed.,

The New Historicism (New York: Routledge, 1989); and Veeser, ed., *The New Historicism Reader* (New York: Routledge, 1994).

3. I borrow the term "micropolitics" from Deleuze and Guattari, who use it in *A Thousand Plateaus* to describe molecular movements, flows, cracks, forces, multiplicities, and their singularities—those hidden histories of becoming that are generally ignored by more traditional accounts of official history. See *A Thousand Plateaus*, 208–31; *Negotiations*, 30–31, 152–53, 159–60, 170–71. Also cf. Michel Foucault's usage of "microphysics" in Alan Sheridan, trans., *Discipline and Punish: Birth of the Prison* (New York: Vintage Books, 1977), 139.

4. See James R. Brandon, ed., *Nō and Kyōgen in the Contemporary World* (Honolulu: University of Hawaii Press, 1997), 10.

5. "Discourse networks" translates Friedrich Kittler's term *Aufschreibesysteme*: a reticulated web of discursive systems and technologies of notation and inscription, which "allow a given culture to select, store, and process relevant data." See Friedrich A. Kittler, *Discourse Networks: 1800/1900*, trans. Michael Metteer (Stanford, Calif.: Stanford University Press, 1990), 369. Cf. Michel Foucault's usage of the term *dispositif*: a historically specific apparatus, arrangement, or system of institutions, discourses, and practices (including instruments, procedures, techniques, mechanisms, strategies, tactics, exercises, and modalities). See Gilles Deleuze, "What Is a *Dispositif*?" in Timothy J. Armstrong, trans., *Michel Foucault, Philosopher* (New York: Routledge, 1992), 159–68.

6. Personal communication from Royall Tyler, 4 October 1995.

7. With a nod to its Latin etymology in the verb *fingere* (to shape, fashion, form, represent, conceive, invent), Foucault makes the following remarks on the "fictioning of history":

> As to the problem of fiction, it seems to me to be a very important one; I am well aware that I have never written anything but fictions. I do not mean to say, however, that truth is therefore absent. It seems to me that the possibility exists for fiction to function in truth, for a fictional discourse to induce effects of truth, and for bringing it about that a true discourse engenders or "manufactures" something that does not as yet exist, that is, "fictions" it. One "fictions" history on the basis of a political reality that makes it true, one "fictions" a politics not yet in existence on the basis of a historical truth.

See Foucault, *Power/Knowledge*, ed. Colin Gordon (New York: Pantheon Books, 1980), 193. Also cf. Philippe Lacoue-Labarthe, "History and Mimesis," in Laurence A. Rickels, ed., *Looking After Nietzsche* (Albany: State University of New York Press, 1990), 218.

8. Nagao Kazuo, "A Return to Essence Through Misconception: From Zeami to Hisao," in Brandon, ed., *Nō and Kyōgen in the Contemporary World*, 111–24. Cf. Foucault on the genealogical demystification of "essence":

> [I]f the genealogist refuses to extend his faith in metaphysics, if he listens to history, he finds that there is "something altogether different" behind things: not a timeless and essential secret, but the secret that they have no essence or that their

essence was fabricated in a piecemeal fashion from alien forms. . . . What is found at the historical beginning of things is not the inviolable identity of their origin; it is the dissension of other things. It is disparity.

See Foucault, "Nietzsche, Genealogy, History," in Paul Rabinow, ed., *The Foucault Reader* (New York: Pantheon Books, 1984), 78–79.

9. I have borrowed this phrase from Jacques Derrida, "Passages—from Traumatism to Promise," in Elisabeth Weber, ed., *Points . . . Interviews, 1974–1994* (Stanford, Calif.: Stanford University Press, 1995), 372. On the problem of "context," also see Derrida, "Signature Event Context," in Alan Bass, trans., *Margins of Philosophy* (Chicago: University of Chicago Press, 1982), 307–30; Derrida, "Some Statements and Truisms About Neo-Logisms, Newisms, Postisms, Parasitisms, and Other Small Seismisms," in David Carroll, ed., *The States of "Theory": History, Art, and Critical Discourse* (New York: Columbia University Press, 1990), 92–93.

Chapter 1: Instituting Noh

1. I have transliterated Japanese texts, terms, titles, and proper names according to the conventional system of Romanization used in Kenkyūsha's *New Japanese-English Dictionary*.

2. *Noh* as a term derives from its usage in *sarugaku no nō* (*sarugaku* performances) and *dengaku no nō* (*dengaku* performances). Here and elsewhere I use the term *noh* as an abbreviation for the *sarugaku* noh developed and refined by Kannami, Zeami, and others, which superseded *dengaku* noh by the mid fifteenth century. On the origins of noh in both the courtly forms of entertainment and popular performing arts (*minzoku geinō*), see Nose Asaji, *Nōgaku genryūkō* (Tokyo: Iwanami Shoten, 1938); Nose Asaji, "Nō no senkō geijitsu," in *Nō no rekishi*, vol. 2 of Nogami Toyoichirō, ed., *Nōgaku zensho* (Tokyo: Sōgensha, 1979–80), 146–63; Gotō Hajime, *Nōgaku no kigen* (Tokyo: Mokujisha, 1975); Gotō Hajime, *Zoku nōgaku no kigen* (Tokyo: Mokujisha, 1981); Omote Akira and Amano Fumio, *Nōgaku no rekishi*, in *Iwanami kōza: Nō kyōgen*, vol. 1 (Tokyo: Iwanami Shoten, 1992); P. G. O'Neill, *Early Nō Drama* (London: Lund Humphries, 1958); Jacob Raz, *Audience and Actors: A Study of Their Interaction in the Japanese Traditional Theatre* (Leiden: E. J. Brill, 1983); Benito Ortolani, *The Japanese Theatre: From Shamanistic Ritual to Contemporary Pluralism* (Leiden: E. J. Brill, 1990).

3. "Institutionality" refers to the network of institutions, discourses, codes, and practices that I have abbreviated above as "discourse network." Cf. Peter L. Berger and Thomas Luckmann's sociological definition of "institutionalization," in *The Social Construction of Reality*: "Institutionalization occurs whenever there is a reciprocal typification of habitualized actions by types of actors. . . . [A]ny such typification is an institution." Berger and Luckmann, *The Social Construction of Reality: A Treatise in the Sociology of Knowledge* (Garden City, N.Y.: Doubleday, 1966), 51.

4. On the "*dengaku* craze" in the early fourteenth century, see Gotō Tanji, Kamada Kisaburō, and Okami Masao, eds., *Taiheiki*, in *Nihon koten bungaku taikei* (Tokyo: Iwanami Shoten, 1960–62), 34: 161–63.

5. Dōami reportedly attributed his own success, in part, to the strong impression

Kannami had made on Yoshimitsu at Imagumano, which paved the way for other troupes to receive shogunal patronage. See Zeami, *Sarugaku dangi*, in Omote Akira and Katō Shūichi, eds., *Zeami, Zenchiku*, in *Nihon shisō taikei* (Tokyo: Iwanami Shoten, 1974), 24: 293, 301.

6. Thomas Blenman Hare, *Zeami's Style: The Noh Plays of Zeami Motokiyo* (Stanford, Calif.: Stanford University Press, 1986), 13.

7. On the emergence of different entertainment and theatrical "troupes" (*za*) and the professionalization of actors in the Kamakura and Muromachi periods, see Omote and Amano, *Nōgaku no rekishi*, 37–41; O'Neill, *Early Nō Drama*, 8–9, 18. Jacob Raz notes the interesting movement toward the professionalization of actors and spectators in noh's early history and then away from professionalization in its later history:

> The early history of geinō, from Heian through Kamakura and early Muromachi periods, faithfully followed the common theory of the linear development of theatre: from religious to secular and from participatory to non-participatory theatre. But the late Muromachi period was on the way towards greater participation in the theatre on the part of its audience. This period also refutes the theoretical connexion between religious theatre and participation. The post-Ōnin sarugaku was not religious—yet it was participative. Spectators took part in performances along with actors, or even without them. . . . Spectators became performers and vice-versa; amateurs shared performances with professionals; even audience classification (and as a result, theatre seating arrangements) became indistinct. (Raz, *Audience and Actors*, 125)

8. See Zeami, *Fūshikaden*, in Omote and Katō, eds., *Zeami, Zenchiku*, 41 (trans. mine).

9. Cf. Omote and Katō, eds., *Zeami, Zenchiku*, 261, 265, 272, 277, 290, 293, 296, 297, 301, 303, 306, 311.

10. See Zeami, *Sarugaku dangi*, in Omote and Katō, eds., *Zeami, Zenchiku*, 267, 272.

11. For an extended comparative analysis of noh and Greek tragedy, see Mae J. Smethurst, *The Artistry of Aeschylus and Zeami: A Comparative Study of Greek Tragedy and Nō* (Princeton, N.J.: Princeton University Press, 1989).

12. See Omote and Katō, eds., *Zeami, Zenchiku*, 305. Drawing lots in medieval Japan was used both to divine the intentions of the gods and to help decide difficult matters. In practice, the lots drawn were small strips of paper or bamboo preinscribed with marks, signs, or phrases indicating good or bad fortune (*kikkyō*), victory or defeat (*shōhai*), or order, class, or rank (*tōkyū*).

13. Ibid., 45 (trans. mine).

14. Ibid., 27–28.

15. See ibid., 298.

16. See Tokyo Daigaku Shiryō Hensanjo, ed., *Gogumaiki*, in *Dai Nihon kokiroku* (Tokyo: Iwanami Shoten, 1980), 17: 267; Kobayashi Shizuo, *Nōgaku shiryō* (Tokyo: Ōkayama Shoten, 1933), 9; Hayashiya Tatsusaburō, *Chūsei geinōshi no kenkyū* (Tokyo: Iwanami Shoten, 1957), 491–92. Cf. Steven D. Carter, introduction to Carter, ed., *Literary Patronage in Late Medieval Japan* (Ann Arbor: University of Michigan Center for Japanese Studies, 1993), 6–7.

17. "Eiwa 4/6/7" designates the fourth year of Eiwa, sixth month, seventh day.

18. O'Neill, *Early Nō Drama*, 59.

19. See Nose, *Nōgaku genryūkō*, 1053–54; O'Neill, *Early Nō Drama*, 70–71; Raz, *Audience and Actors*, 76–77, 85. Yoshimitsu started attending *kanjin* noh performances regularly in 1375. Since records of *kanjin* noh are not well documented in the late fourteenth and early fifteenth centuries, it is difficult to say exactly how many were held. However, available records do seem to indicate that *kanjin* noh became increasingly popular after 1413. *Kanjin* noh were so called because a large percentage of the admission fees, or "subscriptions" (*kanjin*), collected from audience members was contributed to local shrines and temples. Noh troupes that participated in subscription festivals were motivated by the same economic incentives as local religious sponsors, since they, too, received a percentage of the total receipts. In later years, *kanjin* noh were held not only as a fund-raising device to help maintain and repair local shrines and temples, but also in order to collect money for public works projects, such as road and bridge construction. As time went on, money from *kanjin* noh festivals became a primary source of income for many noh troupes, one that helped them to establish greater independence from local shrines and temples.

20. Omote and Katō, eds., *Zeami, Zenchiku*, 27.

21. The medieval noh stage underwent a number of significant changes before taking on the spatial configuration of the modern noh stage, which made its first appearance in the early seventeenth century. The physical dimensions of the typical *kanjin* noh theater were approximately 312 feet in circumference and 100 feet in diameter (see O'Neill, *Early Nō Drama*, 78–83). Reproductions of the earliest extant sketch of a *kanjin* noh theater, depicting the Tadasugawara, *kanjin* theater of 1464 (supported and attended by Ashikaga no Yoshimasa, 1436–90), can be found in *Ihon Tadasugawara kanjin nō sarugakki*, in *Dengaku, sarugaku*, vol. 2 of Geinōshi kenkyūkai, ed., *Nihon shomin bunka shiryō shūsei* (Tokyo: San'ichi Shobō, 1974), 149; Suda Atsuo, *Nihon gekijōshi no kenkyū* (Tokyo: Sagami Shobō, 1966), 168–70; Takahashi Yōji, ed., *Bessatsu taiyō: Nō 25* (Winter 1978): 39; Yokomichi Mario, ed., *Nōgaku zusetsu*, appendix to *Iwanami kōza: Nō kyōgen* (Tokyo: Iwanami Shoten, 1992), 400. Illustrations of the modern noh stage can be found in ibid., 392–400; Nishino Haruo and Hata Akira, eds., *Nō kyōgen jiten* (Tokyo: Heibonsha, 1987), 339–41; and Earl Miner, Odagiri Hiroko, and Robert E. Morrell, eds., *The Princeton Companion to Classical Japanese Literature* (Princeton, N.J.: Princeton University Press, 1985), 333–35.

22. See the description of *sajiki* in Raz, *Audience and Actors*, 83:

> Those who could afford it—that is, high officials, warriors, nobles, high-ranking priests and others—would not only reserve sajiki, but also have them built to their specifications, reflecting their social class. Sometimes a patron would take one or two boxes or more. The shōgun and his retinue occupied at least five boxes. It is clear from the account that the ladies' boxes were covered with curtains, and they were not expected (or not allowed) to show their faces behind them. We might assume that these were very thin curtains, through which they could see the stage and the other spectators.

23. Cf. O'Neill's account of audience violence at noh performances during the Muromachi period:

> Numerous mentions of brawls and killings can still be found, even in records written only within the first sixty years of the fifteenth century. Sometimes when the audience was involved, we are told that "many people, both men and women, were killed," or that although "someone watching was slashed," the performance continued when the disturbance was over. Often the players themselves were directly concerned. They, or the *gakutō* responsible for them, might only be struck for making fun of priests or drunken nobles, or for not putting in an appearance to perform as arranged. But it also happened that they met their deaths fighting, like the head of Yata Sarugaku and a flute player who were cut down in a quarrel after a performance. Similarly, when a dispute arose between Dengaku and Sarugaku players over the former wearing a mask in a performance in Nara, someone who tried to come between them was killed by an arrow. The significance of such stories is that they show how far removed were the performances of Nō in those days from the hushed, solemn atmosphere in which the plays are usually given today. (*Early Nō Drama*, 77–78)

Cf. Kobayashi, *Nōgaku shiryō*, 52, 57, 63, 120, 124, 173.

24. See Konishi Jin'ichi, *A History of Japanese Literature*, 3 vols., trans. Aileen Gatten and Mark Harbison (Princeton, N.J.: Princeton University Press, 1991), 3: 552, 557; Hare, *Zeami's Style*, 230–32.

25. See Raz, *Audience and Actors*, 92–97.

26. See Omote and Katō, eds., *Zeami, Zenchiku*, 184–85.

27. Omote and Katō (ibid., 62) gloss *jibun* as the "fortune of [a given] time" (*toki no un*) and the "rotations of divine fortune and fate" (*ten'un no junkan*).

28. *Fūshikaden*, ibid., 63–64; trans. modified from J. Thomas Rimer and Yamazaki Masakazu, trans., *On the Art of Nō Drama: The Major Treatises of Zeami* (Princeton, N.J.: Princeton University Press, 1984), 61–62.

29. See Omote and Katō, eds., *Zeami, Zenchiku*, 207, 263. Also cf. Omote Akira, *Nōgakushi shinkō* (Tokyo: Wan'ya Shoten, 1979), 1: 489. On the issue of authorship vis-à-vis the plays attributed to Zeami, see Hare, *Zeami's Style*, 41–47.

30. Cf. Linda H. Chance's discussion of literary authors, such as Yoshida Kenkō (ca. 1283–1350/52), and the status of medieval authorship: *Formless in Form: Kenkō, Tsurezuregusa, and the Rhetoric of Japanese Fragmentary Prose* (Stanford, Calif.: Stanford University Press, 1997), 110–14. On the "author-function" in the West, see Michel Foucault, "What Is an Author?" in Donald F. Bouchard, ed., *Language, Counter-Memory, Practice* (Ithaca, N.Y.: Cornell University Press, 1984), 113–38; Donald T. O'Hara, "What Was Foucault?" in Jonathan Arac, ed., *After Foucault: Humanistic Knowledge, Postmodern Challenges* (New Brunswick, N.J.: Rutgers University Press, 1988), 71–96.

31. Monica Bethe and Richard Emmert, trans., *Aoinoue* (Tokyo: National Noh Theatre, 1997), 72–73.

32. Omote and Katō, eds., *Zeami, Zenchiku*, 143; trans. modified from Rimer and Yamazaki, *On the Art of Nō Drama*, 160–61.

33. Konishi, *History of Japanese Literature*, 3: 529. Also cf. P. G. O'Neill, "Music, Dance and Text in *Nō* Drama," in James Redmond, ed., *Drama, Dance, and Music* (Cambridge: Cambridge University Press, 1981), 111–12. I have also profited from reading Thomas Hare's exploration of these issues in "A Separate Piece: Proprietary Claims and Intertexuality in the Rokujō Plays," in Thomas Hare, Robert Borgen, and Sharalyn Orbaugh, eds., *The Distant Isle* (Ann Arbor: University of Michigan Center for Japanese Studies, 1996), 183–203.

34. On "participatory textual production" during the Heian period, see H. Richard Okada, *Figures of Resistance: Language, Poetry, and Narrating in* The Tale of Genji *and Other Mid-Heian Texts* (Durham, N.C.: Duke University Press, 1991), 22, 303, 336. The quotation on reception as creation is from Mitani Eiichi, "Sagoromo monogatari no ihon seiritsu to sono jiki: Maki ichio chūshin to shite," *Kokugakuin Daigaku kiyō* 7 (1967): 277–309.

35. See discussion in Yokomichi, *Nō no kōzō to gihō*, 4: 281–308; Yokomichi, ed., *Nōgaku zusetsu*, 175–205; Hare, *Zeami's Style*, 50–61.

36. For detailed illustrations of the *fue, kotsuzumi, ōtsuzumi*, and *taiko*, see Nishino and Hata, eds., *Nō kyōgen jiten*, 341–44; also see discussion in Yokomichi, *Nō no kōzō to gihō*, 309–28; Yokomichi, ed., *Nōgaku zusetsu*, 207–329.

37. See discussion of *kata* and *mai* in Yokomichi, *Nō no kōzō to gi hō*, 261–80. Also see Yokomichi, ed., *Nōgaku zusetsu*, 331–89; Monica Bethe and Karen Brazell, *Dance in the Nō Theater*, 3 vols. (Ithaca, N.Y.: Cornell University East Asia Program, 1982).

38. See discussion of noh costumes and props in Yokomichi, *Nō no kōzō to gihō*, 93–260; Yokomichi, ed., *Nōgaku zusetsu*, 401–572; Kanze Hisao, "Life with the Nō Mask," *Mime Journal* (1984): 65–73; Monica Bethe, "Okina: An Interview with Takabayashi Kōji," *Mime Journal* (1984): 93–103; Nakamura Yasuo, "Nō Masks: Their History and Development," *Mime Journal* (1984): 114–24; Mark J. Nearman, "Behind the Mask of Nō," *Mime Journal* (1984): 20–64; Monica Bethe, "Nō Costume as Interpretation," *Mime Journal* (1984): 148–55; Monica Bethe, "The Use of Costumes in Nō Drama," in *Five Centuries of Japanese Kimono: On This Sleeve of Fondest Dreams*, Art Institute of Chicago Museum Studies 18, no. 1 (1992): 6–19.

39. See discussion in Yokomichi, *Nō no kōzō to gihō*, 61–92; Yokomichi, *Nōgakuzusetsu*, 391–400.

40. See Omote and Katō, eds., *Zeami, Zenchiku*, 29, 90–91, 190–91, 267–68, 281, 287–88.

41. On the different temporalities of noh, see Komparu Kunio, *The Noh Theater: Principles and Perspectives*, trans. Jane Corddry (New York: Walker/ Weatherhill, 1983), xvii, 81–88.

42. The one exception to this general rule of performativity is the closet noh dramas written during the Edo period. See O'Neill, *Early Nō Drama*, 101.

43. Derrida, "The Double Session," in Barbara Johnson, trans., *Dissemination* (Chicago: University of Chicago Press, 1981), 187, note 14.

44. The *locus classicus* for Plato's conception is the *Sophist* (235d–36c), in which mimesis is differentiated into "eikastic" mimesis—defined as "the making of likenesses

[*eidōla*]" that produce authentic facsimiles of the original model—and "phantastic" mimesis—defined as "the making of semblances [*phantasmata*]" that produce counterfeiting forgeries of the model. Across the Platonic corpus, a complex oscillation between these two forms of mimesis—"good" (or eikastic) mimesis and "bad" (or phantastic) mimesis—ends up producing a crisis of legitimation that forever haunts the very possibility of "representation" and repeatedly undercuts its far-reaching claims. On the forms of mimesis circulating across Plato's textual corpus, see *Sophist* (234b, 235d–36c, 265b–67a), *Republic* (509d–11e, 595a–608b), *Timaeus* (30c–31b), *Parmenides* (132c–33a), and *Cratylus* (389a–91c).

45. The Tokugawa shogunate adopted noh as its official entertainment and music (*shikigaku*) in 1615. Although the five-play taxonomy of role and character representations was not codified and institutionalized until the seventeenth century, the idea had been in circulation at least since 1512, if not earlier. For that reason, it is extremely difficult, if not impossible, to determine precisely when Zeami's conception of the three bodies (*santai*) was reconceived by later actors and playwrights in terms of the five-role representations. See Gotō, *Zoku nōgaku*, 392–94.

46. H. E. Plutschow, *Chaos and Cosmos: Ritual in Early and Medieval Japanese Literature* (Leiden: E. J. Brill, 1990), 247.

47. See Nogami Toyoichirō, ed., *Yōkyoku zenshū* (Tokyo: Chūō Kōronsha, 1935), 1: 20–37; Bethe and Brazell, *Dance in the Nō Theater*, 2: 2–3; Janet Goff, *Noh Drama and The Tale of Genji* (Princeton, N.J.: Princeton University Press, 1991), 48.

48. On the history and theatricality of *kyōgen*, see Koyama Hiroshi, Taguchi Kazuo, and Hashimoto Asao, *Kyōgen no sekai*, in *Iwanami kōza: Nō kyōgen*, vol. 5 (Tokyo: Iwanami Shoten, 1993); Koyama Hiroshi et al., eds., *Kyōgen kanshō annai*, in *Iwanami kōza: Nō kyōgen*, vol. 7 (Tokyo: Iwanami Shoten, 1993); Carolyn Anne Morley, *Transformation, Miracles, and Mischief: The Mountain Priest Plays of Kyōgen* (Ithaca, N.Y.: Cornell University East Asia Program, 1993).

49. Most plays were probably performed in as little as thirty minutes. See O'Neill, *Early Nō Drama*, 88–89.

50. Yokomichi Mario and Omote Akira, eds., *Yōkyokushū*, in *Nihon koten bungaku taikei* (Tokyo: Iwanami Shoten, 1960), 40: 6–8. Yokomichi's classification is actually a further development of a taxonomy introduced earlier by Sanari Kentarō, *Yōkyoku taikan*, 7 vols., 3rd ed. (Tokyo: Meiji Shoin, 1985), 56–61.

51. The *shite*'s act of recounting the story of his or her karmic suffering is probably not unrelated to the Buddhist religio-literary genre of *sange* revelatory tales, in which characters admit to having committed "specific past transgressions that are the cause of present suffering and negative karma." See Margaret H. Childs, "The Influence of the Buddhist Practice of *Sange* on Literary Form: Revelatory Tales," *Japanese Journal of Religious Studies* 14 (1987): 63. Such an admission of past transgressions usually leads to "an awakening in one's heart to the idea that actions and attachments in one's past had kept one in a state of illusion" (ibid.).

52. On the form and functions of religious travel accounts (*michiyuki*) during the medieval period, see Konishi, *History of Japanese Literature*, 3: 359–60, 482–85; and Plutschow, *Chaos and Cosmos*, 196–97.

53. For examples of countercurrents to this antiquarianism, see the essays and interviews included in part three of Brandon, ed., *Nō and Kyōgen in the Contemporary World*, which opens a window into the workshop of contemporary experiments with noh and *kyōgen* across the nexus of intercultural hybridity.

54. Two of the most prevalent misconceptions about the form and function of noh in the medieval period are that it was always performed in cycles of five plays—according to the taxonomy of *gobandate* I outlined above—and that its pace was as slow then as it is now.

55. Engaging discussions of *santai* can be found in Hare, *Zeami's Style*, 65–224, and Kitagawa Tadahiko, "'Monomane no jōjō' kara 'santai' ron e," *Bungaku* 51 (July 1983): 47–56. Hare translates *santai* as the "three modes": the aged mode, the woman's mode, and the martial mode.

56. Zeami's *santai* may be an intertextual reinscription of the "three bodies" (*sanjin*) of Buddha in esoteric Buddhism: (1) *hosshin*: dharma-body, or the suchness of the Buddhist Law; (2) *hōjin*: reward-body, or the bliss of Buddhist enlightenment and bodhisattvahood; (3) *ōjin*: accommodation-body, or the historical manifestations of Buddha for sentient beings. See Nakamura Hajime et al., eds., *Iwanami Bukkyō jiten* (Tokyo: Iwanami Shoten, 1992), 321. Also cf. Zeami's remarks in *Fūshikaden* that the three ceremonial plays collectively known as *Shiki sanban* are *kuden* (orally transmitted secret teachings) of the Buddha's *sanjin*: see Omote and Katō, eds., *Zeami, Zenchiku*, 40.

57. It is instructive that in his discussion in *Fūshikaden* of the maturation of the actor's body around the ages of twenty-four to twenty-five, Zeami uses the word *tai*: "It is the time when the voice will already have adjusted and the body settled" (*koe mo sude ni naori, tai mo sadamaru jibun nari*) (Omote and Katō, eds., *Zeami, Zenchiku*, 71; trans. mine). This usage of *tai* is perfectly in keeping with other texts from the medieval period. Cf. the following feudalistic maxim from book 10 of *Heike monogatari*: "The retainer considers the lord his heart; the lord considers the retainer his body" (*sore omi wa kimi wo motte kokoro to shi, kimi wa omi wo motte tai to su*). See Mizuhara Hajime, ed., *Heike monogatari*, 3 vols., in *Shinchō Nihon koten shūsei*, vols. 25, 37, and 47 (Tokyo: Shinchōsha, 1979–81), 47: 144 (trans. mine). Clearly, in both the *Fūshikaden* and *Heike monogatari* passages, translating *tai* as "body" makes more sense than translating it as "mode," "style," "form," or "type." Other examples of the corporeality of *tai* could be adduced from both Kamakura and Muromachi literature.

58. Omote and Katō, eds., *Zeami, Zenchiku*, 112 (trans. mine). Rimer and Yamazaki overlook this corporeality by translating *jintai* as follows: "By the Three Role Types, I refer to the human forms [*jintai*] that constitute the basis of role impersonation [*monomane*]" (*On the Art of Nō Drama*, 64).

59. Omote and Katō, eds., *Zeami, Zenchiku*, 124–27. The illustrations of the three bodies are also reproduced in Hare, *Zeami's Style*, 67, 133, 187 and Rimer and Yamazaki, *On the Art of Nō Drama*, lii–liv. The oldest extant version of this manuscript is the 1441 edition copied by Konparu Zenchiku. The sketches of the three bodies in the 1441 edition were most likely drawn by Zenchiku, though probably based upon sketches in Zeami's original 1421 manuscript. That this emphasis on the corporeality of noh performativity was not unique to Zeami is clearly evidenced by the large num-

ber of similarly unclad bodies included and discussed in sketches from the Tenshō-era (1573–91) noh treatise *Hachijō kadensho*. See Takemoto Mikio, ed., *Nōgaku shiryōshū*, in *Waseda Daigaku zō shiryō eiin sōsho*, 37 vols. (Tokyo: Waseda Daigaku Shuppanbu, 1988), 21: 263–77. On the history of *Hachijō kadensho*, see Eric C. Rath, "Legends, Secrets, and Authority: *Hachijō Kadensho* and Early Modern Noh," *Monumenta Nipponica* 54, no. 2 (1999): 169–94. In the context of contemporary noh performance, see Richard Emmert's remarks regarding the "physicality" of the noh actor's performance, which he considers the sine qua non of noh. See Emmert, "Expanding Nō's Horizons: Considerations for a New Nō Perspective," in Brandon, ed., *Nō and Kyōgen in the Contemporary World*, 19–35.

60. Zeami uses corporeal tropes to describe other aspects of noh theatricality as well, such as in his description of the "skin, flesh, and bone" (*hi, niku, kotsu*) of noh performance. See Zeami, *Shikadō*, in Omote and Katō, eds., *Zeami, Zenchiku*, 116–17; trans. in Rimer and Yamazaki, *On the Art of Nō Drama*, 69–71.

61. Rimer and Yamazaki translate this as "the general framework for the representation appropriate for an old person." This goes far beyond what Zeami writes. To translate *fūtei* as "appropriate representation" ignores the ontological presuppositions of Zeami's conception of the three bodies.

62. *Minari* does not refer to costume, but rather to body posture, pose, structure, style, and appearance (*karada no kamae*). See Omote and Katō, eds., *Zeami, Zenchiku*, 193.

63. Ibid.; trans. modified from Rimer and Yamazaki, *On the Art of Nō Drama*, 141. Hare writes that "by the 1420's, yūgen had replaced monomane as the primary goal of a performance" (*Zeami's Style*, 229–30). But given the continued importance of *monomane* to Zeami's mature conception of *santai*, as evidenced by its appearance in his 1428 treatise, *Shūgyoku tokka*, it seems more likely that Zeami's later usage of *monomane* was extended to include the ontology of *yūgen* rather than simply being replaced by it.

64. Omote and Katō, eds., *Zeami, Zenchiku*, 192–93; trans. modified from Rimer and Yamazaki, *On the Art of Nō Drama*, 141.

65. Omote and Katō, eds., *Zeami, Zenchiku*, 193; trans. modified from Rimer and Yamazaki, *On the Art of Nō Drama*, 141–42.

66. An art with no owner, an art without internalized mastery.

67. An art with an owner, an art with internalized mastery.

68. Omote and Katō, eds., *Zeami, Zenchiku*, 194; trans. modified from Rimer and Yamazaki, *On the Art of Nō Drama*, 143. Cf. Zeami's *Fūshikaden*:

> In the art of role playing, there is a level at which imitation is no longer sought. When every technique of role playing is mastered, and the actor has truly become one with his impersonation, then the mind that desires to imitate is not there [*sono mono ni makoto ni nariirinureba, nisen to omou kokoro nashi*]. Then, if the actor seeks to enjoy his own performance to its fullest extent, how can the flower not be present? For example, in imitating an old man, the psyche of a truly gifted player will become altogether like that of a real old man, who, perhaps, dresses himself up for some procession or temple entertainment, thinking to dance and make music himself. Now, if from the beginning he is the old man, he cannot have a wish to imitate one [*moto yori ono ga mi ga toshiyori naraba*

toshiyori ni nisen to omou kokoro wa arubekarazu]. (Omote and Katō, eds., *Zeami, Zenchiku*, 194; trans. modified from Rimer and Yamazaki, *On the Art of Nō Drama*, 55)

69. See Omote and Katō, eds., *Zeami, Zenchiku*, 166; trans. in Rimer and Yamazaki, *On the Art of Nō Drama*, 118.

70. Cf. Jean Laplanche and J.-B. Pontalis, *The Language of Psycho-Analysis*, trans. Donald Nicholson-Smith (New York: Norton, 1973), 211. I am employing "virtual" in a Deleuzean sense: "The virtual is real and in reciprocal presupposition with the actual, but does not exist even to the extent that the actual could be said to exist. It *subsists* in the actual or is immanent to it." See Brian Massumi, *A User's Guide to Capitalism and Schizophrenia: Deviations from Deleuze and Guattari* (Cambridge: MIT Press, 1992), 37. Also cf. Gilles Deleuze and Félix Guattari, *What Is Philosophy?*, trans. Hugh Tomlinson and Graham Burchell (New York: Columbia University Press, 1994), 118, 122, 156–57, 160.

71. Watanabe Moriake, quoted in Eugenio Barba and Nicola Savarese, eds., *A Dictionary of Theatre Anthropology: The Secret Art of the Performer*, trans. Richard Fowler (London: Routledge, 1991), 195.

72. A glimpse of the great variety of bodily elements and configurations employed in noh theatricality can be found in Yokomichi, ed., *Nōgaku zusetsu*, 366–89.

73. See Zeami, *Fūshikaden*, in Omote and Katō, eds., *Zeami, Zenchiku*, 23–25.

74. In *Yūgaku shūdō fūken*, Zeami quotes a famous poem by Fujiwara no Teika as an example of the highest level of artistic accomplishment, which the noh actor must emulate if he is to enter the "realm of peerless charm." See Omote and Katō, eds., *Zeami, Zenchiku*, 166; trans. in Rimer and Yamazaki, *On the Art of Nō Drama*, 117–18. Cf. Konishi Jin'ichi, "Hon'i setsu to tōdai shiron," *Kokugo* 1, nos. 2–4 (1953): 100–105; Konishi, *History of Japanese Literature*, 3: 40–43, 159, 192, 200; Robert Brower and Earl Miner, *Japanese Court Poetry* (Stanford, Calif.: Stanford University Press, 1961), 252–59, 505. Brower and Miner describe Teika's conception of *hon'i* as "the quasi-Platonic 'thingness' of an event or experience" (505).

75. Komparu, *The Noh Theater*, 7–8.

76. Komparu, *The Noh Theater*, 227–28; Nakamura Yasuo, *Noh: The Classical Theatre*, trans. Don Kenny (New York: Walker/Weatherhill, 1971), 214.

77. Komparu, *The Noh Theater*, 126.

78. See Kajii Yukiyo, "Nyotai no shite ni tsuite," *Gakuyō* 15 (December 1973): 9–18; Toida Michizō, *Nō: Kami to kojiki no geijutsu* (Tokyo: Serika Shobō, 1972), 83; Thomas Immoos, "The Birth of the Japanese Theater," *Monumenta Nipponica* 24 (1969): 410–12; Akima Toshio, "The Songs of the Dead: Poetry, Drama, and Ancient Death Rituals of Japan," *Journal of Asian Studies* 41 (1982): 506; Kanze, "Life with the Nō Mask," 70; Solrun Hoaas, "Noh Masks: The Legacy of Possession," *Drama Review* 26 (Winter 1982): 83; Plutschow, *Chaos and Cosmos*, 231, 238; Barbara Ruch, "The Other Side of Culture in Medieval Japan," in Kozo Yamamura, ed., *The Cambridge History of Japan* (Cambridge: Cambridge University Press, 1990), 3: 523–24.

79. See Richard B. Pilgrim, "The Japanese Noh Drama in Ritual Perspective," *Eastern Buddhist* 22 (1989): 61.

80. Given Zeami's paucity of remarks on the conventions and functions of masks in Muromachi noh, it is largely a matter of speculation as to how the drama of possessive othering unfolded in the medieval mirror room. Such speculation is based on contemporary practices and assumptions, as well as on Zeami's own delineation of the aesthetics of alterity. My analysis of the reflexivity between self and other in the mirror room is also indebted to Hans Ulrich Gumbrecht's discussion of double eccentricity and multilevel self-reflexivity ("the unity of the difference between self-reference and non-self-reference"), which he presented during a comparative-literature seminar at Stanford University (January–March 1990), entitled "Mysticism: An Impossible Discourse?"

81. See Mark C. Taylor's discussion of Hegel's speculative philosophy vis-à-vis Lacan in *Altarity* (Chicago: University of Chicago Press, 1987), 96–99.

82. Omote and Katō, eds., *Zeami, Zenchiku*, 88; trans. modified from Rimer and Yamazaki, *On the Art of Nō Drama*, 81. While Zeami's conception of self-other reflexivity clearly owes much to esoteric Buddhism and shamanism, Zeami's reflections do not seem to presuppose a particular sectarian allegiance. Zeami's formulations intertwine multiple sectarian strands of Buddhism—Tendai, Shingon, Jōdo, Sōtō Zen, and so on—without necessarily favoring one over another. Zeami's nonsectarian Buddhist stance, as well as his mixture of Buddhist and Shintoist beliefs and tropes, is symptomatic of the generalized syncretism of the medieval Japanese religio-cultural world. See Royall Tyler, "Buddhism in Noh," *Japanese Journal of Religious Studies* 14 (1987): 19–52; Hare, *Zeami's Style*, 31; *pace* Nishio Minoru, *Dōgen to Zeami: Chūseitekina mono no genryū o motomete* (Tokyo: Iwanami Shoten, 1965).

83. See Omote and Katō, eds., *Zeami, Zenchiku*, 88; trans. in Rimer and Yamazaki, *On the Art of Nō Drama*, 117–18. Jacob Raz drastically reduces the complexity of this reflexive play by translating *riken no ken* as "objective viewpoint" and *gaken no ken* as "subjective viewpoint." See Raz, *Audience and Actors*, 106–7. Cf. Komparu, *The Noh Theater*, 27; Yusa Michiko, "*Riken no Ken*: Zeami's Theory of Acting and Theatrical Appreciation," *Monumenta Nipponica* 42 (1987): 331–45; and Frank Hoff, "Seeing and Being Seen: The Mirror of Performance," in James H. Stanford, William R. LaFleur, and Masatoshi Nagatomi, eds., *Flowing Traces: Buddhism in the Literary and Visual Arts of Japan* (Princeton, N.J.: Princeton University Press, 1992), 131–48.

84. Yokomichi and Omote, eds., *Yōkyokushū*, 40: 64 (trans. mine). Cf. Royall Tyler's intertextual analysis of *Matsukaze* in "The Nō Play *Matsukaze* as a Transformation of *Genji monogatari*," *The Journal of Japanese Studies* 20 (Summer 1994): 377–422.

85. The complexities of double cross-dressing are also explored in relation to the noh play *Tomoe* in Chapter 4, below. For an interesting discussion of scenes of double cross-dressing on the English Renaissance stage, see Lesley Ferris, *Acting Women: Images of Women in Theatre* (New York: New York University Press, 1989), 3–8.

86. Paul de Man, "Autobiography as De-Facement," *Modern Language Notes* 94 (1979): 926.

87. Ibid., 927. Also cf. Pierre Fontanier, *Les Figures du discours*, ed. Gérard Genette (Paris: Flammarion, 1968), 404–6; Michael Riffaterre, "Prosopopeia," *Yale French Studies* 69 (1985): 107–23.

88. Yokomichi and Omote, eds., *Yōkyokushū*, 40:64 (trans. mine; emphasis added). Yukihira's poem appears in *Kokinshū*:

> Tachiwakare
> Inaba no Yama no
> Mine ni ouru
> Matsu to shi kikaba
> Ima kaerikomu.

> Though I depart
> to travel to Mt. Inaba,
> with its pine-topped peaks,
> if I hear that you pine for me,
> I will return at once.

See Ozawa Masao, ed., *Kokinwakashū*, in *Nihon koten bungaku zenshū*, vol. 7 (Tokyo: Shōgakkan, 1971), no. 365 (trans. mine).

89. Parallels with this scene from *Matsukaze*, in which a female character becomes her lover by donning his clothes—that is, through an act of cross-dressing—can also be found in such plays as *Izutsu*, *Sotoba Komachi*, and *Kakitsubata*. Cf. Tokue Gensei, *Geinō, Nōgei* (Tokyo: Miyai Shoten, 1979), 90; Plutschow, *Chaos and Cosmos*, 229.

90. This is not the place to rehearse the long and complicated history of the term *yūgen* and its various redactions, since I am primarily concerned here with how *yūgen* was construed by Zeami and his patrons in relation to noh performance. For a brief history of *yūgen* and its various modalities, operating in discourses ranging from the *waka* poetics of Fujiwara no Shunzei (1114–1204) and Kamo no Chōmei (1155–1216) to the noh aesthetics of Zeami and Zenchiku, see Arthur H. Thornhill III, "*Yūgen* After Zeami," in *Nō and Kyōgen in the Contemporary World*, 36–64. For more exhaustive treatments, see Nose Asaji, *Yūgen ron* (Tokyo: Kawade Shobō, 1944), and Nogami Toyoichirō, *Nō no yūgen to hana* (Tokyo: Iwanami Shoten, 1943). Also helpful is Kobayashi Shizuo, "*Yūgen to iu kotoba no imi*," in *Seami* (Tokyo: Hinoki Shoten, 1958), 79–93.

91. Omote and Katō, eds., *Zeami, Zenchiku*, 137–38 (trans. mine); cf. 97. Though most of the plays Zeami singles out for praise for their exemplification of *yūgen* would be categorized today as *mugen* noh plays, *yūgen* is not the exclusive attribute of *mugen* noh, but can also be found in certain *genzai* noh as well.

92. On the indebtedness of Zeami's conception of *yūgen* to the poetics of Nijō Yoshimoto, see Nose, *Yūgen ron*, 145–51. For Zeami's remarks on the stylized depiction of nonaristocratic characters, see Omote and Katō, eds., *Zeami, Zenchiku*, 20.

93. Thornhill, "*Yūgen* After Zeami," 43, 46. On other aspects of Zenchiku's treatises, see Thornhill, *Six Circles, One Dewdrop: The Religio-Aesthetic World of Komparu Zenchiku* (Princeton, N.J.: Princeton University Press, 1993).

94. See Pierre Bourdieu, *In Other Words: Essays Towards a Reflexive Sociology*, trans. Matthew Adamson (Stanford, Calif.: Stanford University Press, 1990), 22. Also see Bourdieu, *The Logic of Practice*, trans. Richard Nice (Stanford, Calif.: Stanford University Press, 1990), 112–21.

95. See Bourdieu, *In Other Words*, 93.

96. Ibid., 111–12.

97. Cf. Bourdieu in *La Noblesse d'état*:

One must be noble in order to behave nobly, but one would cease to be noble if one did not behave as a noble. In other words, social magic has very real effects. To assign somebody to a group with a superior essence (nobles as opposed to commoners, men as opposed to women, cultured people as opposed to unedu- cated people, and so on) operates an objective transformation determining a learning process, which in its turn facilitates a real transformation apt to bring that person closer to the definition that has been bestowed on him.

Quoted in Toril Moi, "The Challenge of the Particular Case: Bourdieu's Sociology of Culture and Literary Criticism," *Modern Language Quarterly* 58, no. 4 (December 1997): 502.

98. Omote and Katō, eds., *Zeami, Zenchiku*, 351.

99. Omote Akira and Itō Masayoshi, eds., *Konparu kodensho shūsei* (Tokyo: Wan'ya Shoten, 1969), 263.

100. Palace Minister Sanjō Kintada criticized *sarugaku* noh actors for exhibiting the "conduct of beggars" (*kotsujiki no shogyō*). See *Gogumaiki*, in Tokyō Daigaku Shiryō Hensanjo, ed., *Dai Nihon kokiroku* (Tokyo: Iwanami Shoten, 1980), 17: 267; Kobayashi, *Nōgaku shiryō*, 9; Hayashiya, *Chūsei geinōshi no kenkyū*, 491–92. On the marginal status of noh actors and their competition for shogunal patronage, see Michele Marra, *Representations of Power: The Literary Politics of Medieval Japan* (Honolulu: University of Hawaii Press, 1993), 105–9.

101. See *Yoshida nikki*, in Morisue Yoshiaki, *Chūsei geinōshi ronkō* (Tokyo: Tōkyōdō Shuppan, 1971), 238.

102. See Nose Asaji, *Nōgaku genryūkō* (Tokyo: Iwanami Shoten, 1938), 716–17; Morisue, *Chūsei geinōshi*, 239–40; Nishino Haruo, "Nōgaku shiryaku nenpyō," in No- gami Toyoichirō, ed., *Nōgaku zensho*, 2: 345; O'Neill, *Early Nō Drama*, 32–33; Raz, *Audience and Actors*, 86–87.

103. Mimetic desire typically involves three stages: (1) *B* desires to be like *A*, tak- ing *A* as its model; (2) in order to better emulate *A*, *B* imitates *A*'s objects of desire; (3) eventually mimetic rivalry erupts between the copy [*B*] and the model [*A*], as each tries to differentiate itself from the other, asserting itself as the true model. On mimetic desire, see René Girard, *Deceit, Desire, and the Novel*, trans. Yvonne Freccero (Baltimore: Johns Hopkins University Press, 1965); Girard, *Violence and the Sacred*, trans. Patrick Gregory (Baltimore: Johns Hopkins University Press, 1977); and *Things Hidden Since the Foundation of the World*, trans. Stephen Bann and Michael Metteer (Stanford, Calif.: Stanford University Press, 1987).

104. See Morisue Yoshiaki, "Nō no hogosha," in Nogami Toyoichirō, ed., *Nōgaku zensho*, 2: 198–235; H. Paul Varley, "Ashikaga Yoshimitsu and the World of Kitayama: Social Change and Shogunal Patronage in Early Muromachi Japan," in John W. Hall and Toyoda Takeshi, eds., *Japan in the Muromachi Age* (Berkeley: University of Cali- fornia Press, 1977); Kenneth A. Grossberg, *Japan's Renaissance: The Politics of the Muro-*

machi Bakufu (Cambridge: Harvard University Press, 1981), 30–38; and Carter, ed., *Literary Patronage in Late Medieval Japan*, 1–17.

Chapter 2: The Politics of Exorcism in Aoi no Ue

1. *Aoi no Ue* has been classified variously as a fourth-category demoness (*kijomono*) and vengeful spirit play (*onryōmono* or *hannyamono*), as a quasi-double-entry phantasmal play (*junfukushiki mugen nō*), and as a large-drum play (*taikomono*). *Aoi no Ue* is considered a *junfukushiki* phantasmal play insofar as the *shite* remains on stage the whole time, as in a single-entry (*tanshiki*) *genzai* noh, but changes costume while on stage and then dramatically discloses the identity of the vengeful spirit of Lady Rokujō in the second half, as in a double-entry (*fukushiki*) *mugen* noh. From a strictly musical perspective, *Aoi no Ue* is sometimes referred to as a *taikomono* because, in addition to employing the instruments commonly used in most noh plays today—including small and large hand drums and flute—*Aoi no Ue* also requires the use of the distinctive *taiko*—a large drum played with drumsticks—in order to rhythmically punctuate the dramatic closing section.

2. Yokomichi and Omote, eds., *Yōkyokushū*, 40: 125. Subsequent references will be quoted parenthetically within the text. All translations are mine unless otherwise indicated and are based upon the 1576 (fourth year of the Tenshō era) *kamigakari* text. I have also consulted (and in some cases, incorporated) Itō Masayoshi, ed., *Yōkyokushū*, 3 vols., in *Shinchō Nihon koten shūsei* (Tokyo: Shinchōsha, 1983), 57: 16–24. See Appendix A for a complete translation of the play. During Muromachi and subsequent periods, *Aoi no Ue* was usually performed in the middle or toward the end of a day-long program of noh performances. Though performance records before 1450 are sketchy at best, it is clear that, at least during the late medieval and early modern periods, *Aoi no Ue* was one of the most popular plays in the noh repertoire—a reputation that continues today. See Nose, *Nōgaku genryūkō*, 1263–99. Other translations of *Aoi no Ue* can be found in Kokusai Bunka Shinkokai, ed., *The Noh Drama* (Tokyo: Kokusai Bunka Shinkokai, 1937), 47–65; Arthur Waley, trans., *The Nō Plays of Japan* (London: George Allen and Unwin, 1954), 179–89; Nippon Gakujutsu Shinkōkai, trans., *Japanese Noh Drama* (Tokyo: Nippon Gakujutsu Shinkōkai, 1959), 2: 89–102; Goff, *Noh Drama and The Tale of Genji*, 134–39; and Bethe and Emmert, trans., *Aoinoue*.

3. See Goff on the intertextual linkages between noh performance texts and fourteenth- and fifteenth-century *Genji monogatari* handbooks such as *Genji kokagami*, *Hikaru Genji ichibu renga yoriai no koto*, *Genji ōkagami*, and *Genji monogatari teiyō*.

4. See sections 12 and 13 of *Murasaki Shikibu nikki*, in Yamamoto Ritatsu, ed., *Murasaki Shikibu nikki, Murasaki Shikibu shū*, vol. 35 of *Shinchō Nihon koten shūsei* (Tokyo: Shinchōsha, 1980); Richard Bowring, trans., *Murasaki Shikibu: Her Diary and Poetic Memoirs* (Princeton, N.J.: Princeton University Press, 1982), 55–57.

5. Abe Akio, Akiyama Ken, and Imai Gen'e, eds., *Genji monogatari*, 6 vols., in *Nihon koten bungaku zenshū* (Tokyo: Shōgakkan, 1970–76), 2: 25 and 2: 14 (hereafter *GM*). All translations are mine. *Genji monogatari* manuscripts are divided into three basic textual lines: (1) the Aobyōshibon recension established by Fujiwara no Teika; (2) the

Kawachibon recension established by Minamoto no Mitsuyuki (1163–1244); and (3) variant texts (*beppon*). In my interpretations and translations of *Genji monogatari* I have used the Aobyōshibon, which is the text most widely used by *Genji* scholars today.

6. See *GM* 2: 32.

7. Text in Nakajima Etsuji, ed., *Gukanshō hyōshaku* (Tokyo: Kokubun Kenkyūkai, 1931), 611–14; translation modified from Delmer M. Brown and Ichirō Ishida, trans., *The Future and the Past* (Berkeley: University of California Press, 1979), 218–21.

8. See Tachibana Kenji, ed., *Ōkagami*, in *Nihon koten bungaku zenshū* (Tokyo: Shōgakkan, 1974), 20: 103–7, 138–39, 184–85, 198–202, 224–25; Helen Craig Mc-Cullough, trans., *Okagami: The Great Mirror* (Princeton, N.J.: Princeton University Press, 1980), 102–4, 118–19, 138, 145–46, 155.

9. "Living spirits" were referred to as *ikiryō, ikisudama, onryō,* or *mono no ke.*

10. "Dead spirits" were known as *shiryō, bōkon, akuryō, goryō, onryō,* or *mono no ke.*

11. See Plutschow, *Chaos and Cosmos*, 204.

12. See ibid., 203–16; Jolanta Tubielewicz, *Superstitions, Magic, and Mantic Practices in the Heian Period* (Warsaw: Wydaw-a UW, 1980), 36–46; and Brown and Ishida, trans., *The Future and the Past*, 219–20. Also see Carmen Blacker, *The Catalpa Bow: A Study of Shamanistic Practices in Japan* (London: Allen and Unwin, 1986).

13. *Rokkon*: eyes, ears, nose, tongue, tactile body, and mind.

14. Also referred to as *yorimashi, miko,* and *reibai.*

15. Plutschow, *Chaos and Cosmos*, 233.

16. Ibid., 234.

17. Omote and Katō, eds., *Zeami, Zenchiku*, 263 (trans. mine).

18. See Hare, *Zeami's Style*, 230–32.

19. Leon Hurvitz, trans., *Scripture of the Lotus Blossom of the Fine Dharma* (New York: Columbia University Press, 1976), 59.

20. Ibid., 59.

21. The repetition of *yaru* in *yareguruma* and *yaru kata naki* polysemically inter-twines at least four different semantic strands: (1) to tear, rend, break down, violate, defeat; (2) to be torn, broken down, dilapidated, tattered, defeated, beaten; (3) to per-form, drive, send, dispatch; and (4) to drive away, dispel, dispose of, banish, clear out. The direct object of *yaru* could be the preceding *yareguruma*, "dilapidated carriage," or it could be something metonymically linked to the "dilapidated carriage," such as Rokujō's burning jealousy of Aoi. On *yaru*, see Kindaichi, ed., *Shin meikai kogo jiten*, 1042.

22. The figure of patterns "flashing across a screen" is borrowed from Hare (per-sonal communication). On the "renga-like" associative progressions in noh, see Hare, *Zeami's Style*, 118; Goff, *Noh Drama and The Tale of Genji*, 84–85. My understanding of the importance of parataxis in noh texts owes much to Hare.

23. For an interesting study of spiritual possession in *Genji monogatari*, see Doris G. Bargen, *A Woman's Weapon: Spirit Possession in The Tale of Genji* (Honolulu: University of Hawaii Press, 1997). Bargen mentions *Aoi no Ue* in passing, but does not give much attention to the revisions performed on the Muromachi stage or their so-ciopolitical implications.

24. Yokomichi and Omote, eds., *Yōkyokushū*, 40: 434, note 56; also cf. Masuda Shōzō, *Nō no hyōgen: Sono gyakusetsu no bigaku* (Tokyo: Chūō Kōronsha, 1971), 74.

25. Ivan Morris, *The World of the Shining Prince* (New York: Penguin, 1964), 190–99, 225–26. On the emergence of the *kana* writing system and its role in the channeling of desire between Japanese men and women in the arena of Heian sexual politics, see Steven T. Brown, "Zur Entstehungsgeschichte der japanischen Schrift," in Hans Ulrich Gumbrecht and K. Ludwig Pfeiffer, eds., *Schrift* (Munich: Wilhelm Fink Verlag, 1994), 183–90.

26. See *GM* 2: 29 and 3: 407; Tamagami Takuya, ed., *Genji monogatari hyōshaku*, 14 vols. (Tokyo: Kadokawa Shoten, 1964–69), 6: 350; Norma Field, *The Splendor of Longing in* The Tale of Genji (Princeton, N.J.: Princeton University Press, 1987), 55; Okada, *Figures of Resistance*, 312.

27. Hare, *Zeami's Style*, 299.

28. For a description of the Aoi Festival's schedule of events, see Ikeda Kikan, *Heian jidai no bungaku to seikatsu* (Tokyo: Shibundō, 1966), 556–60; Akiyama Ken, ed., *Genji monogatari jiten* (Tokyo: Gakutōsha, 1989), 74–75; I. Morris, *The World of the Shining Prince*, 173; and William H. McCullough and Helen Craig McCullough, trans., *A Tale of Flowering Fortunes*, 2 vols. (Stanford, Calif.: Stanford University Press, 1980), 2: 408–9.

29. There were earthquakes in 1344, 1347, 1350–51, 1356, 1358, 1361–62, 1369, 1371, 1383, 1391, 1423, and 1433; pestilence in 1341, 1351, 1361, 1365–66, 1373–74, 1378, 1391, 1421, and 1434; typhoons in 1346, 1353, 1356, 1365, and 1406; droughts and famine in 1362, 1379, 1391, and 1420–21; fires in 1365, 1401, 1426, and 1434; and floods in 1350, 1356, and 1393.

30. Another noh play dealing with Rokujō, *Nonomiya*, also includes references to the *kuruma arasoi*, but focuses on Genji's attempts to meet with Rokujō one more time before her daughter assumes her duties as high priestess at Ise Shrine (as recounted in the "Sakaki" chapter of *Genji monogatari*) rather than Rokujō's possession of Aoi. For a discussion of *Nonomiya*, see Hare, "A Separate Piece," 183–203. Also see Paul Atkins, "The Noh Plays of Komparu Zenchiku (1405–?)," Ph.D. diss., Stanford University, 1999, 193–217.

31. See Nakamura et al., eds., *Iwanami Bukkyō jiten*, 47.

32. Mizuno Kōgen, "Gōsetsu ni tsuite," *Indogaku Bukkyōgaku kenkyū* 2 (1954): 110–20. Cf. the following frequently quoted medieval maxim from *Seppō myōgen ron* (On preaching the law and opening the eyes): "Taking shelter under the same tree, or drawing water from the same stream—these are, one and all, karmic bonds from previous lives" (*ichiju no kage ni yadori, ichiga no nagare wo musubu . . . kore wa mina zense no kechien nari*). See Yokomichi and Omote, eds., *Yōkyokushū*, 40: 427–28, note 14.

33. On the contingency of *gyakuen*, see ibid., 40: 429, note 28.

34. See William R. LaFleur's study of *rokudō* cosmology in medieval literature, poetry, and drama: *The Karma of Words: Buddhism and the Literary Arts in Medieval Japan* (Berkeley: University of California Press, 1983).

35. *Shishō* ("four modes of birth"): birth from the womb (*taishō*), birth from an egg (*ranshō*), birth from moisture (*shisshō*), and birth from metamorphosis (*keshō*) (Nakamura, et al., eds., *Iwanami Bukkyō jiten*, 354).

36. LaFleur, *The Karma of Words*, 118.

37. Yokomichi and Omote, eds., *Yōkyokushū*, 40: 126, note 1.

38. Kindaichi, ed., *Shin meikai kogo jiten*, 609.

39. *Kagerō* involves the homophonic intertwinement of at least four semantic clusters: (1) to become dark, cloudy, obscure; (2) to flash, flicker, flit, or be dazzled; (3) shimmering heat waves; and (4) ephemeral mayflies. See ibid., 229. *Kagerō* also serves as the title of chapter 52 in *Genji monogatari*. Titles from *Genji* woven into the text of *Aoi no Ue* (e.g., "Aoi," "Yūgao," "Kagerō," "Azumaya," "Sawarabi," "Hotaru," etc.) are all examples of the rhetorical device *monozukushi*, which paradigmatically lists types of trees, flowers, birds, and mountains, chapters from *Genji monogatari*, and so forth.

40. Tubielewicz, *Superstitions, Magic, and Mantic Practices*, 92–93. Also see Barbara Ruch on *biwa hōshi* (lute-playing priests) who "seem to have begun by performing rituals to placate unsettled spirits attached to home or village, during which the plucking and striking of the strident-sounding lutelike instrument, the *biwa*, played an important role. Its sound was believed to reach across to the spirit world and dissipate malignant forces (much as was the sounding of the string of an archer's bow in other shamanistic connections)." See Ruch, "The Other Side of Culture in Medieval Japan," 535.

41. *Jōrō* refers to the upper grade of the sovereign's ladies-in-waiting, composed of a select group of women authorized to wear the so-called "forbidden" colors and fabrics (*kinjiki*)—red-and-green jackets made out of the finest damask or brocade and stenciled trains—that were reserved for the highest echelons of the aristocracy. See McCullough and McCullough, trans., *A Tale of Flowering Fortunes*, 1: 225, 2: 822.

42. Punning on the homophones for "to conceal" and "to remember," *shinobiguruma* is both a "concealing carriage" and a "remembrance carriage."

43. Haruo Shirane, *The Bridge of Dreams: A Poetics of* The Tale of Genji (Stanford, Calif.: Stanford University Press, 1987), 144.

44. Ibid., 43–44.

45. Rokujō was known as Rokujō no Miyasudokoro, or "Lady of the Bedchamber from the Sixth Ward," because of her status as consort of the former crown prince. "Miyasudokoro" was not a formal title per se, but rather a general designation applied to imperial consorts below the rank of empress.

46. Field, *The Splendor of Longing*, 45–46. Also see Kawasaki Noboru, "Rokujō miyasundokoro no shinkōteki haikei," *Kokugakuin zasshi* 68 (September 1967): 13–23; Fujimoto Katsuyoshi, "Genji monogatari 'zenbō' 'kofu daijin no onryō' kō," *Nihon bungaku* 32 (August 1983): 54–64; Gondō Yoshikazu, "Nō no yūrei," in Gondō Yoshikazu, Nakagawa Akira, and Tsuyuno Gorō, *Nihon no yūrei: Nō, kabuki, rakugo* (Osaka: Osaka Shoseki, 1983), 28–31; Baba Akiko, *Oni no kenkyū* (Tokyo: Chikuma Shobō, 1992), 196–99; Okada, *Figures of Resistance*, 276, 363; and Wakita Haruko, *Nihon chūsei joseishi no kenkyū: Seibetsu yakuwari buntan to bosei, kasei, seiai* (Tokyo: Tokyo Daigaku Shuppankai, 1992), 223.

47. In this connection, it is probably not insignificant that Rokujō happens to be Aoi's aunt by marriage: that is, Rokujō's deceased husband, the former crown prince, was brother to Princess Ōmiya, who is, in turn, the wife of the Minister of the Left and the mother of Aoi. Besides noting these genealogical linkages and their assumed

relevance to the inter- and intraclan politics of the day, it is difficult to know what conclusions to draw other than that each family branch undoubtedly sought to reinforce and expand its political power and position at the Heian court.

48. Cf. Oasa Yūji on linkages between Rokujō's possessions in *Genji monogatari* and the stories of possession recounted in *Eiga monogatari* (Flowering fortunes). See Oasa Yūji, "Rokujō miyasudokoro no kunō," in Akiyama Ken, Kimura Masanori, and Shimizu Yoshiko, eds., *Kōza Genji monogatari no sekai* (Tokyo: Yūhikaku, 1981), 3: 24.

49. See Yamagishi Tokuhei, ed., *Genji monogatari*, 5 vols., in *Nihon koten bungaku taikei*, vols. 14–18 (Tokyo: Iwanami Shoten, 1958–63), 14: 334; Tubielewicz, *Superstitions, Magic, and Mantic Practices*, 36. Also cf. Takagi Ichinosuke, Gomi Tomohide, and Ono Susumu, eds., *Man'yōshū*, 4 vols., in *Nihon koten bungaku taikei*, vols. 4–7 (Tokyo: Iwanami Shoten, 1957–62), 4: 251, 763; 6: 3427.

50. See Field, *The Splendor of Longing*, 50; also cf. *GM* 2: 33, note 32.

51. See Hare, *Zeami's Style*, 295–96.

52. See Ikeda Yasaburō, *Nihon no yūrei* (Tokyo: Chūō Kōronsha, 1974), 124; Plutschow, *Chaos and Cosmos*, 75, 87. Also cf. J. J. M. de Groot, *The Religious System of China*, vol. 6, bk. 2 (Leiden: E. J. Brill, 1910), 1126.

53. *Hana no en* is also the title of chapter 8 in *Genji monogatari*, "Flower Banquet."

54. Kindaichi, ed., *Shin meikai kogo jiten*, 161–62.

55. *Asagao* is the title of chapter 20 in *Genji monogatari*, "Morning Glory." This line is an intertextual reinscription of a poem from the early-twelfth-century poetry collection *Horikawa hyakushu*:

> Shinonome ni
> Okitsutsu zo mimu
> Asagao wa
> Hikage matsu ma no
> Hodo shinakereba.
>
> At day's break
> I must awaken so that I might gaze
> upon the morning glory,
> since it waits only until
> the sun's rays shine.
> (Yokomichi and Omote, eds.,
> *Yōkyokushū*, 40: 127; trans. mine)

56. *Hikage*: (1) sunlight, sun's rays; (2) out of the sunlight, a shady place; (3) a place or person that has been hidden away, ignored, or discarded by society (Kindaichi, ed., *Shin meikai kogo jiten*, 862).

57. Minemura Fumito, ed., *Shinkokinwakashū*, in *Nihon koten bungaku zenshū*, vol. 26 (Tokyo: Shōgakkan, 1974), no. 1400 (trans. mine).

58. Ozawa Masao, ed., *Kokinwakashū*, no. 823. All translations by the author.

59. For an alternative interpretation of this line, see Yokomichi and Omote, eds., *Yōkyokushū*, 40: 127, note 38. Cf. Itō, ed., *Yōkyokushū*, 57: 20, note 13.

60. This line is sometimes divided up between the *tsure* and the *shite*. See Itō, ed.,

Yōkyokushū, 57: 20–21. "The flames of wrath envelop me" is a reinscription of lines from the Buddhist text *Daishōgonron*: "The self is like dried-up wood, / one's wrath a raging fire; / before it burns others, / it consumes the self" (Yokomichi and Omote, eds., *Yōkyokushū*, 40: 128; trans. mine).

61. Kindaichi, ed., *Shin meikai kogo jiten*, 142; also cf. Hisamatsu Senichi and Satō Kenzō, eds., *Kadokawa shinpan kogo jiten* (Tokyo: Kadokawa Shoten, 1989), 170. See Itō, ed., *Yōkyokushū*, 57: 320–28; Baba Mitsuko, *Hashiru onna: Uta no chūsei kara* (Tokyo: Chikuma Shobō, 1992), 47–51.

62. See Jane Marie Law, *Puppets of Nostalgia: The Life, Death, and Rebirth of the Japanese Awaji Ningyō Tradition* (Princeton, N.J.: Princeton University Press, 1997), 17–49. Law suggests that in addition to serving as "body substitutes," such *ningyō* functioned as "vessels" for "detached spirits" (34). Zeami's advice to the noh actor to turn his body into a "vessel" or "receptacle" (*ki, kimotsu*) is a product of the same socioreligious tradition. See my discussion in Chapter 1. Cf. Yamagami Izumo, *Miko no rekishi* (Tokyo: Yūzankaku, 1984), 26.

63. I. Morris, *The World of the Shining Prince*, 142. Also see Field, *The Splendor of Longing*, 259–62; Tubielewicz, *Superstitions, Magic, and Mantic Practices*, 128; and Nagata Kōkichi, "Ningyō shibai no kigen shiryō," in Honda Yasuji, ed., *Geinō ronshū* (Tokyo: Kinseisha, 1976), 635–37.

64. Ihara Saikaku, *The Life of an Amorous Woman*, ed. Ivan Morris (New York: New Directions, 1963), 165–69 (trans. altered).

65. Cf. ibid., 352–53.

66. David John Lu, ed., *Sources of Japanese History*, vol. 1 (New York: McGraw-Hill, 1974), 32. The Yōrō code was a revision of the Taihō code of 701, Japan's first major *ritsuryō*—that is, penal (*ritsu*) and administrative (*ryō*)—code. The Taihō code itself is no longer extant.

Chapter 3: Lady Rokujō in Aoi no Ue

1. Plutschow, *Chaos and Cosmos*, 240, 232. Cf. Shirane, *The Bridge of Dreams*, 115–16. Also see Saigō Nobutsuna, "*Genji monogatari* no mono no ke ni tsuite," in *Shi no hassei: Bungaku ni okeru genshi, kodai no imi* (Tokyo: Miraisha, 1964), 297–323; and Saigō, "Yume to mono no ke," in *Genji monogatari o yomu tame ni* (Tokyo: Heibonsha, 1983), 124–25.

2. Jacques Derrida, *Glas*, trans. John P. Leavey, Jr., and Richard Rand (Lincoln: University of Nebraska Press, 1986), 134.

3. Ibid., 215.

4. Wakita Haruko, "Marriage and Property in Premodern Japan from the Perspective of Women's History," *Journal of Japanese Studies* 10 (1984): 80. My understanding of the history of female inheritance rights in Japan has also benefited from the following studies: Jeffrey P. Mass, *Lordship and Inheritance in Early Medieval Japan: A Study of the Kamakura Sōryō System* (Stanford, Calif.: Stanford University Press, 1989); Gomi Fumihiko, "Josei shoryō to ie," in Joseishi Sōgō Kenkyūkai, ed., *Nihon joseishi*, 5 vols. (Tokyo: Tokyo Daigaku Shuppankai, 1982), 2: 29–64; Wakita Haruko,

Chūsei ni ikiru onnatachi (Tokyo: Iwanami Shoten, 1995), 111–14; and Wakita, *Nihon chūsei joseishi no kenkyū*, 44, 46, 48, 50, 77, 99.

5. Mass, *Lordship and Inheritance in Early Medieval Japan*, 24.

6. Ibid., 10–11, 18. Also see Fukuo Takeichirō, *Nihon kazoku seidoshi gaisetsu* (Tokyo: Yoshikawa Kobunkan, 1972), 65.

7. Mass, *Lordship and Inheritance in Early Medieval Japan*, 17.

8. Wakita, "Marriage and Property," 81.

9. On the history of premodern marriage practices, see William H. McCullough, "Japanese Marriage Institutions in the Late Heian Period," *Harvard Journal of Asiatic Studies* 27 (1967): 103–67; Wakita, "Marriage and Property," 83–87; Peter Nickerson, "The Meaning of Matrilocality: Kinship, Property, and Politics in Mid-Heian," *Monumenta Nipponica* 48, no. 4 (1993): 429–67; and Tonomura Hitomi, "Re-Envisioning Women in the Post-Kamakura Age," in Jeffrey P. Mass, ed., *The Origins of Japan's Medieval World: Courtiers, Clerics, Warriors, and Peasants in the Fourteenth Century* (Stanford, Calif.: Stanford University Press, 1997), 145–53. More extensive analysis and documentation may be found in the groundbreaking work of Takamure Itsue, *Shōseikon no kenkyū*, 2 vols. (Tokyo: Rironsha, 1966).

10. Wakita, "Marriage and Property," 83 and 87. See Sekiguchi Hiroko, "Nihon kodai no kon'in keitai ni tsuite," *Rekishi hyōron* 311 (March 1976): 34–52. Also cf. Mark Morris: "Women of the courtly elite may in some cases have held title to their own houses and property, but patriarchy held title to the socioeconomic structures that provided the context for the possession and circulation of women and houses." See Morris, "Desire and the Prince: New Work on *Genji monogatari*: A Review Article," *Journal of Asian Studies* 49 (1990): 299.

11. Mass, *Lordship and Inheritance in Early Medieval Japan*, 10–11.

12. Ibid., 18–19.

13. Wakita, "Marriage and Property," 87–88.

14. Ibid., 89–90. Also cf. Amino Yoshihiko, "Chūsei ni okeru kon'in kankei no ichi kōsatsu," *Chihōshi kenkyū* 107 (October 1970): 1–24; and Suzuki Kunihiro, "Chūsei zenki ichizoku ketsugō no kenkyū shikaku," *Nihon rekishi* 281 (October 1971): 13–33.

15. Mass, *Lordship and Inheritance in Early Medieval Japan*, 101.

16. Ibid., 101, 116; Wakita, "Marriage and Property," 90–91.

17. Mass, *Lordship and Inheritance in Early Medieval Japan*, 116.

18. Wakita, "Marriage and Property," 82, 90. Cf. Mass, *Lordship and Inheritance in Early Medieval Japan*, 104; and Hirayama Kōzō, *Wayo no kenkyū* (Tokyo: Yoshikawa Kobunkan, 1964), 201.

19. Both quotations are from Wakita, "Marriage and Property," 92.

20. Ozawa Masao, ed., *Kokinwakashū*, no. 767.

21. On the performativity of vows and promises, see J. L. Austin, *Philosophical Papers* (Oxford: Oxford University Press, 1979), 98–103, 236, 239, 242, 248; Austin, *How to Do Things with Words* (Cambridge: Harvard University Press, 1975), 150–62; Derrida, "Signature Event Context," 321–27; and Shoshana Felman, *The Literary Speech Act: Don Juan with J. L. Austin, or Seduction in Two Languages*, trans. Catherine Porter (Ithaca, N.Y.: Cornell University Press, 1983).

22. Yamamoto, ed., *Murasaki Shikibu nikki, Murasaki Shikibu shū*, 131–32 (trans. mine).

23. Field, *The Splendor of Longing*, 40.

24. See Mitani Kuniaki, "*Genji monogatari* daisanbu no hōhō," *Bungaku* 50 (August 1982): 100–102. Also see Goff, *Noh Drama and* The Tale of Genji, 51; Shirane, *The Bridge of Dreams*, 115. Cf. Mishima Yukio's contemporary rewriting of *Aoi no Ue* for the modern stage. Mishima takes a psychoanalytic approach to the dynamics of power and desire binding the characters of Rokujō Yasuko, Wakabayashi Hikaru (Genji), and Wakabayashi Aoi. See Mishima Yukio, "Aoi no Ue," in *Mishima Yukio shū*, vol. 68 of *Chikuma gendai bungaku taikei* (Tokyo: Chikuma Shobō, 1984), 425–35. Also cf. Masuda Shōzō, *Nō to kindai bungaku* (Tokyo: Heibonsha, 1990), 348–54, 372–73.

25. See Fujii Sadakazu, *Genji monogatari no shigen to genzai*, rev. ed. (Tokyo: Tō-jūsha, 1980), 157–59; Shirane, *The Bridge of Dreams*, 25–27; Field, *The Splendor of Longing*, 56–57.

26. Ferris, *Acting Women*, xi; cf. 19, 29.

27. The *hannya* ("transcendental wisdom" or "enlightenment") mask was named after the Muromachi monk Hannyabō, who is said to have first carved such a mask.

28. *Kushiki*: (1) *genshiki*: visual consciousness; (2) *nishiki*: auditory consciousness; (3) *bishiki*: olfactory consciousness; (4) *zesshiki*: gustatory consciousness; (5) *shinshiki*: tactile consciousness; (6) *ishiki*: thought-consciousness (distinguishes between objects); (7) *manashiki*: ego-consciousness (deluded attachment to one's ego); (8) *arayashiki*: foundation-consciousness (repository of energy for all the manifestations of existence); and (9) *ammarashiki*: pure consciousness (without any defilement or attachment). See Nakamura et al., eds., *Iwanami Bukkyō jiten*, 205; Kindaichi, ed., *Shin meikai kogo jiten*, 322; and Inagaki Hisao, ed., *A Dictionary of Japanese Buddhist Terms* (Kyoto: Nagata Bunshodo, 1988), 9, 94.

29. *Jūjō no yuka* (also referred to as *jūjō kanbō*): a ten-stage method of meditation established by the Tendai sect, which leads to enlightenment: (1) *kanfushigikyō*: meditation on the mysterious realm of absolute reality beyond conceptualization; (2) *hotsu shinshō bodaishin*: awakening an aspiration for enlightenment called the "Bodhi-mind"; (3) *zengyō anjin shikan*: meditation that keeps one's thoughts focused on absolute reality; (4) *habōben*: complete eradication of attachments to all types of delusion by meditating on the triple truth (*santai*) of voidness, transiency, and nonduality; (5) *shikitsūsoku*: determination of paths to and from the triple truth and following the former; (6) *dōbon jōjaku*: selection of suitable practices leading to enlightenment; (7) *taiji jokai*: the elimination of unwholesome thoughts obstructing one's concentration on the triple truth; (8) *chijii*: awareness of one's stage of spiritual development and the removal of any pride that may obstruct further advancement; (9) *nōannin*: maintaining composure in all circumstances; and (10) *muhōai*: nonattachment to spiritual achievement. "The most gifted achieve enlightenment by performing the first of these practices, but others must do two or more. Those who are least gifted must practice all ten" (Inagaki, ed., *A Dictionary of Japanese Buddhist Terms*, 151–52). See Nakamura et al., eds., *Iwanami Bukkyō jiten*, 395.

30. *Yuga*: esoteric meditation practices enabling union between the practitioner

and a Buddhist divinity or absolute reality (Nakamura et al., eds., *Iwanami Bukkyō jiten*, 813; Inagaki, ed., *A Dictionary of Japanese Buddhist Terms*, 363).

31. *Hossui*: Dharma-waters, the holy waters of the Buddhist Law.

32. *Sanmitsu no tsuki*: *sanmitsu* are the three secret or mystic practices by which one becomes one with a Buddha, bodhisattva, or other deity. They include: (1) *shinmitsu*: the formation of symbolic hand gestures (*inzō*; Skt. *mudrâ*); (2) *kumitsu*: the recitation of magic spells and incantations (*shingon*; Skt. *mantra*); and (3) *imitsu*: the contemplation of a deity or its iconographic figurations (*mandara*; Skt. *mandala*) (Nakamura et al., eds., *Iwanami Bukkyō jiten*, 331; Inagaki, ed., *A Dictionary of Japanese Buddhist Terms*, 269). The moon (*tsuki*) is a conventional Japanese poetic image for the goal of enlightenment and Buddhist salvation.

33. Hare, *Zeami's Style*, 300.

34. The rendering of this line is indebted to Nippon Gakujutsu Shinkōkai, *Japanese Noh Drama*, 100.

35. See Nakamura et al., eds., *Iwanami Bukkyō jiten*, 81; Plutschow, *Chaos and Cosmos*, 238; and Hori Ichirō, *Folk Religion in Japan: Continuity and Change* (Chicago: University of Chicago Press, 1968), 78.

36. Plutschow, *Chaos and Cosmos*, 238. Also see Ruch, "The Other Side of Culture," 524; Kajii, "Nyotai no shite ni tsuite," 9–18; Toida, *Nō*, 83; and Akima, "The Songs of the Dead," 506.

37. *Tsugu*: (1) follow, inherit, succeed; (2) connect, join, link together; (3) sew together, suture an incision, graft a tree. See Hisamatsu and Satō, eds., *Kadokawa shinpan kogo jiten*, 789–90; Shinmura Izuru, ed., *Kōjien* (Tokyo: Iwanami Shoten, 1988), 1604.

38. See Nakamura et al., eds., *Iwanami Bukkyō jiten*, 117; Hisamatsu and Satō, eds., *Kadokawa shinpan kogo jiten*, 283.

39. See Nakamura et al., eds., *Iwanami Bukkyō jiten*, 832–33; E. Dale Saunders, *Buddhism in Japan* (Philadelphia: University of Pennsylvania Press, 1964), 162–63. For extensive analysis of the two mandalas, see Elizabeth ten Grotenhuis, *Japanese Mandalas: Representations of Sacred Geography* (Honolulu: University of Hawaii Press, 1999), 33–77.

40. Inagaki, ed., *A Dictionary of Japanese Buddhist Terms*, 305; Hurvitz, trans., *Scripture of the Lotus Blossom*, 38.

41. Hurvitz, trans., *Scripture of the Lotus Blossom*, 180; text in Hosoi Nittatsu, ed., *Shinkun ryōdoku myōhōrengekyō narabini kaiketsu* (Tokyo: Sōka Gakkai, 1970), 394.

42. Nakamura et al., eds., *Iwanami Bukkyō jiten*, 645; Inagaki, ed., *A Dictionary of Japanese Buddhist Terms*, 231.

43. Yokomichi and Omote, eds., *Yōkyokushū*, 40: 130, note 7; Itō, ed., *Yōkyokushū*, 57: 23, note 19. Also cf. Robert Morrell, trans., *Sand and Pebbles* (Albany: State University of New York Press, 1985), 323.

44. Tsunoda Ryusaku, William Theodore de Bary, and Donald Keene, eds., *Sources of Japanese Tradition*, 2 vols. (New York: Columbia University Press, 1964), 1: 153.

45. I. Morris, *The World of the Shining Prince*, 260.

46. The Saving Compassion Spell ("Jikuju") of Fudō. Since the *kanji* used to write this spell are not fixed, its precise meaning is uncertain. For one interpretation, see Itō, ed., *Yōkyokushū*, 57: 23, note 19.

47. The first half of this vow of Fudō is as follows: "Whoever looks upon my body awakens aspiration for enlightenment; whoever hears my name refuses evil and reaps good" (Yokomichi and Omote, eds., Yōkyokushū, 40: 130; trans. mine).

48. The Five Great Wisdom Kings are as follows: (1) Gōzanze: incarnation of Ashuku, the Immovable Buddha of the East, who embodies the wisdom of perfectly reflecting all phenomenal things in a clear mirror (daienkyōchi); (2) Gundari: incarnation of Hōshō, the Treasure Producing Buddha of the South, who embodies the wisdom of discerning the absolute equality of all things (byōdōshōchi); (3) Daiitoku: incarnation of Amida, the Infinite Light Buddha of the West, who embodies the wisdom of recognizing the distinctive features of all phenomena (myōkanzatchi); (4) Kongōyasha: incarnation of Fukūjōju, the Effective Accomplishment Buddha of the North, who embodies the wisdom of accomplishing metamorphoses for the benefit of sentient beings (jōshosachi); and (5) Fudō: incarnation of Dainichi, the Great Illumination Buddha of the Center, who embodies the wisdom of knowing the essence of every existence (hokkaitaishōchi).

49. Nakamura et al., eds., Iwanami Bukkyō jiten, 216, 249–50, 277, 290–91, 542, 706–7.

50. See Hagitani Boku, ed., Murasaki Shikibu nikki zenchūshaku, 2 vols., Nihon koten hyōshaku zenchūshaku sōsho (Tokyo: Kadokawa Shoten, 1971–73), 1: 61–66; Yamamoto, ed., Murasaki Shikibu nikki, 12, note 5.

51. Konishi Jin'ichi views such incantatory elements as historical remnants of noh's derivation from earlier religious dramatic forms such as shushi sarugaku. See Konishi, A History of Japanese Literature, 3: 522.

52. Genshin is also said to be the model for the Bishop of Yokawa (Yokawa no sōzu), who appears in the last two chapters of Genji monogatari as a renowned exorcist able to drive out malign spirits by summoning the Buddha's power (kaji) through spells and incantations. Insofar as the holy man in Aoi no Ue is also from Yokawa and also relies on the transference of Buddha's power to exorcise the vengeful spirit of Rokujō from Aoi, he too is probably loosely modeled after Genshin and/or the Bishop of Yokawa in Genji. But such loose similarities may not add up to much, since the yamabushi from Yokawa in Aoi no Ue aligns himself more with En no Gyōja. Moreover, the Bishop of Yokawa plays no role whatsoever in the unsuccessful attempt to exorcise Rokujō from Aoi in chapter 9 of Genji monogatari. On the Bishop of Yokawa as a Genshin intertext in Genji, see Yamagishi, ed., Genji monogatari, 18: 354.

53. See Yokomichi and Omote, eds., Yōkyokushū, 40: 116.

Chapter 4: Ominameshi and the Politics of Subjection

1. Twenty-four performance records exist for Ominameshi between the years 1429 and 1602. This makes it as popular as Izutsu, one of the most frequently performed plays in the noh repertoire during the premodern period. See Nose, Nōgaku genryūkō, 1301–2.

2. I use the term "husband" here somewhat loosely. Whether the couple was actually married or not seems impossible to confirm on the basis of available evidence

that is ambiguous at best. But since Yorikaze's torture in the hell of adulterers (discussed below) seems more plausible and dramatic if it is assumed that they were married, I have done so throughout. For alternative views on this and other topics relating to the play, see the essays collected in Mae Smethurst, ed., *Ominameshi: A Flower Viewed from Many Directions* (forthcoming).

3. Here I am not interested in determining the "causes" of the discourse of "Otokoyama" so much as I am in describing its complex correlations and collocations with other discourses. As Foucault has argued, the discourse of causality drastically oversimplifies the multifarious relations of dependence and dominance—whether intradiscursive, interdiscursive, or extradiscursive—emerging from a given discourse network. See Michel Foucault, "Politics and the Study of Discourse," in Graham Burchell, Colin Gordon, and Peter Miller, eds., *The Foucault Effect: Studies in Governmentality* (Chicago: University of Chicago Press, 1991), 58–59.

4. These differentiations are my own. I am indebted to Judith Butler's incisive engagement with philosophical aspects of subjection vis-à-vis Hegel, Nietzsche, Freud, Foucault, and Althusser in *The Psychic Life of Power: Theories in Subjection* (Stanford, Calif.: Stanford University Press, 1997).

5. Although often translated into English as "maidenflower," *ominameshi* in Muromachi usage suggests not a maiden or virgin per se, but rather an attractive, sexually active young woman. "Damsel flower" may be a more apt translation, if one understands the connotations implied by its French etymology: *damoiselle* as a young woman of quality and erotic charms. See my translation of the play in Appendix B.

6. Itō, ed., *Yōkyokushū*, 57: 251. All translations of *Ominameshi* are my own.

7. Cf. Yamada Yoshio et al., eds., *Konjaku monogatarishū*, 5 vols., in *Nihon koten bungaku taikei*, vols. 22–26 (Tokyo: Iwanami Shoten, 1959–63), 24: 142–43.

8. Itō, ed., *Yōkyokushū*, 57: 247.

9. Allan G. Grapard, "Religious Practices," in Donald H. Shively and William H. McCullough, eds., *The Cambridge History of Japan* (Cambridge: Cambridge University Press, 1999), 2: 569.

10. Cf. Takeda Yūkichi and Satō Kenzō, trans., *Sandai jitsuroku* (Tokyo: Rinsen Shoten, 1986), 696 (see entry under Jōgan 18/5/28).

11. Christine Guth Kanda, *Shinzō: Hachiman Imagery and Its Development* (Cambridge: Harvard University Press, 1985), 41. This is not to say that Fujiwara regents "owned" imperial power; rather, they exercised the imperial power they had displaced without usurping official "ownership" per se from the imperial line. For further discussion of the "ownership/possession dichotomy" in the Heian period, see Nickerson, "The Meaning of Matrilocality," 449–52.

12. See Omote and Katō, eds., *Zeami, Zenchiku*, 286. Although *Yumi Yawata* was not quite as popular a *waki* noh as *Takasago*, performance records indicate that it was one of the ten most popular plays performed during the Muromachi and Azuchi-Momoyama periods. See Nose, *Nōgaku genryūkō*, 1308, 1314.

13. Otokoyama and Yawatayama are alternate names for the same place, each implying the other in the context of their usage in noh. The distribution of Otokoyama/Yawatayama inscriptions is most concentrated in three plays from the current reper-

toire : (1) *Ominameshi*: 10 (Otokoyama) + 1 (Yawatayama) = 11; (2) *Yumi Yawata*: 3 + 4 = 7; and (3) *Hōjōgawa*: 3 + 2 = 5. See Nonomura Kaizō, ed., *Yōkyoku nihyakugojū-banshū sakuin* (Tokyo: Akaoshōbundō, 1978), 237, 1318.

14. See Nose, *Nōgaku genryūkō*, 1302, 1314.

15. Hare, *Zeami's Style*, 104.

16. Omote and Katō, eds., *Zeami, Zenchiku*, 286 (trans. mine).

17. See Imaizumi Atsuo, ed., *Kyōto no rekishi*, 10 vols. (Tokyo: Gakugei Shorin, 1968–76), 3: 169. Cf. Omote and Katō, eds., *Zeami, Zenchiku*, 286, 498, note 167.

18. Cf. the following poem by the founder of the Ashikaga shogunate, Ashikaga Takauji, included in the *Shingoshūishū* (1383):

Mi wo inoru
Hito yori mo nao
Otokoyama
Sunao naru zo
Mamori to wa kiku.

(no. 1507)

More upright than he
who prays for himself
is he who asks for the protection
of his uprightness
at Man Mountain.

That a poem by the founder of the Ashikaga *bakufu*, praying at Otokoyama for protection, would be included in an imperial collection of *waka* suggests the importance of the Hachiman deity and shrines to the descendants of the Seiwa Genji.

19. Itō, ed., *Yōkyokushū*, 79: 480; Imaizumi, ed., *Kyōto no rekishi*, 3: 167.

20. Sung with minimal inflection in the higher register and without strong underlying rhythm, *sashi shōdan* are typically used to highlight important passages by rendering the text as accessible as possible. See Hare, *Zeami's Style*, 299.

21. Ross Bender, "Metamorphosis of a Deity: The Image of Hachiman in *Yumi Yawata*," *Monumenta Nipponica* 33, no. 2 (1978): 171–72 (trans. altered). Japanese text from Sanari, ed., *Yōkyoku taikan*, 5: 3224–25.

22. Bender, "Metamorphosis of a Deity," 169. Gerry Yokota-Murakami follows Bender's interpretation: see Yokota-Murakami, *The Formation of the Canon of Nō: The Literary Tradition of Divine Authority* (Osaka: Osaka University Press, 1997), 43.

23. Watsuji Tetsurō, "Yōkyoku ni arawareta rinri shisō: Japanese Ethical Thought in the Noh Plays of the Muromachi Period," *Monumenta Nipponica* 24, no. 4 (1969): 473. Also cf. Sanari, ed., *Yōkyoku taikan*, 5: 3222.

24. Omote and Katō, eds., *Zeami, Zenchiku*, 286 (trans. mine).

25. Wakita Haruko, "Nōgaku to tennō Shintō," in *Tennōsei: rekishi oken daijōsai*, ed. Irokawa Daikichi (Tokyo: Kawade Shobō Shinsha, 1990), 132.

26. An alternative way of referring to *sekisho no kado*.

27. Bender, "Metamorphosis of a Deity," 172, note 19; also see Watsuji, "Yōkyoku ni arawareta rinri shisō," 471.

28. Grossberg, *Japan's Renaissance*, 94. Also see Kobayashi Yasuo, "Nanbokuchō-Muromachiki no kasho hakkyū ni tsuite: Muromachi bakufu shikiseishi no kisoteki kōsatsu," in Nagoya Daigaku Bungakubu Kokoshigaku Kenkyūshitsu, ed., *Nagoya Daigaku Nihonshi ronshū 1* (Tokyo:Yoshikawa Kōbunkan, 1975), 391–92.

29. Hare, *Zeami's Style*, 104.

30. This is not to say that such ideological expediency necessarily ensured long-term patronage for Zeami's troupe. Despite the success of *Yumi Yawata*, Zeami's troupe quickly fell out of Yoshinori's favor. A successful performance was obviously no guarantee of continued patronage.

31. In sharp contrast, Yoshimochi rejected this title and discontinued trade with China. On the politics of *Nihon kokuō*, see Sasaki Ginya, *Muromachi bakufu*, in *Nihon no rekishi* (Tokyo: Shōgakkan, 1975), 13: 51–53. Also see Grossberg, *Japan's Renaissance*, 34, 36, 49; and John W. Hall, "The Muromachi Bakufu," in Kozo Yamamura, ed., *The Cambridge History of Japan* (Cambridge: Cambridge University Press, 1990), 3: 192–93.

32. See Hall, "The Muromachi Bakufu," 192.

33. For a fuller account of Yoshinori's assassination and its aftermath, see Imaizumi, ed., *Kyōto no rekishi*, 3: 305–6. On *U no ha*, see Amano Fumio, *Nō ni tsukareta kenryokusha: Hideyoshi nōgaku aikōki* (Tokyo: Kōdansha, 1997), 22–23; and Yokota-Murakami, *The Formation of the Canon of Nō*, 72–75.

34. Itō, ed., *Yōkyokushū*, 57: 250.

35. Ibid., 253.

36. On *Hachiman Usagū Hōjōe engi*, see Jane Marie Law, "Violence, Ritual Reenactment, and Ideology:The *Hōjō-e* (Rite for Release of Sentient Beings) of the Usa Hachiman Shrine in Japan," *History of Religions* 33, no. 4 (1994): 325–57. On *Rokugō kaizan Nimmon daibosatsu hongi*, see Allan G. Grapard, "Lotus in Mountain, Mountain in Lotus: *Rokugō Kaizan Nimmon Daibosatsu Hongi*," *Monumenta Nipponica* 41, no. 1 (1986): 21–50. The present discussion of the ideological implications of the Hōjōe is largely indebted to these studies.

37. Other accounts record the year as Yōrō 4 (720): see Edward Kamens, trans., *The Three Jewels: A Study and Translation of Minamoto Tamenori's Sanboe* (Ann Arbor: University of Michigan, 1988), 345–48.

38. Grapard, "Lotus in Mountain," 43.

39. Law, "Violence, Ritual Reenactment, and Ideology," 335.

40. The earliest recorded performance of the Hōjōe at Usa Hachiman Shrine is 745 (Tenpyō 17). At Iwashimizu Hachiman Shrine, the earliest record is for 939 (Tengyō 2), but it may have been performed as early as 863 (Jōgan 5).

41. Law, "Violence, Ritual Reenactment, and Ideology," 345.

42. Ibid. A similar ideological justification for religio-political violence is included in *Rokugō kaizan Nimmon daibosatsu hongi*: "Because I set my mind on governing the world from generation to generation by means of forced conversion and all-embracing compassion, I have taken many lives. In order to bring these spirits to salvation, a ceremony to return living beings to freedom shall be performed" (Grapard, "Lotus in Mountain," 45).

43. Law, "Violence, Ritual Reenactment, and Ideology," 327.

44. Cf. ibid., 350: "A legend from the region of the Kohyō shrine adds another dimension to the story: at the time of the revolt, the Hayato from the two remaining castles fled into the sea rather than be captured. Each and every one of them drowned, the legend says. At about the same time, all along the coastline, there was a marked increase in snails. It was believed that these Hayato had become snails. Shortly after this, a plague broke out, and it was assumed these two problems were the curse (*tatari*) of the Hayato."

45. Ibid., 327.

46. Itō, ed., *Yōkyokushū*, 57: 255.

47. For an excellent discussion of the *sōmoku jōbutsu* debate, see William R. La-Fleur, "Saigyō and the Buddhist Value of Nature," *History of Religions* 13, no. 2 (1973): 93–126.

48. Itō, ed., *Yōkyokushū*, 57: 255.

Chapter 5: The Multiple Histories of Tomoe

1. Ichiko Teiji, ed., *Heike monogatari*, in *Nihon koten bungaku zenshū*, 2 vols. (Tokyo: Shōgakkan, 1973–75), 30: 193 (hereafter *HM*). All translations by the author unless otherwise indicated.

2. For further discussion of the range of female performers circulating in medieval Japan, see the essays included in Steven T. Brown and Sara Jansen, eds., *Performing Japanese Women*, special issue of *Women and Performance* 12, no. 1, issue 23 (2001).

3. Biographical details have been drawn from the following sources: Tomikura Tokujirō, *Heike monogatari zen chūshaku*, 4 vols. (Tokyo: Kadokawa Shoten, 1966–68), 3: 60–62; Hosokawa Ryōichi, *Onna no chūsei: Ono no Komachi, Tomoe, sono ta* (Tokyo: Nihon Editāsukūru Shuppanbu, 1989), 2–33; Baba Akiko, "Tomoe Gozen," in *Genpei sōranki no josei*, vol. 3 of Enchi Fumiko, ed., *Jinbutsu Nihon no joseishi*, 12 vols. (Tokyo: Shūeisha, 1977), 109–38; and Itō Masayoshi, *Yōkyoku zakki* (Tokyo: Izumi Sensho, 1989), 89–93.

4. Tomikura, *Heike monogatari zen chūshaku*, 3: 62.

5. See Mizuhara Hajime, ed., *Shintei Genpei seisuiki*, 6 vols. (Tokyo: Shin Jinbutsu Ōraisha, 1988–91), 4: 311.

6. See Ichiko Teiji, ed., *Heike monogatari hikkei* (Tokyo: Gakutōsha, 1967), 153.

7. See Tomikura, *Heike monogatari zen chūshaku*, 3: 50.

8. Ibid., 61.

9. See Derrida, "Signature Event Context."

10. Cf. Jacques Derrida, "'This Strange Institution Called Literature': An Interview with Jacques Derrida," in Derek Attridge, ed., *Acts of Literature* (New York: Routledge, 1992), 62, 70.

11. Sugimoto, trans., *Heike monogatari*, 90.

12. Nishida Naotoshi, *Heike monogatari no buntaironteki kenkyū* (Tokyo: Meiji Shoin, 1978), 108.

13. Quoted in Itō, *Yōkyoku zakki*, 91.

14. On Tomoe's role in the dissemination of the Yoshinaka *setsuwa*, see Mizuhara

Hajime's "Yoshinaka setsuwa no keisei" and "Tomoe no densetsu, setsuwa," in *Heike monogatari no keisei* (Tokyo: Katō Chūdōkan, 1971), 43–60, 61–74, as well as his entry in Ichiko, ed., *Heike monogatari hikkei*, 153–56.

15. On *gozen* usage, see Hisamatsu and Satō, eds., *Kadokawa shinpan kogo jiten*, 470. Also see Tomikura, *Heike monogatari zen chūshaku*, 3: 61; and Hosokawa, *Onna no chūsei*, 8.

16. Quoted in Hosokawa, *Onna no chūsei*, 10.

17. Given its inclusion in both *Jika denshō* and *Nōhon sakusha chūmon*, Itō (*Yōkyoku zakki*, 89) speculates that *Tomoe* must have already existed in the Eishō or Taiei eras: that is, between 1504 and 1528. If Kobayashi's dating of *Jika denshō* is correct, then *Tomoe* was probably written before 1516.

18. For *Kinu Kazuki Tomoe*, see Haga Yaichi and Sasaki Nobutsuna, eds., *Kōchū yōkyoku sōsho*, 3 vols., 2nd ed. (Tokyo: Rinsen Shoten, 1987), 1: 553–56. For *Katami Tomoe*, see Tanaka Makoto, ed., *Mikan yōkyokushū*, 31 vols. (Tokyo: Koten Bunko, 1987), 16: 65–70.

19. For *Genzai Tomoe* and *Konjō Tomoe*, see Haga and Sasaki, eds., *Kōchū yōkyoku sōsho*, 1: 686–87 and 806–9.

20. Itō, *Yōkyoku zakki*, 90.

21. Ibid.

22. For the current Kanze version of this passage, see *Tomoe*, in Yokomichi and Omote, eds., *Yōkyokushū*, 41: 315. Translations of the play into English may be found in Royall Tyler, "Tomoe: The Woman Warrior," in Chieko Irie Mulhern, ed., *Heroic with Grace: Legendary Women of Japan* (Armonk, N.Y.: M. E. Sharpe, 1991), 129–61; and Chifumi Shimazaki, *Warrior Ghost Plays from the Japanese Noh Theater* (Ithaca, N.Y.: Cornell University East Asia Program, 1993), 165–83.

23. Itō, *Yōkyoku zakki*, 90.

24. Yokomichi and Omote, eds., *Yōkyokushū*, 41: 315.

25. Itō (*Yōkyoku zakki*, 92) thinks it likely that *Genpei seisuiki* served as the *honzetsu* (source) for the noh play *Tomoe*.

26. Tokue Motomasa, "Shizuka Gozen no kaikoku," *Kokugakuin zasshi* 61, no. 1 (1960): 42.

27. Sunagawa Hiroshi, *Heike monogatari shinkō* (Tokyo: Bijutsu, 1982), 154.

28. Quoted in Tomikura, *Heike monogatari zen chūshaku*, 3: 61.

29. Yokomichi and Omote, eds., *Yōkyokushū*, 41: 317.

30. This phonetic play is repeated again a few lines later in "Tomoe wa tomokaku mo."

31. Yokomichi and Omote, eds., *Yōkyokushū*, 41: 317. Itō (*Yōkyoku zakki*, 92) thinks this passage bears the imprint of *Genpei seisuiki*.

32. Haga and Sasaki, eds., *Kōchū yōkyoku sōsho*, 1: 686, 807 (emphasis mine).

33. Yokomichi and Omote, eds., *Yōkyokushū*, 41: 318.

34. Ibid.

35. See the illustration of a *shirabyōshi* dancer in the early-sixteenth-century text of Iwasaki Kae et al., eds., *Shichijūichiban shokunin utaawase*, in *Shin Nihon koten bungaku taikei* (Tokyo: Iwanami Shoten, 1993), 61: 98.

36. Kajihara Masaaki, ed., *Gikeiki*, in *Nihon koten bungaku zenshū* (Tokyo: Shō-

gakkan, 1971), 31: 233–34. For an excellent overview of *shirabyōshi* and other types of female entertainer, see Ruch, "The Other Side of Culture," 525–31.

37. The costume of the *nochijite* in *Tomoe* includes a young woman's *zō* mask, man's *nashiuchi eboshi* hat, white *hachimaki* headband, *karaori* robe over a *surihaku kitsuke* and *ōkuchibakama* divided skirt, *naginata*, and sword.

38. Tomoe's act of cross-dressing on the noh stage does not duplicate that of a *shirabyōshi*. After all, Tomoe dons a *kosode*, not a *suikan*, robe. Moreover, at no time does Tomoe perform the sort of *imayō* song one would expect from a *shirabyōshi* performer. Nevertheless, I would argue that Tomoe's donning of Yoshinaka's robe and sword at the very least gestures toward the figure of the *shirabyōshi*.

39. Cf. Thomas Laqueur, *Making Sex: Body and Gender from the Greeks to Freud* (Cambridge: Harvard University Press, 1990), 24. Also see Susan Klein's provocative reading of gender and sexuality vis-à-vis the demonized *shirabyōshi* of *Dōjōji* in her essay "Woman as Serpent: The Demonic Feminine in the Noh Play *Dōjōji*," in Jane Marie Law, ed., *Religious Reflections on the Human Body* (Bloomington: Indiana University Press, 1994), 100–136.

40. Yokomichi and Omote, eds., *Yōkyokushū*, 41: 316.

41. See William McDuff, "Beautiful Boys in Nō Drama: The Idealization of Homoerotic Desire," *Asian Theatre Journal* 13, no. 2 (1996): 248–58.

42. See Watanabe Shōgo, *Geinō bunkashi jiten [chūsei hen]* (Tokyo: Meicho Shuppan, 1991), 271.

Epilogue: Staging Hideyoshi in Postmedieval Noh

1. My discussion of Hideyoshi's patronage and performance of noh is indebted to the following studies: Hata Hisashi, "Kinsaku nō, kindai nō, gendai nō no sakusha to sakuhin," in Yokomichi Mario, Nishino Haruo, and Hata Hisashi, *Nō no sakusha to sakuhin*, in *Iwanami kōza: Nō kyōgen*, vol. 3 (Tokyo: Iwanami Shoten, 1992), 301–7; George Elison, "Hideyoshi, the Bountiful Minister," in George Elison and Bardwell L. Smith, eds., *Warlords, Artists, & Commoners: Japan in the Sixteenth Century* (Honolulu: University of Hawaii Press, 1981), 223–44; Araki Yoshio, *Azuchi Momoyama jidai bungakushi* (Tokyo: Kadokawa Shoten, 1969), 195–96, 231–32, 389–401; Morisue, "Nō no hogosha," 2: 211–26; Omote and Amano, *Nōgaku no rekishi*, 80–88; Amano, *Nō ni tsukareta kenryokusha*; and Raz, *Audience and Actors*, 126–29.

2. Mary Elizabeth Berry, *Hideyoshi* (Cambridge: Harvard University Press, 1982), 6, 177.

3. Tenshō 13/7/11, 14/12/19, and 19/12/27, respectively. On the historical precedent of Ashikaga Yoshimitsu, see Elison, "Hideyoshi," 231–33; Hayashiya Tatsusaburō, "Kyoto in the Muromachi Age," in John Whitney Hall and Toyoda Takeshi, eds., *Japan in the Muromachi Age* (Berkeley: University of California Press, 1977), 19; Berry, *Hideyoshi*, 184–87.

4. Elison, "Hideyoshi," 239, 243. On Yoshimitsu's cultural dominance during Kitayama, see Varley, "Ashikaga Yoshimitsu and the World of Kitayama," 183–84.

5. Bunroku 2 (1593)/9/16. See Omote and Amano, *Nōgaku no rekishi*, 84–86.

6. Ibid., 81.

7. Tenshō 13/7/13. See ibid., 81; and Elison, "Hideyoshi," 241.

8. See Ose Hoan, *Taikōki*, ed. Kuwata Tadachika (Tokyo: Shin Jinbutsu Ōraisha, 1971), 372–73; Elison, "Hideyoshi," 242; Adriana Boscaro, ed., *101 Letters of Hideyoshi: The Private Correspondence of Toyotomi Hideyoshi*, Monumenta Nipponica Monograph 54 (Tokyo: Sophia University, 1975), 51.

9. Nakamura, *Noh*, 126–27.

10. Zeami, *Fūshikaden*, in Omote and Katō, eds., *Zeami, Zenchiku*, 40 (trans. mine).

11. As Elison so aptly puts it: "In the historical play composed by Hideyoshi, the leading *bushi* actors were cast in the roles of *kuge*." See Elison, "Hideyoshi," 229. Cf. the following statement attributed to Hideyoshi: "These days many military men have ascended to high posts, but their appearance in court dress is utterly ignoble, so that they must all practice Nō." See *Akumabarai* and *Kitaryū hijisho*, quoted in Elison, "Hideyoshi," 243.

12. For a chronological chart of Hideyoshi's involvement with noh, see Hata, "Kinsaku nō, kindai nō," 302–3. For individual performance records and programs, see Hanawa Hokinoichi, ed., *Zoku gunsho ruijū*, vol. 19 (2) (Tokyo: Zoku Gunsho Ruijū Kanseikai, 1925), 240–41.

13. For brief biographical essays on Ōmura Yūko, see Ichiko Teiji et al., eds., *Nihon koten bungaku daijiten*, 6 vols. (Tokyo: Iwanami Shoten, 1983–85), 1: 460; and Donald Keene, *Some Japanese Portraits* (Tokyo: Kodansha International, 1978), 63–70.

14. See Nonomura Kaizō, ed., *Yōkyoku sanbyakugojūbanshū* (Tokyo: Kōbunsha, 1928), 675–76, 684–89, 704–6. Although the plays were not originally designated according to the taxonomy of *gobandate*, I have followed the categorization of Nonomura. As this study was going to press, a sixth Hideyoshi play was discovered, entitled *Kono hana* (This flower), which compares Hideyoshi to the emperor of China. For a facsimile of the play itself and a discussion of the circumstances surrounding its discovery, see *Konparu geppō* 20, no. 11 (2000): 11–18.

15. On the revisionist history of the *Tenshōki*, see Berry, *Hideyoshi*, 222.

16. Nonomura, ed., *Yōkyoku sanbyakugojūbanshū*, 675 (trans. mine).

17. After the trip, the play was performed again during the third month of 1594 (Bunroku 3/3/15) at Osaka Castle and perhaps later at the imperial palace. See Omote and Amano, *Nōgaku no rekishi*, 84; Hata, "Kinsaku nō, kindai nō," 303; Araki, *Azuchi Momoyama jidai bungakushi*, 389. Hideyoshi probably reprised his role as Zaō Gongen at the imperial palace: see Elison, "Hideyoshi," 243–44. Hideyoshi also commissioned a pair of screens by Kanō Mitsunobu (1565–1608) to commemorate the event. A detail from the Kanō screens, entitled *Yoshino no hanami*, is reproduced in Michael Cooper, *The Southern Barbarians* (Tokyo: Kodansha International, 1971), 83. The original screens are contained in the Hosomi collection in Osaka.

18. Ose, *Taikōki*, 437.

19. See Alicia Matsunaga and Daigan Matsunaga, *Foundation of Japanese Buddhism* (Los Angeles: Buddhist Books International, 1976), 1: 245.

20. Nonomura, ed., *Yōkyoku sanbyakugojūbanshū*, 676.

21. See Michael Cooper, *Rodrigues the Interpreter: An Early Jesuit in Japan and China* (New York: Walker/Weatherhill, 1974), 185.

22. Genna 5/9. See Imaizumi, ed., *Kyōto no rekishi* (Tokyo: Gakugei Shorin, 1970), 5: 42–43.

23. Berry argues persuasively that "the growing emphasis on status and its requirements" in the late-sixteenth-century world of Momoyama Japan led to a sociopolitical order that "was increasingly associated with the clarification of roles and their symbols" (*Hideyoshi*, 146).

24. Nonomura, ed., *Yōkyoku sanbyakugojūbanshū*, 687.

25. Donald Keene, *Nō: The Classical Theatre of Japan* (Tokyo: Kodansha International, 1973), 41.

26. Nakamura, *Noh*, 127.

27. Whether Hideyoshi's self-staging owes anything to contemporaneous Jesuit productions of Christian mystery plays (*autos sacramentales*), or vice-versa, remains unclear. Cf. Thomas F. Leims's investigation of cross-cultural linkages between Jesuit forms of theatricality and the early history of Kabuki in *Die Entstehung des Kabuki: Transkulturation Europa-Japan im 16. und 17. Jahrhundert* (Leiden: E. J. Brill, 1990). Also see C. R. Boxer's description of *autos* performances in Japan during the mid sixteenth century: *The Church Militant and Iberian Expansion, 1440–1770* (Baltimore: Johns Hopkins University Press, 1978), 58–59.

28. See my translation of the play in Appendix C.

29. Bunroku 3/3/15. See Hata, "Kinsaku nō, kindai nō," 303. That Hideyoshi actually performed in all five plays, as he clearly intended to do, is likely though uncertain. See Elison, "Hideyoshi," 338, note 84.

30. See Nonomura, ed., *Yōkyoku sanbyakugojūbanshū*, 684. Cf. Hideyoshi's remarks to the Jesuits in 1593 at Nagoya: "When I was born, a sunbeam fell on my chest, and when the diviners were asked about this, they told me that I was to be the ruler of all that lies between east and west." See Michael Cooper, ed., *They Came to Japan: An Anthology of European Reports on Japan, 1543–1640* (Berkeley: University of California Press, 1965), 111. On the politics of "Heaven's Mandate," see George Elison, *Deus Destroyed: The Image Of Christianity in Early Modern Japan* (Cambridge: Harvard University Press, 1988), 5–6.

31. Friedrich Nietzsche, *The Gay Science*, trans. Walter Kaufmann (New York: Vintage Books, 1974), aph. 361.

32. As Elison remarks: "Theatricality marked his person—perhaps justly so, for his career was dramatic." See Elison, "Hideyoshi," 241.

33. See Raz, *Audience and Actors*, 129. Cf. Conrad Totman on "the mingling of elite and commoner culture" in Momoyama Japan: Totman, *Early Modern Japan* (Berkeley: University of California Press, 1993), 88.

34. *Henry V*, prologue, 1–4; also cf. 1.2.105–10.

35. Quoted in Christopher Pye, *The Regal Phantasm: Shakespeare and the Politics of Spectacle* (London: Routledge, 1990), 43. For an interesting discussion of the theatricality of royal progresses by the British monarchy, see David Cannadine, "The Context, Performance and Meaning of Ritual: The British Monarchy and the 'Invention

of Tradition,' c. 1820–1977," in Eric Hobsbawm and Terence Ranger, eds., *The Invention of Tradition* (Cambridge: Cambridge University Press, 1983), 101–64.

36. See Bourdieu, *In Other Words*, 111–12.

37. According to a contemporaneous account by Pedro Bautista Blanquez, "It is said that people only dare tell him [Hideyoshi] what he wants to hear." See Cooper, *They Came to Japan*, 112.

38. On audience response, see Boscaro, *101 Letters of Hideyoshi*, 67; *Tokiyoshikyōki*, Naikaku Bunko ms. *washo* 35402/72 (6), box no. 159–211; entries for Bunroku 2/10/5–7, cited in Elison, "Hideyoshi," 242.

39. *Tamon'in nikki*, quoted in Elison, "Hideyoshi," 229.

40. Quoted in James Murdoch, *A History of Japan* (New York: Greenberg, 1926), 1: 305.

41. Quoted in Berry, *Hideyoshi*, 208.

42. In a letter dated Bunroku 2/5/27, Hideyoshi relates to his wife his interest in performing noh for the Ming envoys. See Boscaro, *101 Letters of Hideyoshi*, 57.

Appendix A: Lady Aoi

1. This translation is based upon the text of *Aoi no Ue* in Yokomichi and Omote, eds., *Yōkyokushū*, 40: 124–30. I have also consulted (and in some cases, incorporated) Itō, ed., *Yōkyokushū*, 57: 16–24.

2. Here I follow Itō, ed., *Yōkyokushū*, 57: 20.

3. Ibid., 22.

4. Ibid., 23.

Appendix B: Damsel Flower

1. This translation is based upon the text of *Ominameshi* in Itō, ed., *Yōkyokushū*, 57: 246–55.

2. Maruoka Katsura, *Koken yōkyoku kaidai*, ed. Nishino Haruo (Tokyo: Kokon Yōkyoku Kankokai, 1984), 262.

Appendix C: Conquest of Akechi

1. This translation is based upon the text of *Akechi uchi* in Nonomura, ed., *Yōkyoku sanbyakugojūbanshū*, 684–85; and Haga and Sasaki, eds., *Kōchū yōkyoku sōsho*, 1: 20–22. Given the relative inaccessibility of the play in both Japanese and English, I have provided annotations to assist the reader.

2. *Hima no koma*: An intertextual reinscription of a Chinese saying from *Shih Chi* (Records compiled by the historian; 145?–86 B.C.E.), which compares the fleeting passage of time and the brevity of human life to the blur of a passing white horse as seen through a crevice in a wall. Variations on this intertext can be found in noh plays as diverse as *Ema*, *Seiōbo*, *Yorimasa*, *Kinuta*, *Hyakuman*, and *Kirikane Soga*.

3. Hashiba is the surname employed by Hideyoshi from 1573 until he adopted the Toyotomi surname in 1586. It was formed by taking one Chinese character each

from the surnames of Niwa Nagahide (1535–85) and Shibata Katsuie (1522–83), two of Oda Nobunaga's (1534–82) highest-ranking generals.

4. Chikuzen no Kami is an honorary court title. Chikuzen province was located in the northwestern part of present-day Fukuoka prefecture.

5. In an effort to solidify his national hegemony, Nobunaga had entrusted Hideyoshi in 1578 with the task of subduing Mōri Terumoto (1553–1625) and his army, which controlled twelve provinces on Honshū.

6. The year 1582.

7. Western region of present-day Okayama prefecture.

8. On his way to Takamatsu to provide reinforcements to Hideyoshi, Nobunaga stopped at Honnōji Temple in Kyoto, where he was treacherously attacked by Mitsuhide's men. Outnumbered and taken by surprise, Nobunaga is reported to have committed suicide behind Honnōji's closed doors.

9. Southeastern region of present-day Okayama prefecture.

10. Hideyoshi is said to have transported the head and body of Mitsuhide back to Honnōji in order to appease Nobunaga's spirit. See Berry, *Hideyoshi*, 72.

11. Before attacking, Hideyoshi tried first to negotiate the surrender of Takamatsu by offering an enormous bribe.

12. Dispatched by Mitsuhide to the Mōri, the secret informant was intercepted by Hideyoshi before he could deliver word of Nobunaga's death. See Berry, *Hideyoshi*, 71–72.

13. Shimizu Muneharu (1537–82), lord of Takamatsu Castle, was compelled to commit suicide after Hideyoshi inundated the castle compound by diverting rain water and the Ashimori River by means of an elaborate network of channels and dikes.

14. *Harakiri* is used here, instead of the more formal term *seppuku*, to show disrespect toward Shimizu's act of suicide.

15. After reaching an agreement with the Mōri for the surrender of Takamatsu Castle, Hideyoshi's army broke camp and raced back to the capital to confront Mitsuhide.

16. Hsiang Yü, the mighty general who, with the help of Liu Pang, overthrew the Ch'in dynasty and appointed himself overlord of a confederacy of nineteen minor kingdoms in 206 B.C.E. Soon thereafter, his ally Liu Pang became his rival for power, and the two engaged each other in a military chess match of battles and broken agreements. In his last battle at Kai-hsia in 202 B.C.E., Hsiang Yü found himself outnumbered, and committed suicide at Wu Jiang River by means of self-decapitation. See Michael Loewe, "The Former Han Dynasty," in Denis Twitchett and Michael Loewe, eds., *The Cambridge History of China* (Cambridge: Cambridge University Press, 1986), I: 111–19.

17. Wu Jiang River.

18. A literalizing pun on the Chinese characters that form the name of Minase River: that is, "river without water" (*mizu no nai kawa*).

19. Located in present-day Miyazaki prefecture.

20. Located in Yamazaki province.

21. In fact, Mitsuhide was slain by a group of peasants in the village of Ogurusu, located in the eastern part of Fushimi ward in southern Kyoto. See Berry, *Hideyoshi*, 72.

Bibliography

Abe Akio, Akiyama Ken, and Imai Gen'e, eds. *Genji monogatari*. 6 vols. In *Nihon koten bungaku zenshū*, vols. 12–17. Tokyo: Shōgakkan, 1970–76.

Akima Toshio. "The Songs of the Dead: Poetry, Drama, and Ancient Death Rituals of Japan." *Journal of Asian Studies* 41 (1982): 485–509.

Akiyama Ken, ed. *Genji monogatari jiten*. Tokyo: Gakutōsha, 1989.

Amano Fumio. *Nō ni tsukareta kenryokusha: Hideyoshi nōgaku aikōki*. Tokyo: Kōdansha, 1997.

Amino Yoshihiko. "Chūsei ni okeru kon'in kankei no ichi kōsatsu." *Chihōshi kenkyū* 107 (October 1970): 1–24.

Araki Yoshio. *Azuchi Momoyama jidai bungakushi*. Tokyo: Kadokawa Shoten, 1969.

Armstrong, Timothy J., trans. *Michel Foucault, Philosopher*. New York: Routledge, 1992.

Atkins, Paul. "The Noh Plays of Komparu Zenchiku (1405–?)." Ph.D. diss., Stanford University, 1999.

Austin, J. L. *How to Do Things with Words*. Cambridge: Harvard University Press, 1975.

———. *Philosophical Papers*. Oxford: Oxford University Press, 1979.

Baba Akiko. *Oni no kenkyū*. Tokyo: Chikuma Shobō, 1992.

———. "Tomoe Gozen." In *Genpei sōranki no josei*. Vol. 3 of Enchi Fumiko, ed., *Jinbutsu Nihon no joseishi*, 12 vols., 109–38. Tokyo: Shūeisha, 1977.

Baba Mitsuko. *Hashiru onna: Uta no chūsei kara*. Tokyo: Chikuma Shobō, 1992.

Barba, Eugenio, and Nicola Savarese, eds. *A Dictionary of Theatre Anthropology: The Secret Art of the Performer*. Trans. Richard Fowler. London: Routledge, 1991.

Bargen, Doris G. *A Woman's Weapon: Spirit Possession in* The Tale of Genji. Honolulu: University of Hawaii Press, 1997.

Bender, Ross. "Metamorphosis of a Deity: The Image of Hachiman in *Yumi Yawata*." *Monumenta Nipponica* 33, no. 2 (1978): 165–78.

Berger, Peter L., and Thomas Luckmann. *The Social Construction of Reality: A Treatise in the Sociology of Knowledge*. Garden City, N.Y.: Doubleday, 1966.

Berry, Mary Elizabeth. *Hideyoshi*. Cambridge: Harvard University Press, 1982.

Bethe, Monica. "Nō Costume as Interpretation." *Mime Journal* (1984): 148–55.

———. "Okina: An Interview with Takabayashi Kōji." *Mime Journal* (1984): 93–103.

———. "The Use of Costumes in Nō Drama." In *Five Centuries of Japanese Kimono: On This Sleeve of Fondest Dreams*. Art Institute of Chicago Museum Studies 18, no. 1 (1992): 6–19.

Bethe, Monica, and Karen Brazell. *Dance in the Nō Theater*. 3 vols. Ithaca, N.Y.: Cornell University East Asia Program, 1982.

Bethe, Monica, and Richard Emmert, trans. *Aoinoue*. Tokyo: National Noh Theatre, 1997.

Blacker, Carmen. *The Catalpa Bow: A Study of Shamanistic Practices in Japan*. London: Allen and Unwin, 1986.

Boscaro, Adriana, ed. *101 Letters of Hideyoshi: The Private Correspondence of Toyotomi Hideyoshi*. *Monumenta Nipponica* Monograph 54. Tokyo: Sophia University, 1975.

Bourdieu, Pierre. *In Other Words: Essays Towards a Reflexive Sociology*. Trans. Matthew Adamson. Stanford, Calif.: Stanford University Press, 1990.

———. *The Logic of Practice*. Trans. Richard Nice. Stanford, Calif.: Stanford University Press, 1990.

Bowring, Richard, trans. *Murasaki Shikibu: Her Diary and Poetic Memoirs*. Princeton, N.J.: Princeton University Press, 1982.

Boxer, C. R. *The Church Militant and Iberian Expansion, 1440–1770*. Baltimore: Johns Hopkins University Press, 1978.

Brandon, James R., ed. *Nō and Kyōgen in the Contemporary World*. Honolulu: University of Hawaii Press, 1997.

Brower, Robert, and Earl Miner. *Japanese Court Poetry*. Stanford, Calif.: Stanford University Press, 1961.

Brown, Delmer M., and Ichirō Ishida, trans. *The Future and the Past*. Berkeley: University of California Press, 1979.

Brown, Steven T. "Zur Entstehungsgeschichte der japanischen Schrift." In Hans Ulrich Gumbrecht and K. Ludwig Pfeiffer, eds., *Schrift*, 183–90. Munich: Wilhelm Fink Verlag, 1994.

Brown, Steven T., and Sara Jansen, eds. *Performing Japanese Women*. Special issue of *Women and Performance* 12, no. 1, issue 23 (2001).

Butler, Judith. *The Psychic Life of Power: Theories in Subjection*. Stanford, Calif.: Stanford University Press, 1997.

Cannadine, David. "The Context, Performance, and Meaning of Ritual: The British Monarchy and the 'Invention of Tradition,' c. 1820–1977." In Eric

Hobsbawm and Terence Ranger, eds., *The Invention of Tradition*, 101–64. Cambridge: Cambridge University Press, 1983.

Carter, Steven D., ed. *Literary Patronage in Late Medieval Japan*. Ann Arbor: University of Michigan Center for Japanese Studies, 1993.

Chance, Linda H. *Formless in Form: Kenkō, Tsurezuregusa, and the Rhetoric of Japanese Fragmentary Prose*. Stanford, Calif.: Stanford University Press, 1997.

Childs, Margaret H. "The Influence of the Buddhist Practice of *Sange* on Literary Form: Revelatory Tales." *Japanese Journal of Religious Studies* 14 (1987): 53–66.

Cooper, Michael. *Rodrigues the Interpreter: An Early Jesuit in Japan and China*. New York: Walker/Weatherhill, 1974.

———. *The Southern Barbarians*. Tokyo: Kodansha International, 1971.

———, ed. *They Came to Japan: An Anthology of European Reports on Japan, 1543–1640*. Berkeley: University of California Press, 1965.

De Groot, J. J. M. *The Religious System of China*. 6 vols. Leiden: E. J. Brill, 1910.

Deleuze, Gilles. *Negotiations: 1972–1990*. Trans. Martin Joughin. New York: Columbia University Press, 1995.

———. "What Is a *Dispositif*?" In Timothy J. Armstrong, trans., *Michel Foucault, Philosopher*, 159–68. New York: Routledge, 1992.

Deleuze, Gilles, and Félix Guattari. *A Thousand Plateaus: Capitalism and Schizophrenia*. Trans. Brian Massumi. Minneapolis: University of Minnesota Press, 1987.

———. *What Is Philosophy?* Trans. Hugh Tomlinson and Graham Burchell. New York: Columbia University Press, 1994.

De Man, Paul. "Autobiography as De-Facement." *Modern Language Notes* 94 (1979): 919–30.

Derrida, Jacques. "Double Session." In Barbara Johnson, trans., *Dissemination*, 173–286. Chicago: University of Chicago Press, 1981.

———. *Glas*. Trans. John P. Leavey, Jr., and Richard Rand. Lincoln: University of Nebraska Press, 1986.

———. "Passages—from Traumatism to Promise." In Elisabeth Weber, ed., *Points . . . Interviews, 1974–1994*, 372–95. Stanford, Calif.: Stanford University Press, 1995.

———. "Signature Event Context." In Alan Bass, trans., *Margins of Philosophy*, 307–30. Chicago: University of Chicago Press, 1982.

———. "Some Statements and Truisms About Neo-Logisms, Newisms, Postisms, Parasitisms, and Other Small Seismisms." In David Carroll, ed., *The States of "Theory": History, Art, and Critical Discourse*, 63–94. New York: Columbia University Press, 1990.

———. "'This Strange Institution Called Literature': An Interview with Jacques Derrida." Interviewed by Derek Attridge. In Derek Attridge, ed., *Acts of Literature*, 33–75. New York: Routledge, 1992.

Elison, George. *Deus Destroyed: The Image Of Christianity in Early Modern Japan*. Cambridge: Harvard University Press, 1988.

———. "Hideyoshi, the Bountiful Minister." In George Elison and Bardwell L.

Smith, eds., *Warlords, Artists, and Commoners: Japan in the Sixteenth Century*, 223–44. Honolulu: University of Hawaii Press, 1981.

Emmert, Richard. "Expanding Nō's Horizons: Considerations for a New Nō Perspective." In James R. Brandon, ed., *Nō and Kyōgen in the Contemporary World*, 19–35. Honolulu: University of Hawaii Press, 1997.

Felman, Shoshana. *The Literary Speech Act: Don Juan with J. L. Austin, or Seduction in Two Languages*. Trans. Catherine Porter. Ithaca, N.Y.: Cornell University Press, 1983.

Ferris, Lesley. *Acting Women: Images of Women in Theatre*. New York: New York University Press, 1989.

Field, Norma. *The Splendor of Longing in* The Tale of Genji. Princeton, N.J.: Princeton University Press, 1987.

Fontanier, Pierre. *Les Figures du discours*. Ed. Gérard Genette. Paris: Flammarion, 1968.

Foucault, Michel. *Discipline and Punish: Birth of the Prison*. Trans. Alan Sheridan. New York: Vintage Books, 1977.

———. "Nietzsche, Genealogy, History." In Paul Rabinow, ed., *The Foucault Reader*, 76–100. New York: Pantheon Books, 1984.

———. "Politics and the Study of Discourse." In Graham Burchell, Colin Gordon, and Peter Miller, eds., *The Foucault Effect: Studies in Governmentality*, 53–72. Chicago: University of Chicago Press, 1991.

———. *Power/Knowledge*. Ed. Colin Gordon. New York: Pantheon Books, 1980.

———. "What Is an Author?" In Donald F. Bouchard, ed., *Language, Counter-Memory, Practice*, 113–38. Ithaca, N.Y.: Cornell University Press, 1984.

Fujii Sadakazu. *Genji monogatari no shigen to genzai*. Rev. ed. Tokyo: Tōjūsha, 1980.

Fujimoto Katsuyoshi. "Genji monogatari 'zenbō' 'kofu daijin no onryō' kō." *Nihon bungaku* 32 (August 1983): 54–64.

Fukuo Takeichirō. *Nihon kazoku seidoshi gaisetsu*. Tokyo: Yoshikawa Kobunkan, 1972.

Girard, René. *Deceit, Desire, and the Novel*. Trans. Yvonne Freccero. Baltimore: Johns Hopkins University Press, 1965.

———. *Things Hidden Since the Foundation of the World*. Trans. Stephen Bann and Michael Metteer. Stanford, Calif.: Stanford University Press, 1987.

———. *Violence and the Sacred*. Trans. Patrick Gregory. Baltimore: Johns Hopkins University Press, 1977.

Goff, Janet. *Noh Drama and* The Tale of Genji. Princeton, N.J.: Princeton University Press, 1991.

Gomi Fumihiko. "Josei shoryō to ie." In Joseishi Sōgō Kenkyūkai, ed., *Nihon joseishi*, 5 vols., 2: 29–64. Tokyo: Tokyo Daigaku Shuppankai, 1982.

Gondō Yoshikazu, Nakagawa Akira, and Tsuyuno Gorō. *Nihon no yūrei: Nō, kabuki, rakugo*. Osaka: Osaka Shoseki, 1983.

Gotō Hajime. *Nōgaku no kigen*. Tokyo: Mokujisha, 1975.

———. *Zoku nōgaku no kigen*. Tokyo: Mokujisha, 1981.

Gotō Tanji, Kamada Kisaburō, and Okami Masao, eds. *Taiheiki*. 3 vols. In *Nihon koten bungaku taikei*, vols. 34–36. Tokyo: Iwanami Shoten, 1960–62.

Grapard, Allan G. "Lotus in Mountain, Mountain in Lotus: *Rokugō Kaizan Nimmon Daibosatsu Hongi.*" *Monumenta Nipponica* 41, no. 1 (1986): 21–50.

———. "Religious Practices." In Donald H. Shively and William H. McCullough, eds., *The Cambridge History of Japan*, 2: 517–75. Cambridge: Cambridge University Press, 1999.

Greenblatt, Stephen. *Shakespearean Negotiations: The Circulation of Social Energy in Renaissance England*. Berkeley: University of California Press, 1988.

———, ed. *Representing the English Renaissance*. Berkeley: University of California Press, 1988.

Grossberg, Kenneth A. *Japan's Renaissance: The Politics of the Muromachi Bakufu*. Cambridge: Harvard University Press, 1981.

Grotenhuis, Elizabeth ten. *Japanese Mandalas: Representations of Sacred Geography*. Honolulu: University of Hawaii Press, 1999.

Haga Yaichi and Sasaki Nobutsuna, eds. *Kōchū yōkyoku sōsho*. 3 vols. 2nd ed. Tokyo: Rinsen Shoten, 1987.

Hagitani Boku, ed. *Murasaki Shikibu nikki zenchūshaku*. In *Nihon koten hyōshaku zenchūshaku sōsho*. Tokyo: Kadokawa Shoten, 1971–73.

Hall, John W. "The Muromachi Bakufu." In Kozo Yamamura, ed., *The Cambridge History of Japan*, 3: 175–230. Cambridge: Cambridge University Press, 1990.

Hall, John W., and Toyoda Takeshi, eds. *Japan in the Muromachi Age*. Berkeley: University of California Press, 1977.

Hanawa Hokinoichi, ed. *Zoku gunsho ruijū*. Vol. 19 (2). Tokyo: Zoku Gunsho Ruijū Kanseikai, 1925.

Hare, Thomas Blenman. "A Separate Piece: Proprietary Claims and Intertexuality in the Rokujō Plays." In Thomas Hare, Robert Borgen, and Sharalyn Orbaugh, eds., *The Distant Isle*, 183–203. Ann Arbor: University of Michigan Center for Japanese Studies, 1996.

———. *Zeami's Style: The Noh Plays of Zeami Motokiyo*. Stanford, Calif.: Stanford University Press, 1986.

Hata Hisashi. "Kinsaku nō, kindai nō, gendai nō no sakusha to sakuhin." In Yokomichi Mario, Nishino Haruo, and Hata Hisashi, *Nō no sakusha to sakuhin*, in vol. 3 of *Iwanami kōza: Nō kyōgen*, 301–62. Tokyo: Iwanami Shoten, 1992.

Hayashiya Tatsusaburō. *Chūsei geinōshi no kenkyū*. Tokyo: Iwanami Shoten, 1957.

———. "Kyoto in the Muromachi Age." In John W. Hall and Toyoda Takeshi, eds., *Japan in the Muromachi Age*, 15–36. Berkeley: University of California Press, 1977.

Hirayama Kōzō. *Wayo no kenkyū*. Tokyo: Yoshikawa Kobunkan, 1964.

Hisamatsu Senichi and Satō Kenzō, eds. *Kadokawa shinpan kogo jiten*. Tokyo: Kadokawa Shoten, 1989.

Hoaas, Solrun. "Noh Masks: The Legacy of Possession." *Drama Review* 26 (Winter 1982): 82–86.

Hoff, Frank. "Seeing and Being Seen: The Mirror of Performance." In James H. Stanford, William R. LaFleur, and Masatoshi Nagatomi, eds., *Flowing Traces: Buddhism in the Literary and Visual Arts of Japan*, 131–48. Princeton, N.J.: Princeton University Press, 1992.

Hori Ichirō. *Folk Religion in Japan: Continuity and Change.* Chicago: University of Chicago Press, 1968.

Hosoi Nittatsu, ed. *Shinkun ryōdoku myōhōrengekyō narabini kaiketsu.* Tokyo: Sōka Gakkai, 1970.

Hosokawa Ryōichi. *Onna no chūsei: Ono no Komachi, Tomoe, sono ta.* Tokyo: Nihon Editāsukūru Shuppanbu, 1989.

Hurvitz, Leon, trans. *Scripture of the Lotus Blossom of the Fine Dharma.* New York: Columbia University Press, 1976.

Ichiko Teiji, ed. *Heike monogatari.* 2 vols. In *Nihon koten bungaku zenshū,* vols. 29–30. Tokyo: Shōgakkan, 1973–75.

———, ed. *Heike monogatari hikkei.* Tokyo: Gakutōsha, 1967.

Ichiko Teiji, et al., eds. *Nihon koten bungaku daijiten.* 6 vols. Tokyo: Iwanami Shoten, 1983–85.

Ihara Saikaku. *The Life of an Amorous Woman.* Ed. Ivan Morris. New York: New Directions, 1963.

Ihon Tadasugawara kanjin nō sarugakki. In *Dengaku, Sarugaku,* vol. 2 of Geinōshi kenkyūkai, ed., *Nihon shomin bunka shiryō shūsei.* Tokyo: San'ichi Shobō, 1974.

Ikeda Kikan. *Heian jidai no bungaku to seikatsu.* Tokyo: Shibundō, 1966.

Ikeda Yasaburō. *Nihon no yūrei.* Tokyo: Chūō Kōronsha, 1974.

Imaizumi Atsuo, ed. *Kyōto no rekishi,* 10 vols. Tokyo: Gakugei Shorin, 1968–76.

Immoos, Thomas. "The Birth of the Japanese Theater." *Monumenta Nipponica* 24 (1969): 403–14.

Inagaki Hisao, ed. *A Dictionary of Japanese Buddhist Terms.* Kyoto: Nagata Bunshodo, 1988.

Irokawa Daikichi. *Tennōsei: Rekishi oken daijōsai.* Tokyo: Kawade Shobō Shinsha, 1990.

Itō Masayoshi, ed. *Yōkyokushū.* 3 vols. In *Shinchō Nihon koten shūsei,* vols. 57, 73, and 79. Tokyo: Shinchōsha, 1983–88.

———. *Yōkyoku zakki.* Tokyo: Izumi Sensho, 1989.

Iwasaki Kae, et al., eds. *Shichijūichiban shokunin utaawase.* In *Shin Nihon koten bungaku taikei,* vol. 61. Tokyo: Iwanami Shoten, 1993.

Kajihara Masaaki, ed. *Gikeiki.* In *Nihon koten bungaku zenshū,* vol. 31. Tokyo: Shōgakkan, 1971.

Kajii Yukiyo. "Nyotai no shite ni tsuite." *Gakuyō* 15 (December 1973): 9–18.

Kamens, Edward, trans. *The Three Jewels: A Study and Translation of Minamoto Tamenori's* Sanboe. Ann Arbor: University of Michigan Center for Japanese Studies, 1988.

Kanda, Christine Guth. *Shinzō: Hachiman Imagery and Its Development.* Cambridge: Harvard University Press, 1985.

Kanze Hisao. "Life with the Nō Mask." *Mime Journal* (1984): 65–73.

Kawasaki Noboru. "Rokujō miyasundokoro no shinkōteki haikei." *Kokugakuin zasshi* 68 (September 1967): 13–23.

Keene, Donald. *Nō: The Classical Theatre of Japan.* Tokyo: Kodansha International, 1973.

———. *Some Japanese Portraits*. Tokyo: Kodansha International, 1978.

Kindaichi Haruhiko, ed. *Shin meikai kogo jiten*. 2nd ed. Tokyo: Sanseidō, 1977.

Kitagawa Tadahiko. "'Monomane no jōjō' kara 'santai' ron e." *Bungaku* 51 (July 1983): 47–56.

Kittler, Friedrich A. *Discourse Networks: 1800/1900*. Trans. Michael Metteer. Stanford, Calif.: Stanford University Press, 1990.

Klein, Susan B. "Woman as Serpent: The Demonic Feminine in the Noh Play *Dōjōji*." in Jane Marie Law, ed., *Religious Reflections on the Human Body*, 100–136. Bloomington: Indiana University Press, 1994.

Kobayashi Shizuo. *Nōgaku shiryō*. Tokyo: Ōkayama Shoten, 1933.

———. *Seami*. Tokyo: Hinoki Shoten, 1958.

Kobayashi Yasuo. "Nanbokuchō-Muromachiki no kasho hakkyū ni tsuite: Muromachi bakufu shikiseishi no kisoteki kōsatsu." In Nagoya Daigaku Bungakubu Kokoshigaku Kenkyūshitsu, ed., *Nagoya Daigaku Nihonshi ronshū 1*. Tokyo: Yoshikawa Kōbunkan, 1975.

Kokusai Bunka Shinkokai, ed. *The Noh Drama*. Tokyo: Kokusai Bunka Shinkokai, 1937.

Komparu Kunio. *The Noh Theater: Principles and Perspectives*. Trans. Jane Corddry. New York: Walker/Weatherhill, 1983.

Konishi Jin'ichi. *A History of Japanese Literature*. 3 vols. Trans. Aileen Gatten and Mark Harbison. Princeton, N.J.: Princeton University Press, 1984–91.

———. "Hon'i setsu to tōdai shiron." *Kokugo* 1, nos. 2–4 (1953): 100–105.

Koyama Hiroshi, Taguchi Kazuo, and Hashimoto Asao. *Kyōgen no sekai*. In *Iwanami kōza: Nō kyōgen*, vol. 5. Tokyo: Iwanami Shoten, 1993.

Koyama Hiroshi et al., eds. *Kyōgen kanshō annai*. In *Iwanami kōza: Nō kyōgen*, vol. 7. Tokyo: Iwanami Shoten, 1993.

Lacoue-Labarthe, Philippe. "History and Mimesis." In Laurence A. Rickels, ed., *Looking After Nietzsche*, 209–31. Albany: State University of New York Press, 1990.

LaFleur, William R. *The Karma of Words: Buddhism and the Literary Arts in Medieval Japan*. Berkeley: University of California Press, 1983.

———. "Saigyō and the Buddhist Value of Nature." *History of Religions* 13, no. 2 (1973): 93–126.

Laplanche, Jean, and J.-B. Pontalis. *The Language of Psycho-Analysis*. Trans. Donald Nicholson-Smith. New York: Norton, 1973.

Laqueur, Thomas. *Making Sex: Body and Gender from the Greeks to Freud*. Cambridge: Harvard University Press, 1990.

Law, Jane Marie. *Puppets of Nostalgia: The Life, Death, and Rebirth of the Japanese Awaji Ningyō Tradition*. Princeton, N.J.: Princeton University Press, 1997.

———. "Violence, Ritual Reenactment, and Ideology: The *Hōjō-e* (Rite for Release of Sentient Beings) of the Usa Hachiman Shrine in Japan." *History of Religions* 33, no. 4 (1994): 325–57.

———, ed. *Religious Reflections on the Human Body*. Bloomington: Indiana University Press, 1994.

Leims, Thomas F. *Die Entstehung des Kabuki: Transkulturation Europa-Japan im 16. und 17. Jahrhundert.* Leiden: E. J. Brill, 1990.

Loewe, Michael. "The Former Han Dynasty." In Denis Twitchett and Michael Loewe, eds., *The Cambridge History of China*, 1: 103–222. Cambridge: Cambridge University Press, 1986.

Lu, David John, ed. *Sources of Japanese History.* 2 vols. New York: McGraw-Hill, 1974.

Marra, Michele. *Representations of Power: The Literary Politics of Medieval Japan.* Honolulu: University of Hawaii Press, 1993.

Maruoka Katsura. *Kokon yōkyoku kaidai.* Ed. Nishino Haruo. Tokyo: Kokon Yōkyoku Kaidai Kankōkai, 1984.

Mass, Jeffrey P. *Lordship and Inheritance in Early Medieval Japan: A Study of the Kamakura Sōryō System.* Stanford, Calif.: Stanford University Press, 1989.

Massumi, Brian. *A User's Guide to Capitalism and Schizophrenia: Deviations from Deleuze and Guattari.* Cambridge: MIT Press, 1992.

Masuda Shōzō. *Nō no hyōgen: Sono gyakusetsu no bigaku.* Tokyo: Chūō Kōronsha, 1971.

———. *Nō to kindai bungaku.* Tokyo: Heibonsha, 1990.

Matsunaga, Alicia, and Daigan Matsunaga. *Foundation of Japanese Buddhism.* Los Angeles: Buddhist Books International, 1976.

McCullough, Helen Craig, trans. *Ōkagami: The Great Mirror.* Princeton, N.J.: Princeton University Press, 1980.

McCullough, William H. "Japanese Marriage Institutions in the Late Heian Period." *Harvard Journal of Asiatic Studies* 27 (1967): 103–67.

McCullough, William H., and Helen Craig McCullough, trans. *A Tale of Flowering Fortunes.* 2 vols. Stanford, Calif.: Stanford University Press, 1980.

McDuff, William. "Beautiful Boys in Nō Drama: The Idealization of Homoerotic Desire." *Asian Theatre Journal* 13, no. 2 (1996): 248–58.

Minemura Fumito, ed. *Shinkokinwakashū.* In *Nihon koten bungaku zenshū*, vol. 26. Tokyo: Shōgakkan, 1974.

Miner, Earl, Hiroko Odagiri, and Robert E. Morrell, eds. *The Princeton Companion to Classical Japanese Literature.* Princeton, N.J.: Princeton University Press, 1985.

Mishima Yukio. "Aoi no Ue." In *Mishima Yukio shū*, vol. 68 of *Chikuma gendai bungaku taikei*, 425–35. Tokyo: Chikuma Shobō, 1984.

Mitani Eiichi. "Sagoromo monogatari no ihon seiritsu to sono jiki: Maki ichio chūshin to shite." *Kokugakuin Daigaku kiyō* 7 (1967): 277–309.

Mitani Kuniaki. "*Genji monogatari* daisanbu no hōhō." *Bungaku* 50 (August 1982): 76–104.

Mizuhara Hajime. *Heike monogatari no keisei.* Tokyo: Katō Chūdōkan, 1971.

———, ed. *Heike monogatari.* 3 vols. In *Shinchō Nihon koten shūsei*, vols. 25, 37, and 47. Tokyo: Shinchōsha, 1979–81.

———, ed. *Shintei Genpei seisuiki.* 6 vols. Tokyo: Shin Jinbutsu Ōraisha, 1988–91.

Mizuno Kōgen. "Gōsetsu ni tsuite." *Indogaku Bukkyōgaku kenkyū* 2 (1954): 110–20.

Moi, Toril. "The Challenge of the Particular Case: Bourdieu's Sociology of Culture and Literary Criticism." *Modern Language Quarterly* 58, no. 4 (December 1997): 497–508.

Morisue Yoshiaki. *Chūsei geinōshi ronkō.* Tokyo: Tōkyōdō Shuppan, 1971.

———. "Nō no hogosha." In *Nō no rekishi,* vol. 2 of Nogami Toyoichirō, ed., *Nōgaku zensho,* 198–235. Tokyo: Sōgensha, 1979–81.

Morley, Carolyn Anne. *Transformation, Miracles, and Mischief: The Mountain Priest Plays of Kyōgen.* Ithaca, N.Y.: Cornell University East Asia Program, 1993.

Morrell, Robert, trans. *Sand and Pebbles.* Albany: State University of New York Press, 1985.

Morris, Ivan. *The World of the Shining Prince.* New York: Penguin, 1964.

Morris, Mark. "Desire and the Prince: New Work on *Genji monogatari*: A Review Article." *Journal of Asian Studies* 49 (1990): 291–304.

Murdoch, James. *A History of Japan.* Vol. 1. New York: Greenberg, 1926.

Nagao Kazuo. "A Return to Essence Through Misconception: From Zeami to Hisao." In James R. Brandon, ed., *Nō and Kyōgen in the Contemporary World,* 111–24. Honolulu: University of Hawaii Press, 1997.

Nagata Kōkichi. "Ningyō shibai no kigen shiryō." In Honda Yasuji, ed., *Geinō ronshū.* Tokyo: Kinseisha, 1976.

Nakajima Etsuji, ed. *Gukanshō hyōshaku.* Tokyo: Kokubun Kenkyūkai, 1931.

Nakamura Hajime et al., eds. *Iwanami Bukkyō jiten.* Tokyo: Iwanami Shoten, 1992.

Nakamura Yasuo. "Nō Masks: Their History and Development." *Mime Journal* (1984): 114–24.

———. *Noh: The Classical Theatre.* Trans. Don Kenny. New York: Walker/Weatherhill, 1971.

Nearman, Mark J. "Behind the Mask of Nō." *Mime Journal* (1984): 20–64.

Nickerson, Peter. "The Meaning of Matrilocality: Kinship, Property, and Politics in Mid-Heian." *Monumenta Nipponica* 48, no. 4 (1993): 429–67.

Nietzsche, Friedrich. *The Gay Science.* Trans. Walter Kaufmann. New York: Vintage Books, 1974.

Nippon Gakujutsu Shinkōkai, trans. *Japanese Noh Drama.* Vol. 2. Tokyo: Nippon Gakujutsu Shinkōkai, 1959.

Nishida Naotoshi. *Heike monogatari no buntaironteki kenkyū.* Tokyo: Meiji Shoin, 1978.

Nishino Haruo. "Nōgaku shiryaku nenpyō." In *Nō no rekishi,* vol. 2 of Nogami Toyoichirō, ed., *Nōgaku zensho,* 341–61. Tokyo: Sōgensha, 1979–81.

Nishino Haruo and Hata Akira, eds. *Nō kyōgen jiten.* Tokyo: Heibonsha, 1987.

Nishio Minoru. *Dōgen to Zeami: Chūseitekina mono no genryū o motomete.* Tokyo: Iwanami Shoten, 1965.

Nogami Toyoichirō. *Nō no yūgen to hana.* Tokyo: Iwanami Shoten, 1943.

———, ed. *Nōgaku zensho.* 7 vols. 2nd rev. ed. Tokyo: Sōgensha, 1979–81.

———, ed. *Yōkyoku zenshū.* Tokyo: Chūō Kōronsha, 1935, 1: 20–37.

Nonomura Kaizō, ed. *Yōkyoku nihyakugojūbanshū sakuin.* Tokyo: Akaoshōbundō, 1978.

———, ed. *Yōkyoku sanbyakugojūbanshū.* Tokyo: Kōbunsha, 1928.

Nose Asaji. *Nōgaku genryūkō*. Tokyo: Iwanami Shoten, 1938.

———. "Nō no senkō geijitsu." In *Nō no rekishi*, vol. 2 of Nogami Toyoichirō, ed., *Nōgaku zensho*, 146–63. Tokyo: Sōgensha, 1979–81.

———. *Yūgen ron*. Tokyo: Kawade Shobō, 1944.

Oasa Yūji. "Rokujō miyasudokoro no kunō." In Akiyama Ken, Kimura Masanori, and Shimizu Yoshiko, eds., *Kōza Genji monogatari no sekai*, vol. 3. Tokyo: Yūhikaku, 1981.

O'Hara, Donald T. "What Was Foucault?" In Jonathan Arac, ed., *After Foucault: Humanistic Knowledge, Postmodern Challenges*, 71–96. New Brunswick, N.J.: Rutgers University Press, 1988.

Okada, H. Richard. *Figures of Resistance: Language, Poetry, and Narrating in* The Tale of Genji *and Other Mid-Heian Texts*. Durham, N.C.: Duke University Press, 1991.

Omote Akira. *Nōgakushi shinkō*. Vol. 1. Tokyo: Wan'ya Shoten, 1979.

Omote Akira and Amano Fumio. *Nōgaku no rekishi*. Vol. 1 of *Iwanami kōza: Nō kyōgen*. Tokyo: Iwanami Shoten, 1992.

Omote Akira and Itō Masayoshi, eds. *Konparu kodensho shūsei*. Tokyo: Wan'ya Shoten, 1969.

Omote Akira and Katō Shūichi, eds. *Zeami, Zenchiku*. Vol. 24 of *Nihon shisō taikei*. Tokyo: Iwanami Shoten, 1974.

O'Neill, P. G. *Early Nō Drama*. London: Lund Humphries, 1958.

———. "Music, Dance, and Text in Nō Drama." In James Redmond, ed., *Drama, Dance and Music*, 103–21. Cambridge: Cambridge University Press, 1981.

Origuchi Shinobu. "Nukata no Ōkimi." In Origuchi Hakase Kinen Kodai Kenkyūjo, ed., *Origuchi Shinobu zenshū*, 9: 444–60. Tokyo: Chūō Kōronsha, 1976.

Ortolani, Benito. *The Japanese Theatre: From Shamanistic Ritual to Contemporary Pluralism*. Leiden: E. J. Brill, 1990.

Ose Hoan. *Taikōki*, ed. Kuwata Tadachika. Tokyo: Shin Jinbutsu Ōraisha, 1971.

Ozawa Masao, ed. *Kokinwakashū*. Vol. 7 of *Nihon koten bungaku zenshū*. Tokyo: Shōgakkan, 1971.

Pilgrim, Richard B. "The Japanese Noh Drama in Ritual Perspective." *Eastern Buddhist* 22 (1989): 54–70.

Plutschow, Herbert E. *Chaos and Cosmos: Ritual in Early and Medieval Japanese Literature*. Leiden: E. J. Brill, 1990.

Pye, Christopher. *The Regal Phantasm: Shakespeare and the Politics of Spectacle*. London: Routledge, 1990.

Rabinow, Paul, ed. *The Foucault Reader*. New York: Pantheon Books, 1984.

Rath, Eric C. "Legends, Secrets, and Authority: *Hachijō Kadensho* and Early Modern Noh." *Monumenta Nipponica* 54, no. 2 (1999): 169–94.

Raz, Jacob. *Audience and Actors: A Study of Their Interaction in the Japanese Traditional Theatre*. Leiden: E. J. Brill, 1983.

Riffaterre, Michael. "Prosopopeia." *Yale French Studies* 69 (1985): 107–23.

Rimer, J. Thomas, and Yamazaki Masakazu, trans. *On the Art of Nō Drama: The Major Treatises of Zeami*. Princeton, N.J.: Princeton University Press, 1984.

Ruch, Barbara. "The Other Side of Culture in Medieval Japan." In Yamamura

Kozo, ed., *The Cambridge History of Japan*, 3: 500–43. Cambridge: Cambridge University Press, 1990.

Saigō Nobutsuna. *Genji monogatari o yomu tame ni.* Tokyo: Heibonsha, 1983.

————. *Shi no hassei: Bungaku ni okeru genshi, kodai no imi.* Tokyo: Miraisha, 1964.

Sanari Kentarō, ed. *Yōkyoku taikan.* 7 vols. 3rd ed. Tokyo: Meiji Shoin, 1985.

Sasaki Ginya. *Muromachi bakufu.* Vol. 13 of *Nihon no rekishi.* Tokyo: Shōgakkan, 1975.

Saunders, E. Dale. *Buddhism in Japan.* Philadelphia: University of Pennsylvania Press, 1964.

Sekiguchi Hiroko. "Nihon kodai no kon'in keitai ni tsuite." *Rekishi hyōron* 311 (March 1976): 34–52.

Shimazaki, Chifumi. *Warrior Ghost Plays from the Japanese Noh Theater.* Ithaca, N.Y.: Cornell University East Asia Program, 1993.

Shinmura Izuru, ed. *Kōjien.* Tokyo: Iwanami Shoten, 1988.

Shirane, Haruo. *The Bridge of Dreams: A Poetics of* The Tale of Genji. Stanford, Calif.: Stanford University Press, 1987.

Shively, Donald H., and William H. McCullough, eds. *The Cambridge History of Japan.* Vol. 2. Cambridge: Cambridge University Press, 1999.

Smethurst, Mae. *The Artistry of Aeschylus and Zeami: A Comparative Study of Greek Tragedy and Nō.* Princeton, N.J.: Princeton University Press, 1989.

————, ed. *Ominameshi: A Flower Viewed from Many Directions.* Forthcoming.

Suda Atsuo. *Nihon gekijōshi no kenkyū.* Tokyo: Sagami Shobō, 1966.

Sugimoto Keizaburō, trans. *Heike monogatari.* Tokyo: Kōdansha, 1988.

Sunagawa Hiroshi. *Heike monogatari shinkō.* Tokyo: Bijutsu, 1982.

Suzuki Kunihiro. "Chūsei zenki ichizoku ketsugō no kenkyū shikaku." *Nihon rekishi* 281 (October 1971): 13–33.

Tachibana Kenji, ed. *Ōkagami.* Vol. 20 of *Nihon koten bungaku zenshū.* Tokyo: Shōgakkan, 1974.

Takagi Ichinosuke, Gomi Tomohide, and Ono Susumu, eds. *Man'yōshū.* 4 vols. In *Nihon koten bungaku taikei*, vols. 4–7. Tokyo: Iwanami Shoten, 1957–62.

Takahashi Yōji, ed., *Bessatsu Taiyō: Nō* 25 (Winter 1978).

Takamure Itsue. *Shōseikon no kenkyū*, 2 vols. Tokyo: Rironsha, 1966.

Takeda Yūkichi and Satō Kenzō, trans. *Sandai jitsuroku.* Tokyo: Rinsen Shoten, 1986.

Takemoto Mikio., ed. *Nōgaku shiryōshū.* Vol. 21 of *Waseda Daigaku zō shiryō eiin sōsho*, 37 vols. Tokyo: Waseda Daigaku Shuppanbu, 1988.

Tamagami Takuya, ed. *Genji monogatari hyōshaku.* 14 vols. Tokyo: Kadokawa Shoten, 1964–69.

Tanaka Makoto, ed. *Mikan yōkyokushū.* 31 vols. Tokyo: Koten Bunko, 1987.

Taylor, Mark C. *Altarity.* Chicago: University of Chicago Press, 1987.

Thornhill, Arthur H., III. *Six Circles, One Dewdrop: The Religio-Aesthetic World of Komparu Zenchiku.* Princeton, N.J.: Princeton University Press, 1993.

————. "*Yūgen* After Zeami." In James R. Brandon, ed., *Nō and Kyōgen in the Contemporary World*, 36–64. Honolulu: University of Hawaii Press, 1997.

Toida Michizō. *Nō: Kami to kojiki no geijutsu.* Tokyo: Serika Shobō, 1972.

Tokue Gensei. *Geinō, Nōgei.* Tokyo: Miyai Shoten, 1979.

Tokue Motomasa. "Shizuka Gozen no kaikoku." *Kokugakuin zasshi* 61, no. 1 (1960).

Tokyō Daigaku Shiryō Hensanjo, ed. *Gogumaiki.* Vol. 17 of *Dai Nihon kokiroku.* Tokyo: Iwanami Shoten, 1980.

Tomikura Tokujirō. *Heike monogatari zen chūshaku.* 4 vols. Tokyo: Kadokawa Shoten, 1966–68.

Tonomura Hitomi. "Re-Envisioning Women in the Post-Kamakura Age." In Jeffrey P. Mass, ed., *The Origins of Japan's Medieval World: Courtiers, Clerics, Warriors, and Peasants in the Fourteenth Century,* 138–69. Stanford, Calif.: Stanford University Press, 1997.

Totman, Conrad. *Early Modern Japan.* Berkeley: University of California Press, 1993.

Tsunoda Ryusaku, William Theodore de Bary, and Donald Keene, eds. *Sources of Japanese Tradition,* 2 vols. New York: Columbia University Press, 1964.

Tubielewicz, Jolanta. *Superstitions, Magic, and Mantic Practices in the Heian Period.* Warsaw: Wydaw-a UW, 1980.

Tyler, Royall. "Buddhism in Noh." *Japanese Journal of Religious Studies* 14 (1987): 19–52.

———. "The Nō Play *Matsukaze* as a Transformation of *Genji monogatari.*" *Journal of Japanese Studies* 20 (Summer 1994): 377–422.

———. "Tomoe: The Woman Warrior." In Chieko Irie Mulhern, ed., *Heroic with Grace: Legendary Women of Japan,* 129–36. Armonk, N.Y.: M. E. Sharpe, 1991.

Varley, H. Paul. "Ashikaga Yoshimitsu and the World of Kitayama: Social Change and Shogunal Patronage in Early Muromachi Japan." In John W. Hall and Toyoda Takeshi, eds., *Japan in the Muromachi Age,* 183–204. Berkeley: University of California Press, 1977.

Veeser, H. Aram, ed. *The New Historicism.* New York: Routledge, 1989.

———, ed. *The New Historicism Reader.* New York: Routledge, 1994.

Wakita Haruko. *Chūsei ni ikiru onnatachi.* Tokyo: Iwanami Shoten, 1995.

———. "Marriage and Property in Premodern Japan from the Perspective of Women's History." *Journal of Japanese Studies* 10 (1984): 77–99.

———. *Nihon chūsei joseishi no kenkyū: Seibetsu yakuwari buntan to bosei, kasei, seiai.* Tokyo: Tokyo Daigaku Shuppankai, 1992.

———. "Nōgaku to tennō Shintō." In Irokawa Daikichi, ed., *Tennōsei: rekishi oken daijōsai,* 126–32. Tokyo: Kawade Shobō Shinsha, 1990.

Waley, Arthur, trans. *The Nō Plays of Japan.* London: George Allen and Unwin, 1954.

Watanabe Shōgo. *Geinō bunkashi jiten [chūsei hen].* Tokyo: Meicho Shuppan, 1991.

Watsuji Tetsurō. "*Yōkyoku ni arawareta rinri shisō*: Japanese Ethical Thought in the Noh Plays of the Muromachi Period." *Monumenta Nipponica* 24, no. 4 (1969): 467–98.

Yamada Yoshio, et al., eds. *Konjaku monogatarishū.* 5 vols. In *Nihon koten bungaku taikei,* vols. 22–26. Tokyo: Iwanami Shoten, 1959–63.

Yamagami Izumo. *Miko no rekishi.* Tokyo: Yūzankaku, 1984.

Yamagishi Tokuhei, ed. *Genji monogatari.* 5 vols. In *Nihon koten bungaku taikei,* vols. 14–18. Tokyo: Iwanami Shoten, 1958–63.

Yamamoto Ritatsu, ed. *Murasaki Shikibu nikki, Murasaki Shikibu shū.* In *Shinchō Nihon koten shūsei,* vol. 35. Tokyo: Shinchōsha, 1980.

Yamamura, Kozo, ed. *The Cambridge History of Japan.* Vol. 3. Cambridge: Cambridge University Press, 1990.

Yokomichi Mario. *Nō no kōzō to gihō.* Vol. 4 of *Iwanami kōza: Nō kyōgen.* Tokyo: Iwanami Shoten, 1993.

Yokomichi Mario, Nishino Haruo, and Hata Hisashi. *Nō no sakusha to sakuhin.* Vol. 3 of *Iwanami kōza: Nō kyōgen.* Tokyo: Iwanami Shoten, 1992.

Yokomichi Mario and Omote Akira, eds. *Yōkyokushū.* 2 vols. In *Nihon koten bungaku taikei,* vols. 40 and 41. Tokyo: Iwanami Shoten, 1960 and 1963.

Yokomichi Mario, ed. *Nōgaku zusetsu.* Appendix to *Iwanami kōza: Nō kyōgen.* Tokyo: Iwanami Shoten, 1992.

Yokota-Murakami, Gerry. *The Formation of the Canon of Nō: The Literary Tradition of Divine Authority.* Osaka: Osaka University Press, 1997.

Yusa Michiko. "*Riken no Ken*: Zeami's Theory of Acting and Theatrical Appreciation." *Monumenta Nipponica* 42 (1987): 331–45.

Index

In this index an "f" after a number indicates a separate reference on the next page, and an "ff" indicates separate references on the next two pages. A continuous discussion over two or more pages is indicated by a span of page numbers. *Passim* is used for a cluster of references in close but not consecutive sequence.